REASSESSING THE SIXTIES

REASSESSING THE SIXTIES

Debating the Political and
Cultural Legacy

STEPHEN MACEDO

Editor

W · W · NORTON & COMPANY

New York   London

First Edition

The text of this book is composed in Times Roman, with the display set in
Perpetua. Composition and manufacturing by The Maple-Vail Book
Manufacturing Group. Book design by Jacques Chazaud.

Library of Congress Cataloging-in-Publication Data
Reassessing the sixties : debating the political and cultural legacy /
Stephen Macedo, editor.
p. cm.
Includes bibliographical references
ISBN 0-393-03940-4
1. United States—History—1961–1969.   2. Social movements—United
States—History—20th century.   I. Macedo, Stephen, 1957–
E841.R43   1996
973.922—DC20   96-23185
CIP

W. W. Norton & Company, Inc., 500 Fifth Avenue, New York, N.Y. 10110
http://www.wwnorton.com
W. W. Norton & Company Ltd., 10 Coptic Street, London WC1A 1PU

1 2 3 4 5 6 7 8 9 0

Contents

REASSESSING THE SIXTIES

Foreword

GEORGE F. WILL

The sixties, you may well feel, have been too much with us. Since the sixties our national life has been a running argument about, and with, the sixties. As the strongly argued essays in this volume prove, the argument is far from running out of steam. And the essays prove something else: that it was not a radical decade, as the term "radical" is commonly used in connection with that decade. It was not a decade of the left ascendant. Rampant, perhaps, but not ascendant. Rather, the decade was radicalizing; that, subsequent decades have shown, is different. Politically the decade invigorated the right more than the left. But of course politics is not everything. In fact three decades down the road from the sixties, the nation's political discourse may be driven by conservatives, but they, although by many measures triumphant, seem aggrieved because politics seems peripheral to, and largely impotent against, cultural forces and institutions permeated with what conservatives consider the sixties sensibilities.

Treating a decade as a discrete episode obviously makes the assumption that history during that decade had an obliging tidiness, opening with a decisive and tone-setting episode and closing with a suitably climactic event. History rarely accommodates that assumption. Such a treatment of a decade also makes the equally dubious assumption that the decade in question had a clearly dominant tone or profile. So the 1920s were the decade of jazz, flappers, the birth of sports celebrity (Babe Ruth, Red Grange, Jack Dempsey), the Lost Generation, Sacco and Vanzetti, and . . . Warren Harding, Calvin Coolidge, and Herbert Hoover.

Or consider another measurement. What would you say was the American "book of the decade" for the 1930s, the emblematic publishing event? Many, perhaps most Americans would name John Steinbeck's novel *The Grapes of Wrath,* published in 1939. Today it is thought to have expressed the general, or at least the most significant, social experience and political consciousness of the Depression decade. However, it is at least arguable that two other books, taken singly or together, constitute the publishing event of that decade. Those two would be Douglas Southall Freeman's Pulitzer Prize-winning four-volume biography *R. E. Lee,* the final two volumes of which were published in 1935, and Margaret Mitchell's novel *Gone with the Wind,* published in 1936. These widely read and remarkably durable works reflected, and helped shape, a sensibility that was, to say no more, unlike that of Steinbeck's novel.

So let us stipulate this: A decade, even one as intensely felt at the time and as hotly debated afterward as the sixties were and are, can come to seem, when recollected in tranquillity, quite unlike the decade as it felt at the time and unlike the decade as it is portrayed by people with an emotional or political investment in portraying it a particular way.

It is arguable that we should think of the sixties as beginning in November 1963 and ending in October 1973. That is, the years we associate with the tumultuousness associated with the phrase "the sixties" began with the assassination of a president and ended with the Yom Kippur War and the energy crisis. The assassination shattered (or at least many people say it did) the nation's sunny postwar disposition; it supposedly "ended American innocence." It is unclear how innocent was this nation, which had been made possible by Puritans, had been founded by such innocents as Benjamin Franklin, John Adams, and James Madison, had been born in the bloodshed of what actually was not only the American Revolution but also America's first civil war, had been preserved by the worst civil war the world had until then seen . . . you get the picture. The sixties as a decade of "lost innocence"? Please. The 1973 oil embargo, which produced a sense of national vulnerability and pervasive limits, did seem to bring down a curtain on something. But on what?

Perhaps on a sense of limitlessness. In the middle of the 1960s the United States, or at least the leading members of its political class, acknowledged few limits on the nation's power or their competence. The United States could fight a war, and engage in "nation building" in the nation where the war was being fought, and build a Great Society at home, simultaneously. And the 1960s counterculture, which fancied itself at daggers drawn with the "establishment," partook of the same central assumption: that limits, sometimes known as hang-ups or repressions or bourgeois values, were to be ignored, confronted, transcended, abolished. The makers of the nation's Vietnam policy may have had more in common with their most vociferous critics than either the policy makers or critics could comfortably admit.

Of course the 1950s were pregnant with the 1960s. In the beginning there was not the word but the sound: rock and roll, the vocabulary of a self-conscious and soon self-confident youth cohort. Rock and roll was nowhere in 1950 and was here to stay in 1960. Indeed, the first crashing intimation of what was to come ten years later was the first chord of the sound track of the movie *The Blackboard Jungle* (1955), Bill Haley and the Comets playing "Rock around the Clock." The subject of that movie was juvenile delinquency. "Delinquency." How quaint that word seems in the era of Bloods and Crips and other gangbangers. How quaint that the nation's leading musical light Leonard Bernstein would recast *Romeo and Juliet* as a story of delinquents on Manhattan's West Side. The 1960s took part of the 1950s and stirred in danger—sex, drugs, and rock and roll.

Another 1950s cohort, a small one, the beats, anticipated

the large cohort of adversarial intellectuals in the 1960s. Of course many of the beats, unlike their 1960s children (if members of the 1960s "counterculture" can be so regarded), were passionate lovers of America—its cars, its beckoning spaces, and the sense of no limits that those cars and spaces intimated. But the beats also had that sense of generational uniqueness and of being set upon by an unfeeling world that was to characterize those who were pleased to be called the sixties generation. Remember Allen Ginsberg's "Howl" from 1956:

> *I saw the best minds of my generation destroyed by madness, starving hysterical naked,*
> *dragging themselves through the negro streets at dawn looking for an angry fix.* . . .

Lots of people were to find lots of fixes soon enough. Some of those people would be trying to fix their sense of being "jailed in the prison air of other people's habits" and to express "a disbelief in the socially monolithic ideas of the single mate, the solid family and the respectable love life." What was coming, said the author of those words, was "a psychically armed rebellion whose sexual impetus may rebound against the antisexual foundation of every organized power in America," a rebellion demanding "that every social restraint and category be removed, and the affirmation implicit in the proposal is that man would then prove to be more creative than murderous and so would not destroy himself." So said Norman Mailer in "The White Negro," a peek over the horizon into the future when we would indeed be liberated from the tyranny of the single mate and the solid family and would stay off the streets at night. Mailer's essay was published in *Dissent* magazine in 1957 and republished in pamphlet form at 1562 Grant Avenue in San Francisco, by City Lights Books.

But the 1960s as a decade of dissent did not begin where the "beat generation"—that word "generation" again—supposedly did, at the City Lights bookstore in San Francisco's North Beach section. (Talk about quaint. Only in America could a bookstore be the Finland Station of what fancied itself a revolutionary movement.) Neither did it begin in 1964 at Sproul Plaza on the Berkeley campus, with Mario Savio and the free speech movement. Rather, the decade of dissent began at a place not famous as an locus of tumult, the podium of a Republican National Convention.

In the beginning was Barry Goldwater. In 1960 in Chicago the junior senator from Arizona, seething with the ancient (well, by American standards) and accumulated grievances of the American West against the American East, thundered to the convention that he was mad as hell at Nelson Rockefeller and his ilk and was not going to take it anymore: "Let's grow up, conservatives. We want to take this party back, and I think some day we can. Let's get to work." Four years later he and his people had control of the party. Eight years later the Nixon-Wallace share of the popular vote was 57 percent. In fact, the most remarkable example of "people power"—a favorite incantation of the left in the 1960s—was the achievement of George Wallace's ragtag army in getting him on the ballot in all fifty states in 1968, when laws impeding third-party candidates were much more onerous than they now are.

Thirty-five years after Goldwater became the first potent dissenter of the decade of dissent, it seems that the foremost fecundity of the sixties radicalism of the left, particularly on campuses, was in manufacturing a conservative movement, including a cadre of conservative intellectuals. It is an unanswerable question who was angrier in the 1960s, the Goldwater (and later the Wallace) right or the left. But there can be no argument about which one was more serious about, and successful regarding, the acquisition of power.

The radicalism of the left did not seek power; it purported to despise power. Whereas the left in the 1930s exhorted its adherents to organize, the left in the 1960s celebrated spontaneity. The left in the 1930s was produced by hard material conditions. In the 1960s social abundance and personal affluence were the prerequisites for, and contributing causes of, the campus-based radicalism. That radicalism sought a revolution in "consciousness," sometimes with chemical assistance.

Which is not to say that the radicalism of the left was otherwise sterile. By acts of bravery and skill and perseverance, acts that have not lost their power to take one's breath away, the legal edifice of racial injustice was dismantled. Whatever one thinks of the other consequences of the decade, the decade is redeemed by what was done in bus terminals, at lunch counters, in voter registration drives on ramshackle porches along dangerous back roads and by all the other mining and sapping of the old system. But a revolution interested primarily in "consciousness" is bound to be self-absorbed—each revolutionary looking inward, fascinated by the supposed malleability of his or her "self." The shaping of the "self" is apt to be a more fascinating project for the "consciousness revolutionary" than any mere social reform.

So, then, who won? That is, which of the two antagonistic tendencies activated by the radicalizing decade? It is too soon to say. Politically—or, more precisely and narrowly, in the contest for political offices—the right has won. But conservatives are not happy because they sense the primacy of cultural forces and feel that the culture is still shaped by the forces that have lost in electoral politics, by people who believe what the left believed in the sixties: that the social order is an infringement on freedom rather than freedom's foundation. Society is the crucible in which the citizen's character is formed, and conservatives in their elective offices are dismayed by the formative power of the society they're supposedly governing.

So powerful were—are—the energies let loose in the sixties there cannot now be, and may never be, anything like a final summing-up. After all, what is the "final result" of the Civil War? It is too soon to say. But regarding the unfolding consequences of the sixties, there is much that is important to say, as this volume shows.

Introduction to
Reassessing the Sixties

STEPHEN MACEDO

It seems possible that the 1990s will be remembered as the antisixties, so frequent and so fervent have become the denunciations of that notable decade. This is especially so in the wake of the 1994 congressional elections and the widely quoted efforts of Congressman Newt Gingrich to portray them as a referendum on the "Great Society, counterculture, McGovernik" legacy of the sixties. Our voluble House Speaker has indeed helped intensify the ferment against the sixties, and his remarks have not gone unnoticed by the contributors to this volume. Nevertheless, the intellectual contest over the legacy of the sixties predates the recent ascendancy of the congressional Republicans.

The loudest and the broadest salvos in the debate over the sixties' legacy have been fired by conservatives. This is hardly surprising, for, as Sheldon Wolin remarks, that era, especially its later years, stands for a set of "searing defeats" for conservatism in America. Yet while conservatives have railed against the sixties since the sixties (and have railed against its characteristic liberalism for much longer), their ire intensified noticeably during what should have been a period of triumph and exhilaration for the right—namely, the second term of the Reagan administration. All one need do is recall the remarkable popularity of Allan Bloom's *Closing of the American Mind,* which was nothing if not a scathing indictment of the cultural forces unleashed (or hastened along) by the 1960s.

Bloom's book, published in 1987, was a surprise best seller, an achievement probably not resulting from the book's lengthy exploration of the dire influence of German philosophy. It is, indeed, not immediately clear why so fulsome an indictment of American popular culture should have aroused such widespread interest in 1987, when conservatives had ample cause to rest on their laurels, cheering on the penultimate year of their champion's tenure in the White House.

The very nature of Ronald Reagan's success may help explain Bloom's popularity. The Reagan years were the high tide of conservative optimism, an era of faith in the limitless potential of American power, a power based on economic growth, individual freedom, and military might. The two great achievements of the Reagan years were a huge surge in economic activity and a vast growth in military might that prepared the way for the final confrontation with communism. Gratifying as all this must have been, conservatives had reason to worry that all was far from well on the domestic front.

In the 1980s the scourge of AIDS reared its head, while teen pregnancy, abortion, divorce, and drug use continued to escalate or remained high. While some significant political battles were being won for the right, the booming economy and triumphs abroad left untouched larger cultural shifts of vast significance for the future of the regime.

Of course Reagan paid lip service to the need to restore traditional values—to bring God back into the classroom and to protect fetal life, for example—and he did succeed in making the Supreme Court decidedly less solicitous of the rights of dissenters and minorities. Nevertheless, the state of the moral culture was hardly at the top of Reagan's political agenda. To increasing numbers of conservatives, Reagan's preoccupation with free markets and his sunny optimism about the future must have seemed more and more a distraction from the titanic shifts of cultural forces that had been going badly awry for some time, most especially in the 1960s. Indeed, if Bloom and others were right, the Reagan revolution's oft-stated faith in individual freedom must have seemed increasingly part of the problem.

Bloom and other conservative critics gave voice to a set of cultural anxieties that the Reagan revolution barely addressed, anxieties that no amount of economic growth or military might could really salve. Conservatives increasingly warned of the threats to our moderate commercial democracy posed by the permissiveness and easy self-indulgence that were undermining the (sometimes) hard disciplines of family life and sexual restraint. It seems doubtful that such anxieties were ever far from the surface of the popular mind, even if some intellectuals have been apt to forget them. Of course conservatives were far from alone in arguing that even a government of limited powers and broad individual rights depends upon patterns of self-restraint, civility, and prudence that are nurtured (or not) by families, and local communities, and the culture more broadly.

Bloom was neither the first nor the only important contributor to this widening concern with America's moral culture. His sudden and unexpected celebrity helped show, however, that Reaganite optimism was being supplanted by a decided alarm at the state of the moral culture. Conservatives increasingly worried that, as another astute observer of the contemporary scene had pointed out a few years before, American statecraft was badly neglecting the necessary, if difficult and uncomfortable, task of soulcraft.[1]

By the late 1980s, therefore, conservatives had reason to worry that they had hardly begun to address the task of reversing changes in the moral and political culture that had already degraded and could destroy the American constitutional order. The political enemies for more and more conservatives were not economic sluggishness and military timidity but the erosion of a culture that supported the subordination of self-indulgence to family welfare and the bourgeois virtues of hard work.

To some readers, this may sound too melodramatic an account of what conservative critics of the 1960s are up to. Those readers will not have to proceed far beyond this introduction, however, to see just how fervent and far-reaching is the desire for counterrevolution against the legacy of the 1960s.

These essays are about liberal democracy in America and about whether the distinctive turn taken by our regime in and around the 1960s was for good or ill. They are not, however, about public policy in any narrow sense. Rather, these are broad-gauged essays the aim of which is to uncover and assess the shifts in our moral and political culture that we associate with the 1960s. These shifts no doubt encouraged and reflected the influence of important legislative and judicial acts, but the trends on which our essayists focus suffused the life of the nation and continue to be as much a matter of changing patterns of private life as of public policy. The essays are about our political and moral culture in the broadest sense.

There is much, no doubt, that our contributors agree upon. The aim in assembling a roster of contributors was not to debate all the major political developments of the 1960s when viewed in historical perspective. It was, rather, to focus attention on those aspects of the legacy of the 1960s that seem most controversial and most deserving of critical reassessment today.

I should also emphasize that the essays were largely written independently of one another, and all were written for this volume.[2] All our contributors are academics; they are political scientists, philosophers, law professors, and sociologists. All have long been concerned with the moral dimensions of American citizenship. Our contributors are not simply distinguished professors, however; nearly all have also written for broader reading publics, and several have participated in major political controversies related to the matters of concern to this volume.

Given the extent to which the sixties represent the last (as in most recent) period of liberal ascendancy, it is unsurprising that the essays in this volume with the sharpest rhetorical edges issue from the right. "A comprehensive disaster for America" is the way that Harvey Mansfield's pungent essay describes the late sixties. It is in the spirit of "unremitting hostility" and in order to summon others to "comprehensive counterrevolution" that not only Mansfield but also Jeremy Rabkin and Walter Berns set out to canvass the various aspects of what they regard as a calamitous era and to identify its most basic principles.

It is no short catalog of sixties sins and vices that two of our conservatives, Mansfield and Rabkin, compile in their essays in our first section, "Family, Sex, and Gender": a foreign policy hobbled by failure in Vietnam, widespread drug use and crime, welfare dependency, the politicization of education, and more. Rising above them all are an interconnected set of pathologies associated with sexual liberationism, the collapse of the stable two-parent family, and feminism, which Rabkin calls "a showcase for the least attractive impulses" of sixties radicalism. The feminist movement has, Rabkin charges, bred incivility, extremism, narcissism, and a greatly exaggerated account of women's oppression. This volume's conservatives pull no punches.

But has feminism exaggerated women's oppression? There certainly are grounds for arguing that only in the 1960s was the American commitment to freedom and equality for all finally extended to women. Whereas Rabkin argues that the feminist movement spawned by the sixties was a "revolt of the privileged and overprivileged," Martha Nussbaum highlights the great good done by what she calls the "liberal revolution" of the 1960s. If Mansfield is right to suggest that traditional family relations depend on a double standard "by which more is expected of women," then Nussbaum insists that we not underestimate the moral costs of the tradition. The "immaculate lawns" and "carefully sprayed hairstyles," Nussbaum says, concealed "much depression and self-contempt, much aimless sadness, much diffuse and unfocused anger."

Of course, the sixties' revolution in family relations was far from complete. A children's rights movement grew out of the liberationist enthusiasms of the late sixties and early seventies. Children did gain greater rights of self-expression and due process, but as Martha Minow reminds us, the traditional deference to parental authority was never really eclipsed.

Given the extent to which campus radicalism was a hallmark of the sixties, it is hardly surprising that our essays in Part 2, "The Universities and Education," display a vigor equal to what we have already sampled. Both Sheldon Wolin and Walter Berns observed the campus conflicts at first hand. Berns was with Bloom at Cornell, while Wolin was an observer, and a participant, in the events at Berkeley that were so central to the sixties.

For Wolin, as for Nussbaum, the sixties were a time when old ideals of freedom and democracy were finally made real for many people. At Berkeley, Wolin argues, democracy was converted from "a rhetorical to a working proposition." Thanks to a new "zest for politics," people demanded not just equal rights but "access to power in workplaces, schools, neighborhoods, and local communities."

Conservatives of course take a rather different view of student activism. For them the universities of the sixties and early seventies were not bastions of democratic idealism but forerunners of a shameless politicization at odds with the pursuit of truth. Berns charges that "under pressure from gunbearing students," Cornell University administrators jettisoned "every vestige of academic integrity." In its spineless concessions to political demands, as well as in its pioneering of affirmative action, the Cornell of the sixties paved the way for today's "speech codes and political correctness."

Several of our contributors draw connections between the political radicalism of the sixties and the more intellectual radicalisms of today's academy, such as the approach to the study of literature known as deconstructionism. But does deconstructionism represent a continuation of the project of the sixties or its derailment? Berns emphasizes the similarities:

Today's deconstructionists advance the view popularized by sixties student radicals—namely, that the humanities as traditionally conceived have nothing important to teach. Alan Wolfe, on the other hand, emphasizes that much of today's academic radicalism betrays the reformism of the early sixties. Early sixties radicals turned away from university careers because they saw that the academic departments and professions were cliquish and inbred; "neutrality and objectivity" masked "an unargued preference for the status quo." Wolfe applauds the promise of a university finally opened to talent and merit without regard to old-boy cronyism. The problem is that too many sixties radicals, now ensconced in powerful university positions, have replicated (if not perfected) the worst forms of professionalism: the "hermetic isolation from criticism, self-conscious mandarinism, a propensity to distinguish between the in-group and the out-group." Deconstructionists deconstructed everything except departments, professional associations, annual meetings, conferences, and specialization.

The rhetorical urgency of a number of the essays in the first two parts of this volume reflects something of the fire that so often surrounds debates in the political arena over "values" and the state of our moral culture. Some readers will wonder if it is possible to look back on the sixties with a measure of ambivalence and cool moderation. One might expect that these qualities would be hardest to muster in essays on America's most enduringly divisive problem, that of race. Yet the essays in the third part of this volume display a striking ambivalence (which, admittedly, some will regard as wishy-washiness).

Anita Allen's ambivalence is very much of a piece with her own experiences in the sixties and early seventies. Allen grew up in southern military communities that were full of "integrated housing, schools, churches, swimming pools," and friendships. She later found herself a "second-wave black integrator" at Baker High School in Columbus, Georgia, the alma mater of none other than Newt Gingrich. Allen chronicles the frustrations and hope surrounding the unfulfilled promise of integration.

To recall such hopes is to pose the question of why the civil rights movement led to the harder hostilities of black power? Randall Kennedy describes the frustration and anger that led many blacks to reject the civil rights movement in favor of black power. He shows that it is possible to sympathize with this desperate anger while rejecting the racial pride to which it gave rise. Kennedy, like Allen, displays what might be thought of as an old-fashioned civil rights–era faith in the ultimate value of minimizing racial differences.

This same faith is defended and amplified by the concluding essayist, Cass Sunstein. Sunstein argues that the 1960s' civil rights movement "was mostly conservative and backward-looking," an attempt "to reform American practices by reference to long-standing American ideals." He reminds us that there are ways of thinking about the legacy of sixties activism that avoid the more extreme forms of leveling egalitarianism against which this volume's conservatives warn.

Everyone who debates the 1960s, here or elsewhere, agrees on one thing: Its controversies directly engaged fundamental American ideals of freedom and equality with a vigor and depth rarely matched before and not matched since. The question, all agree, is whether the changes associated with that notable decade represent a fuller realization of American ideals or their betrayal. Since the legacy of the 1960s poses so vital a question, it is no surprise that the ensuing debate—on the political hustings, in the academy, or within a collection such as this—is fraught with controversy and division.

What, finally, should we make of the rhetorical intensity of so many attempts to account for the legacy of the 1960s? Moderation, comity, and the like are sometimes rather bland virtues, and when great things are at stake, they may not be virtues at all. Barry Goldwater, the godfather of Reaganite conservatism, was not altogether wrong to insist—in his failed campaign to abort the sixties—that "moderation in the pursuit of justice is no virtue." How often is it, though, that justice is all on one side? Even the staunchest conservative in this volume is prepared to admit that justice may not be altogether on the side of those moral institutions—such as the traditional family—on which the health of our society allegedly depends.

The conservatives in this volume, as in the broader polity, have most of the fire. Those who more or less defend the sixties' revolution are, here as elsewhere, willing to concede at least some of its shortcomings. While conservatives issue their fulsome attacks on the sixties, liberal reformers seem to muster no more than qualified defenses.

Perhaps in the end this is only because so much of the reformism of the 1960s is now taken for granted, both in this volume and in the polity as a whole. In 1968 it was still possible to doubt that a divorced man could be elected president. Twelve years later Reagan's divorce mattered not a whit. Who today even knows that Bob Dole had a wife before Liddy? As for Newt Gingrich, is it conceivable that for all his hyperbole, he would really take on the sexual revolution of the 1960s?

Conservatives are levying serious charges against the world that the sixties hath wrought. Conservatives are, however, children of the sixties to a greater degree than their rhetoric suggests. The fact is that the sixties' revolution has sweepingly reconstituted the shape of lives across the political spectrum and the nation. It is simply not plausible to imagine a truly radical counterrevolution. Returning once again to Newt Gingrich, I would suggest that it is inconceivable that a truly radical revolution against the cultural changes wrought by the 1960s would be led by a House Speaker whom we might so easily imagine having breakfast with his second wife, lunch with gay Republican Congressman Steve Gunderson, and dinner with Justice Clarence Thomas and his white spouse. We should not let the unremitting urgency and sweep of the conservative attack on the sixties obscure the extent to which the legacy of the sixties is a patrimony to us all, one unlikely to be altogether renounced any time soon.

NOTES

1. As George F. Will argues in his book, *Statecraft as Soulcraft:* New York (1983), among the other conservative intellectuals developing such themes were Irving Kristol, James Q. Wilson, and Charles Murray.
2. Alan Wolfe took the opportunity to pen a draft of his essay "Books: What Cognitive Elite?", in *Lingua Franca* 5, no. 2 (January 1, 1995), p. 61.

PART ONE

———

GENDER ROLES, SEXUALITY, AND THE FAMILY

The Legacy
of the Late Sixties

HARVEY C. MANSFIELD

"Counterculture McGoverniks" is the label that Newton Gingrich placed on Mr. and Mrs. William J. Clinton, president and first lady of the United States, just after the election that made him (Mr. Gingrich) Speaker of the House of Representatives—and he did not mean to praise. In response came a lofty editorial of the *New York Times* "in praise of the counterculture," revealing by its very appearance in the nation's most prestigious newspaper how far the counterculture had become regnant. The fight is still on, and it is still both cultural and political, the site of battle being cultural, but the decision to be made politically.

If I begin by saying that the late sixties were a comprehensive disaster for America, the reader will be advised not to expect a nonjudgmental treatment framed in the weasel words of social science. I reserve my calm to measure the disaster as a whole. In describing its parts, I may occasionally be carried away. I suffered through the sixties and now live with their legacy at a university I once admired, and I feel a personal loss that sharpens the edge of my anger over what was done to our country. I do not propose to call any unfortunate individuals by the name Speaker Gingrich has used, but my sympathies are on his side.

The late sixties produced a shock throughout the Western world, but I will speak only of America, where the movement, as it was known, was active on all fronts. My purpose is to list its aspects, describe their legacy today, and connect them in concluding.

A quick survey will focus our inquiry. America is, or has been until recently, a country dominated by liberals, yet since the late sixties there have been few liberals—i.e., traditional New Deal liberals—in America. There are conservatives, radicals, and these few liberals. The conservatives are aware of the weakness of liberalism and want to correct it. Their problem is deciding whether conservatism is an entire alternative to liberalism or a mere correction. Is it necessary to make a revolution in reverse or is it better to fix things up? The radicals are also aware of the weakness—to be identified later—but they want to aggravate it. Since the late sixties they have taken over liberalism and are now the ones usually known as liberals. The few genuine liberals are unaware of the weakness of their doctrine and of the radical takeover that has made them increasingly obsolete. As Aristotle said, a regime needs to have its supporters stronger than its opponents, and the liberal regime is not meeting that test now.

Looking quickly at the state of the liberal union without liberals, we may assess the economy as good, politics as bad (until recently—November 8, 1994, to be exact), and culture much worse. The economy is in good shape partly because of the Republican presidents elected since the late sixties, especially the notable Ronald Reagan, a man who is much stupider than all professors. But mostly the economy has prospered because of foreign competition and the influx of women into the labor force, which have lowered labor costs and reduced the power of labor unions, the most reactionary force in American society.

America is a hardworking country on the whole, and on the whole that is good. A small fraction of the people live off the rest without working, the welfare dependents. But sympathy for them is salted with disdain, and almost everyone will agree to the need for "ending welfare as we know it." Working hard is not the highest virtue (unless we specify what one is working *at*), nor is it the most necessary in every society; but it is *our* virtue, the virtue of a liberal society in the generic sense of "liberal." We depart from it at our peril, and we should criticize it with great care. One should look at the economy in terms of virtue—does it put people to work and keep them saving?—rather than judge the economy in purely economic terms. Thankfully that virtue has continued strong despite the radicals of the late sixties, who despised the virtue of hard work as bourgeois false consciousness. They mounted a political and cultural assault that failed, fortunately for them, because the strength of the American economy has nourished the legacy of the radicals elsewhere in society. Had the radicals succeeded with their attack on the economy, a crisis would have ensued, and people would long ago have looked less favorably on their noneconomic prescriptions, as they have now begun to do.

Such counterrevolutionary thought that has occurred has been imperfect and incomplete, with the exception of Allan Bloom's *The Closing of the American Mind*. And amazingly popular as that book was, many who agreed with its tendency could not swallow his criticism of rock music. They were still in the grasp of that assertive era, which pretended to liberate and actually enthralled. It is with a view to a comprehensive counterrevolution, and in a spirit of unremitting hostility, from which only the Beatles will be excepted—and they only partially—that I begin a survey, seeking a principle in all the parts. Here, in a list, are the nasty things that were done in the late sixties and transmitted to us. Most or all of them had their origins well before that time, but they came into the open then with public justifications, assertions, and displays. Today they are neither so outrageous nor so violent as at first. The poison has worked its way into our souls, the effects becoming less visible to us as they become more ordinary. Even those who reject the sixties unconsciously concede more than they know to the vicious principle of liberation that once was shouted into the street microphones.

1. THE SEXUAL REVOLUTION

Any survey of the meaning of the period has to begin with its promise of sexual liberation, at once the most and the least successful of its promises. It was the most successful because it was the most avidly adopted and has had the most consequence. The promise arose from an illicit, forced union between Freud and Marx in which Mr. Marx was compelled to yield his principle that economics, not sex, is the focus of liberation, and Mr. Freud was required to forsake his insistence that liberation from human nature is impossible. So we have the importance of sex grossly magnified, as if it were the be-all and end-all of life (to be more precise, the be-*in*), and since that is not enough, it is combined with the notion that all restraint in sex is mere irrational inhibition, unconnected to the protection of anything good in human nature. Moderation or modesty is neither good in itself nor productive of good by permitting us to pursue higher pleasures than sex. On the contrary, the ideal of sexual liberation makes moderation or modesty seem foolish, prudish, and ridiculous.

Although sexual liberation has been powerful to mislead, it has failed utterly to produce better sex or more liberation. It has not brought more pleasure, either bodily or psychic. No new modes or new positions have been discovered, as one can see in the sameness of pornography in the new age and the old. The main difficulty in pornography now is to re-create Victorian conventions so as to have something inhibiting to violate. It's no fun always to encounter, in imagination, someone who knows as much as you do. Since innocence is gone, the only remaining barrier to cross is the consent of the other party, but since both are liberated, why should that be withheld? No wonder, then, that freer sex has produced more rape, just as the prudes would have predicted. No wonder too that it has worked to the advantage of men over women, the less aggressive sex. Sexual liberation has liberated the desire for power rather than sex.

The ideal of polymorphous perversity—that is, sex uninhibited by any notion of the shameful or of what is fitting—has received a rude shock from the emergence of AIDS. Perhaps you should listen more carefully to the vague menaces of your mother, if she is sufficiently unenlightened, about what happens to people who do funny things for sex. Of course this is not the official response to AIDS, which is confined to sympathy for those affected. But the lesson is too obvious to be missed by anyone but a professional in the field. Since the sixties feminine modesty has reasserted itself, though partly in the guise of feminism. There are now plenty of nice girls (and perhaps there always were), but they are confused, apologetic, and unsupported by social norms. What they get for advice is "safe sex."

Sex without inhibition is loveless as well as shameless, because love is felt as a constraint. Love limits one's options. It is better to harden up a bit so as to be able to take off when morning comes. With this attitude you forget that if you desire sex rather than conquest, you can equal the record of Don Giovanni by being and staying happily married. And to do this, you do not have to be either wealthy or an aristocrat. In fact it helps not to be either. But Don Giovanni sang beautiful songs to deceive his women. With sexual liberation there is no deceit, no seduction, no play, no nuance, no courting, no romance, and Mick Jagger instead of Mozart. There may be condoms, if you are lucky.

2. THE VIETNAM SYNDROME

The Vietnam War was America's, to be sure, but in Europe too, general hostility to the policies and even to the very idea of self-defense by liberal democracies was voiced by the activists of the late sixties and accepted by their passive followers, at least whenever it came time to act. "Make love, not war" was a slogan of the time, so we must now look at what was being rejected while the sexual gymnasts were performing their stunts.

Opposition to the war in Vietnam was not merely to that

war, nor was it general pacifism. It was wrong to carry on that war, the radicals said, because the Communists in Vietnam were not our enemy; they were nationalists, and not merely benign but progressive. The United States' effort was not just imprudent—it was not, as a general said at the time, the wrong war at the wrong time in the wrong place—but morally (meaning "absolutely") wrong, and the American military was deservedly defeated. Adorning that conclusion were certain professorial doctrines of civil disobedience and selective conscientious objection (being a pacifist only when confronting Communists) that are best buried in oblivion, even though some of them merit mention in the annals of special pleading. Other disgracefully unpatriotic statements from that time require being confessed and forgiven. Moderate opponents of the war, who were embarrassed by the radicals but went along with them can judge themselves.

The notion that communism was healthy nationalism was decisively refuted by the boat people, who left Vietnam after we did. They nobly risked their lives to escape after Americans had departed the premises. The scenes of our flight from Saigon constitute an indelible stain on our national honor, and without the aid of a monument, they will last as long as the memory of our sacrifices. We knew enough to be ashamed of that sickening event as it transpired, but now, with hindsight, we have a better view of the entire Vietnam War. We can see it as an episode in a long cold war beginning in 1945 and lasting until the sudden, unexpected collapse of the Communists in 1989.

The Communist collapse was a great victory for the West and above all for the United States, and though it was a surprise, it was not altogether unplanned or undeserved. Democratic republics have difficulty in maintaining a consistent foreign policy, said Tocqueville, yet during the post–World War II period the United States conceived and followed a consistent policy of containment against its main enemy that was wise and moderate—not too much pressure, not too little. Notwithstanding challenges, disputes and errors along the way, the policy was kept by all presidents from Harry Truman to George Bush and by both parties. The only serious opposition to the policy came from the antiwar activists of the late sixties, who did their best to destroy it but succeeded only in hobbling it with the "Vietnam syndrome." From this harmful inhibition we were freed, one hopes, by the determined action of George Bush in the Gulf War in 1991.

3. FEMINISM

Feminism, a phenomenon of the seventies and thereafter, was a child, or rather an ugly stepchild, of the late sixties. Although feminism came to view in a popular book by Betty Friedan in 1963, it started from a more serious book, Simone de Beauvoir's *The Second Sex* (first American edition in 1953). Its fundamental premises derive from three male philosophers: that sex is power (Freud and Nietzsche), that sex roles are not fixed by nature but are interchangeable (Marx), and that identity is self-creation (Nietzsche). The early feminists were mostly Marxists, or, better to say, neo-Marxists. They were radically at odds with the bourgeoisie, they believed.

Feminism began partly as a reaction against the sexual revolution, which was, as we have seen, indeed primarily for males, or rather male predators. Women were to be liberated from the kitchen and the nursery, only to be confined to the bedroom. What's in it for us?, women asked reasonably. Insofar as women wanted to be liberated from womanhood, they found some theoretical advantage in the ideology of sexual liberation. More practically, college women eagerly embraced the new idea that it was acceptable, and even desirable, for a nice girl to have sex before marriage. Since marriage was postponed by the need to start a career (= "find one's identity"), it was, apart from ideology, just too long to wait.

What feminism wants is that women be exchangeable with men. As indicated by the use of he/she for the impersonal pronoun, everywhere there's a he, there can be a she; and everywhere a she, there can be a he. In this way a woman can create her own identity liberated from the expectations that go with "woman," to say nothing of "lady." She can become independent, just like a man. What starts as opposition to manliness, machismo, and male chauvinism ends as a complete surrender to those things when it appears that the only objection to them was envy at being excluded. So feminists give themselves over to careerism and success, the same phony "autonomy," or other-directed conformity posing as self-directed creativity, that was scornfully rejected when it was labeled "bourgeois." Gone, or at least forgotten, are the feminine qualities of loyalty, tenderness, loving, mothering, and sexiness—all of which presuppose a certain withdrawal from petty career ambition. Gone too is the traditional woman's skepticism about manly achievements that had always served as a healthy corrective to the vanity of big shot males. If women do not have a nature, neither do men. The complementarity of men and women, which enables and requires them to live together and rewards them when they do, is denied or overlooked. What we get is a jumble of pushy women competing with aggressive males and sensitive men deferring to complaining females, with no sense that anything is out of whack.

Or is all this radical feminism unfairly taken for the whole of feminism? Most women are moderate feminists (and all women today are feminists of some sort). Whereas radical feminists are opposed to the family, moderates believe that it is possible to have both career and family. Their womanly nature asserts itself and is sometimes even recognized as such in the "second wave" feminism of women who do not care to insult men, still less live without them. But the moderates want the advantages of aggression without the stress of feeling and displaying aggression; they complain about a "hostile work environment" and the "glass ceiling" as if success were owed to merit without the trouble of claiming it. When success does not come to those who sit and wait for it, these independent women call in the aid of the government, and affirmative action comes to the rescue. Moderate feminism is some relief from the incivility of the radical variety, but it is less perspicacious because it is based on the delusion that you can have it both ways. Treating women as interchangeable with men has never been tried before by any society, so far as we know. It is essentially a radical idea, and all women should be aware of the fact and should look on its adoption as a risky experiment.

To sum up feminism, it has in my view produced more justice and less happiness. More justice comes from allowing greater scope and recognition to capable women than before. It is marred by the injustice of affirmative action and offset to some extent by the dubiousness of the kind of recognition that comes from the world at large rather than from one's familiars. Less happiness comes from being liberated into a *job*. Congratulations, women, on getting what you asked for! What begins as choice among pleasing possibilities ends as the necessity to earn one's living unsupported. For divorce comes easily with independence. In case of difficulty, or boredom, or attraction elsewhere, your man will readily believe what the feminists have been telling him: that you can take care of yourself. Behind every liberated woman is a liberated man.

And what of men? The feminists have mounted an attack on manliness and have attempted, by methods reminding of Tocqueville's "mild despotism," to transform it into sensitivity. "Tut-tut!" they say, you must learn to behave yourself like a woman or we will send you to a seminar to have your consciousness raised. ("Raising consciousness" is a phrase of neo-Marxist provenance.) Whether such wimps will in the event prove satisfactory to women is perhaps the question of our time. Feminism is now so well established that women do not feel the need to call themselves feminists. But will they ever reject it? Only women can undo what women have done to create sensitive males. At present manliness is allowed only to black males, but in such exaggerated form as to make it look ridiculous.

4. THE COLLAPSE OF THE FAMILY

The American family is now in an advanced state of collapse, showing unprecedented rates of illegitimacy, one-parent families, divorce, and abortion. The percentage of illegitimate births of all races has risen from 5.3 in 1960 to 28 in 1990; single-parent families have gone from 9.1 in 1960 to 28.6 in 1991; divorces have risen from 9.2 per thousand married women in 1960 to 20.9 in 1991; and abortions have gone up from an unknown figure prior to legalization in 1973 to 24.6 in 1990 as a percentage of total pregnancies. What Daniel Patrick Moynihan reported in 1965 as very bad news about black families is now also true of whites. It is hard to see how this frightening development can be unconnected to the doctrine just discussed, which urges women not to stay at home. Why cannot men stay at home half the time? you may ask. But merely to put that question shows an attitude careless of children.

The large number of abortions in recent years reveals women disposing of "unwanted children," a new concept that would be difficult to explain to the children they happen to want. What it says is that life is at someone's convenience, and it is easy to see how that idea can be extended to the care of children. That women continue nonetheless to care for their children, despite being abandoned by the fathers, shows the strength of a natural inclination that does not figure in the ideology of "choice." Nor does the abandonment of feminine modesty, in order to be equal to males, have much regard for those prudent silences and concealments which even the most confident husband has need of. My suggestion, hardly inventive but bold as crazy, is that the collapse of the American family comes from the collapse of the double standard that was intended to uphold the family, by which more is expected of women. Whatever has been subtracted from their responsibility has not been replaced by sensitive, caring males or by day care.

The radicals of the late sixties wanted to do away with

bourgeois conventions supporting the family. What they succeeded in doing was replacing those conventions with other bourgeois conventions of independence and competition once thought suitable only for the workplace and now brought into the home. The attempt to do away with conventions as such has been a total failure. Nor has any substitute been found for what is now called the traditional family. The traditional family *is* the family, undermined and diminished by being called traditional. The hippie communes of the radical era were a complete flop and are no longer heard of. We do hear frequently of same-sex marriage. Here is recognition of the family in the same idea that continues the erosion of the family, for it separates the family from children, from the complementarity of the sexes, and from shame. Same-sex marriage represents a surrender to respectability on the part of homosexuals who used to scoff at it, and still mock it—and not so wrongly either. Our conventions do need skeptics and critics because we often need reform and always need relief from the impositions of duty. But the attempt to have respectability without any accompaniment of shame is impossible.

5. DRUGS AND CRIME

The use of drugs is a plague that we cannot blame on nature or God. We have to blame ourselves. But which of us and when? You guessed it, the radicals of the late sixties. They did not invent drugs, but they justified the use of drugs as a way to free oneself from conventions. They claimed that drugs were "mind-expanding," a delusion so pathetic that one can hardly credit that it was once held. The phrase means something grander than merely opening a mind previously closed by prejudice or superstition. It means actually expanding what the mind can grasp and conveys the excitement—or, more than that, the *will to power*—in freeing oneself not only from conventions but even from one's nature. Man is an animal that naturally lives by conventions, so denying his conventions is denying his nature and replacing it with the desire to go beyond whatever has been fixed, crossing all boundaries, breaking all rules. The appeal of drugs is that of infinite power together with infinite desire. No doubt there is in human nature a yearning to rise above conventions, on occasion to get high. Previously this was thought necessary to control; now it was let loose among the young of the elite and invested with the moral superiority that comes from knowing that the system was corrupt.

The doctrine of the will to power was conceived by Nietzsche and was brought to America in a form so democratized as to make it seem bracing but still innocent. In such form the will to power lacks any appeal to a higher standard or call to redemption. Nietzsche for the American masses avoids the Nazi *Führerprinzip,* but that is because it avoids *any* demanding principle and recommends liberation understood as just letting loose. Still, the violence in the will to power remains, and it has erupted in crime. The psychedelic nonsense of the drug culture, more or less harmless for the upper middle class, was transmitted to fatherless youths in the black ghettos. To it was added the sentiment that they were justified in "ripping off" the white society—in fact, mostly fellow blacks—that had mistreated them. The added sentiment was inconsistent because the will to power knows nothing of justice, but the combination was volatile, to say the least. America has had a frightening, demoralizing increase in crime that has caught everyone's attention but is as yet unchecked.

Not only is crime more frequent among blacks, but for many of them it also has become, through the indulgence of whites, their specialty—or, in sixties lingo, their identity. Crime makes blacks threateningly, hence thrillingly different. Its romanticization by sixties whites lingers on in the diminished form of sympathy or at least toleration for criminals. How can those who experiment with drugs reproach those who are addicted except for going too far on the same path? In fact the addicts do wholeheartedly what others dare only to taste. They are guilty of "substance abuse," an accusation that confuses drug addiction with alcoholism in order to make it seem a time-honored human failing (while at the same time giving an added slap to those who hit the bottle). But alcoholism is far less destructive than drug addiction, and it is easier to control since it is the abuse of a good thing and not a plunge into measureless delusion. Alcohol is a substance for sure, but its abuse is an admitted fault that has never been defended by an ideology. Or shall we compare Falstaff on the virtues of sack to Timothy Leary on LSD?

6. ENVIRONMENTALISM

We have cleaner air and water since the late sixties, but whether *because* of the late sixties is doubtful. Nonetheless we can be thankful that the ideologues of environmentalism have not done harm to the environment and that through the costly exertions of the corporations they attacked, the pollution of nature has much diminished.

But that success was produced at the cost of an understanding of human nature. It is the *ism,* the doctrine, in environmentalism that is objectionable. Contemporary environmentalism dates from the 1962 publication of Rachel Carson's *Silent Spring,* a book of vast exaggeration beginning with the title. It was, however, Charles Reich's *The Greening of America,* another best seller published in 1970, that set forth the doctrine of the movement in "Consciousness III." Touted by Reich as the successor to conservatism (I) and liberalism (II), Consciousness III has by our time been largely absorbed by liberalism, or has absorbed much of liberalism, while Reich himself is forgotten. In his book he uses the Marxist term "consciousness" to describe a state of mind hostile to liberal progress arising from the exercise of power against nature: the conquest of nature by science or technology. Power against nature easily transfers to violence against society, and not so much in crime as in war. In Consciousness III protest of the Vietnam War was connected to protest against destruction of the environment, a link made plausible by the American Army's use of defoliative chemicals to expose enemy forces in the jungle.

To be at peace with nature was to be at peace with other men. But what about human rights? Commonly we think of human rights as claims to equality among human beings, claims that we know may have to be vindicated on occasion by the use of violence in self-defense against oppressors. Human rights are also asserted, however, in the sense of superiority human beings casually assume when they appropriate some part of nature for their use—for example, when they eat. How far is that superiority justified? It is reflected in the very term "environment," which refers anthropomorphically to what surrounds human beings as if they were nature's aristocrats, as if what matters is *their* environment. Environmentalists worry about future generations—of what? Cockroaches? It seems that man is neither so far above nature that he can forget the home where he must live nor so deeply embedded in it that he has no right to consider himself superior. By itself the environmental outlook seems as one-sided as the technological. It views nature as having no place for man, as providing no home for a mere despoiler, while in the technological outlook nature is ready to be despoiled. The two views are opposite sides of the same coin, both lacking appreciation of any problem in the relationship of man and nature. In our public schools today, thanks to the sixties, environmentalism is instilled with more fervor and authority than religion used to be. The reason is that environmentalism is dressed up as science, and in that guise it tolerates no contrary faith. It is indeed a form of *pantheism,* the diseased kind of religion demeaning to humanity and endemic to democracy that Tocqueville warned against. Environmentalism is school prayer for liberals.

Environmentalists often speak as if they wanted to make the whole world look like Yellowstone Park, but of course Yellowstone Park needs the protection of government and not only the friendly ministrations of the charming young people who work as park rangers. Despite their disdain for human artifice, itself rather artificial, in politics environmentalists are for all the devices of Big Government as America has come to know it since the sixties. Legislation on clean air, clean water, and toxic waste has produced a contradictory jumble of regulation under which businesses must pay fines for damage retrospectively declared wrongful, to escape which they must consult the government for much, most, or everything they want to do. Lest the bureaucracies prove too soft on human error, environmental organizations stand ready to flick on the engine of judicial activism, which is primed to start at a touch. Courts have imposed solutions and even selected the management to effect them with little or no regard to the cost. The standard for what is "clean" is to make the environment not usable but riskless, or nearly so. One could say that environmentalism is the name under which the present generation proposes to repeat the follies of socialism, but as usual with a sixties twist. Instead of nationalizing the modes of production, society will litigate corporations into submission. If corporations were the dragons of the sixties, lawyers were the heroes. But in practice the purpose was to distract, not slay, the dragon. Capitalism can be retained as long as it is inefficient, and government will be considered limited if only it is clumsy.

7. Rock Music

Rock achieved its dominance in the late sixties, crowding out both the classical and the popular music that had been coexisting in mutual toleration in the preceding era. To say that rock is vulgar, crude, and noisy cannot be denied, but it will be. That I know, as I said, from the reception given to the chapter on rock music in Bloom's *The Closing of the American Mind,* the most brilliant but also the least acceptable part of the book for those otherwise well disposed to listen. The reaction bears testimony to Bloom's statement of the role of rock in gaining and holding the allegiance of the young to sixties values. For we find it easier to change our opinions and even to reform our morals than to admit to having bad taste.

Rock music glorifies sex to adolescent children who are not ready for it in any way except physically. The words of the songs say what the cavorting performers indicate, both with the crudeness necessary for maximum explicitness. The deafening loudness of the music signifies a demand for total absorption and the exclusion of adults and their authority. Rock is directed to kids and against their parents, reversing the older generation's view that young love is merely puppy love imitating mature love. "Kids" is a category much enlarged during the sixties to include college and even graduate students under the mantle of adolescence, where they can claim they have not yet been spoiled by money and status. Their purity is expressed in the language and gestures of the gutter, teaching the "sexually active," as social workers call them, how to strut. Rock is sex on parade. Although it is aggressively male, even the feminists are caught up in it. They do not dare to denounce it for fear of appearing to be modest or out of step.

Beside rock, even pornography looks elegant, but what a contrast with the popular songs of the thirties at their best, say, in Cole Porter: romantic, allusive, subtle, witty, and tuneful! The Beatles are tuneful, to be sure, but they paved the way for others, like Mick Jagger, who did not try to be charming. In our time rock has descended still further to rap, consisting of stupid rhymes and foul words without a tune. While rock is mainly white, rap is a special contribution of blacks to American cultural degeneration. After having enriched music with jazz and the blues, blacks can hardly take pride in this late, untoward development.

8. POSTMODERN LITERATURE AND FILM

At first it might seem that nothing is more distant from the heady, self-righteous absolutism of the late sixties than the self-conscious, laid-back, ironic postmodernism that pervades American culture today. Yet the one has led to the other. The absolutism of the sixties was not very serious politically. From the SDS (Students for a Democratic Society) there was a call for "power to the people," also known as participatory democracy. At the same time a radical assertion of individuality made itself heard in the desire to say no to all impositions from outside oneself. "I want to control what affects me," said the draft protesters in the democratic version of Nietzsche's will to power discussed above. Here was a contradiction that reflected the amalgam of liberalism and democratism in our liberal democracy, but without reflecting *on* it. The sixties' revolution was more a rebellion of children against parents than of citizens against the government. Its assertiveness was more in style than in substance, more longhair and working-class duds than a new form of government. The New Left, rejecting the establishment, did not have an alternative; it lacked the organizational skills, the staying power, and the ruthlessness of the Old Left. It hoped to change politics by transforming culture rather than through the dictatorship of the proletariat.

Thus for all its certitude those who put their faith in style left their principle to individual creativity or whim. Of course in practice whim was fashion, as it just so happened that all the little rebels put on the same clothes, read the same comics, and lurched to the same rhythms. A stylized revolution, when it lost its first steam, soon became relativized. The counterculture made its peace with bourgeois comfort and capitalist marketing, all the while realizing it was doing so. The irony of a merely cultural revolution that left capitalism in place became apparent, and the yuppie was born. A revolution that did not believe in itself began to believe in style and its intellectual equivalent, the point of view.

This is not the place to analyze postmodernism; let it suffice to mention some qualities of modernity according to one's point of view. We now see many movies about movies, to make us aware of the politics of the moviemakers. Clint Eastwood's *Unforgiven,* for example, is a western about westerns in which the hero gets away with murder. The hero, typically, does not demand our admiration but only makes us aware of the relativity of heroism. As a reflection on westerns this movie is also a reflection on America, suggesting that the West—for which one can read the New World of liberal modernity—was not won justly for the sake of civilization but unjustly for the powerful. Postmodernism is all irony, heavy and obtrusive. Nothing is meant seriously, and everything is said in quotation marks, with self-conscious deprecation. In our day many people have lost the ability to make a straightforward statement of fact, and they answer the simplest question about everyday things they certainly know in an interrogative tone as if open to challenge from a contrary point of view. Behind all the effortful intellectualizing of postmodern culture in rock music and film are thoughtful works of literature that show the need to escape from the point of view. Don DeLillo's *White Noise* is an impressive example. Martin Amis's *The Information* is another. But the point of view of the point of view leaves no distinction between art and life, hence no elevation of art over ordinary life, and no refinement either. The result is democracy in celebration of the quirky in contrast with the commonplace, a culture of self-satisfied dissatisfaction calling itself a counterculture and living off its proclaimed enemy.

9. THE UNDERCLASS

Poverty is nothing new, but Lyndon Johnson's War on Poverty was new. Here was an attempt to do away with an endemic human condition by means of government programs that would pay, house, and employ the formerly poor. The ambition shown in the attempt to do something never done before no doubt accounts for Johnson's name for the enterprise, the Great Society. But because the Great Society did not call for greatness on the part of the benefactors, still less the beneficiaries—because in fact it tried to make life easier all around—the name is a misnomer. The Great Society was a revamping of the New Deal, which had already been directed to the relief of the needy without any provision that they also be worthy. This failure to require or even to encourage any sense of independence or responsibility in the poor, while making them gifts, was a feature of Johnson's program too. Responsibility would come to the poor unforced and unbidden after they had ceased to be poor.

But there was a special contribution from the acolytes of the late sixties, which was to insist that the poor should not feel embarrassed about going on the dole. The work of debasing the morality of the poor was the special office of young lawyers and social workers who helped the poor overcome their inhibitions against signing up for benefits. The poor were given to understand that honesty and pride in work were malicious conventions of the bourgeoisie and that they had an entitlement from a caring government to be lifted out of poverty without being obliged to take any action of their own. Thus the poor became an underclass of government dependents, increasingly both hapless and vicious as the various programs designed to remedy their poverty failed, one by one and together. At present the streets of American cities are decorated with beggars, degraded unfortunates who are living memorials to the welfare state and its moral teachers.

10. THE POLITICIZATION OF EDUCATION

Speaking of teachers reminds me of the corruption of American education that was produced by the sixties' ideologues. The loss of standards has been evident at all levels, but the rot began at the top, in higher education. The turn occurred when professors sympathetic to students protesting the Vietnam War began to conduct "teach-ins" to express their solidarity with those draft-deferred student victims. At first such meetings were held outside regular classes, but soon those classes too became teach-ins in effect. At first too the practice was confined to a few radical professors, but it spread to the moderates, who bowed to the radicals' demand that education become *relevant*.

Relevance meant relevant to the students' lives that were dominated by the potential compulsion to fight in a war they did not believe in. But more generally the demand for relevance began from an accusation that the objectivity of scholars in refusing to take, or even to declare, sides in a moral or political debate had served to reinforce the status quo. Objective scholars were "complicit" in the crimes being committed against the Vietnamese people or, more generally, in the oppression they claimed merely to observe. Here was Nietzsche's perspectivism at work, destroying the role of the university as an independent critic of democratic society. It now became the university's role to advance democracy—that is, to make democracy more democratic—which it proceeded to do after the war was over by promoting feminism. With the imposition of the feminist agenda relevance was transformed into sensitivity. Women are too prudent to want to rely on exhibition and strident rhetoric for making their point; such behavior also makes them uncomfortable. It is much better to get men to correct themselves by raising their consciousness and making them sensitive. So the raucous hubbub in the universities during the late sixties has been succeeded by unnatural quiet in the decades following. But the cause of the quiet was the same as of the uproar: the politicization of education, which soon descended from universities to schools. Politicization leads immediately to the lowering of standards in education because standards are meant to be objective measures. If a teacher believes that such measures are in principle impossible, or not relevant, he has insufficient motive to insist on them even though the discrimination of more able from less able students seems to be central to his daily life of teaching. The grade inflation that dates from the late sixties is the clearest sign that teachers do not take their jobs seriously. Since an appreciative eye is always a critical eye, one could even say that despite their claims, teachers under the regime of grade inflation do not care for their students.

At present the greatest respect for merit in American society has to be found not in the universities but in sports, the least intellectual arena. Of course much brainpower goes into the game in all its phases, but not for the sake of celebrating the mind. Still, the college football team is the most honest part of the university: It cheats only to improve itself. In sports no one thinks of affirmative action. No one except relatives of the players watches female sports because the athletes are not as good as males. People do watch women in sports such as gymnastics, in which the activities reveal a particularly feminine grace as opposed to doing the same thing as men less well.

11. AFFIRMATIVE ACTION

Why did the protest of the late sixties come when it did? Since the movement was worldwide, a full answer would have to draw from the world. But in America one factor in the explanation would have to be the example set by the civil rights revolution in the early and middle sixties. The civil rights revolution showed that protest against unjust laws can succeed without violence, indeed by provoking violence from the authorities defending injustice. Compulsion exercised by the federal government against the states was more evident to the states than to the revolutionaries. To the latter, the moral and political lesson of the civil rights movement was the severance of law from justice, thus the delegitimation of law. Judicial activism from the same period taught the further lessons that law would always adjust to whatever seems just and that protesters did not have to gain the consent of the majority. One could ignore law when it obstructed morality and then use it without restraint in the service of morality.

Affirmative action is an instance of law both delegitimated and overused. It says that law against discrimination does not work, yet the government applies more coercion to force it to work. As now appears increasingly to be understood, affirmative action is a corruption of civil rights. Instead of providing a right that is then the responsibility of the individual to exercise with his own abilities, affirmative action gives the recipient a helping hand, a preference that substitutes for the exercise of a right on one's own. Thus affirmative action transforms responsible individuals who deserve rights because of their capabilities into beneficiaries who deserve them to compensate for (it is hoped) temporary incapacity. The demeaning effect is obvious, and indeed, affirmative action is more harmful for its injury to pride than for its injustice.

Affirmative action had its start under Lyndon Johnson in 1965 but received its great impetus from the Nixon administration. Its principle comes from the sixties' belief, once again having its origin in Nietzsche, that human beings are historically created. Humans do not have fixed natures or faculties that supply them with the equipment to rise on their own, once freed from oppression, nor do they have an inner, natural spark of freedom that fires their indignation and ambition without help from outside. Those made by history are determined by history, and the result for blacks is: Once a slave, always a slave. That point is never made explicitly, of course, but it is conveyed by the patronizing liberal welfare state, which reserves places for its less capable dependents, those who could not compete for what they get. To be defined by one's history is to be defined by one's "roots," a term now in vogue. That definition turns attention from where one is heading to where one has been. No wonder, then, that the sixties' designation of "blacks," associated with "black power" and self-affirmation, has degenerated into "African Americans," a name that reminds blacks of their descent and their former servitude. What starts out as self-affirmation for blacks ends as being affirmed by someone else and as victims to boot.

12. EGALITARIANISM

A more general evil coming from the sixties is to have converted the American Constitution into an engine of egalitarianism. All parts of the government have shared in this perversion, but the federal judiciary has been in the lead. Here there is room only to discuss briefly the principle under which the change was made. The principle says that equality does not mean equal rights, but rather equal *exercise* of rights, or equal *power* to exercise rights. For it claims that rights are not equal unless the power to exercise them is equal. But if people have equal power, then they do not need equal rights because the result of exercising one's right is already guaranteed in the primary condition of equal power. That is why this equality is known as equality of result, in contrast with equality of opportunity. Then, in order to reach an equality of result, those without equal power must be *equalized*. To equalize becomes the first duty of government.

The idea of equalizing opposes the *formalism* of rights under liberalism, a quality altogether essential to them. The formality of a right protects the freedom to exercise it, for if the content of a right is specified, one is no longer free to use it as one wills. For example, a right to free speech cannot specify what is to be said, nor can a right to vote say how one must vote. If the government tries to equalize the speakers so that each has equal power with his speech, or the same with the vote, then the government curtails or takes away the right by trying to prescribe how it must be exercised. A right is no longer a right if its exercise is prescribed so as to make all rights equal in fact and all citizens equal in power. The equality of rights in liberalism requires, and resides in, a toleration of their *unequal exercise*. A voting rights act that seeks to give minorities equal voting power, or the demand for sensitive speech to equalize respect for women and men, are examples of sixties egalitarianism hostile to liberalism. When Karl Marx denounced the formality of the rights of man, disparaging them as merely rights of the bourgeois, he knew he was attacking liberalism. But our complacent liberals swallow his criticism and think themselves unaffected.

With these strong words I have emerged temporarily from my normal modest seclusion to give an idea of the measureless harm that came from the late sixties, especially from the principles of the late sixties. Admittedly I have not shown sufficiently why those principles were so attractive; I leave that task to others in this volume. It is not that people now practice those principles in their most extreme form. But they do not know why the principles are wrong, and often they do not even recognize them in their moderate form. One needs to think about the radical ideas in order to judge them when they are diluted and widely held.

I can now summarize. The twelve items listed have in common the loss of distinction or distinctiveness in our culture and politics: between permissible and impermissible sex; between democracy and communism; between men and women; between respectability and the lack of it; between reasonable relaxation and getting stoned; between humanity and nature; between music and noise, or between children and adults; between art and life; between freedom and dependency; between education and propaganda; between having dignity and being patronized; and between an equal individual and an equalized automaton.

Distinctiveness requires inequality, as nothing is distinctive unless it has more or less than something else. The same is true of "diversity," today's approved term that tries vainly to describe variety without admitting inequality. But there is no diversity without inequality. Nor can there be diversity if people are not willing to make distinctions—to be "judgmental." Nor can diversity exist if toleration is expanded to mean "inclusion"—that is, approval or respect of everyone and everything. One cannot approve of everything unless all is the same.

Our liberal democracy is a mixture of equality and inequality, with the accent on equality to be sure. We hold to the practice of equal rights, but the meaning of such rights is the freedom of unequal exercise. The weakness of liberalism to which I alluded at the beginning is that of necessity it seems to promise more equality than it can deliver, more than it can *want* to deliver. Hence liberal society always needs to be governed sensibly, reasonably, and moderately in the spirit of liberalism. There can be no liberalism without liberals; its weakness prevents it from working automatically. It needs people who can understand the weakness and turn it into strength, because a strong, free people is one that is always working at freedom.

Where are the liberals? Today most of them are called conservatives, a fact probably connected to a thirteenth item I could have mentioned, the takeover of the Democratic party by McGoverniks in 1969–70. The McGoverniks are still in evidence, the open, active legacy of the sixties. The rest of it is working its way through the system and, let us hope, out of it, like a powerful toxic waste. Nature's purgation operates through the conservatives of various kinds who have recently come to the fore. The so-called liberals are being defeated by their enemies, but liberalism is being saved.

Feminism: Where the Spirit of the Sixties Lives On

JEREMY RABKIN

Bob Dylan, who certainly knew a lot about "the sixties," said it was ultimately "about clothes." It was about dressing up—or dressing down. As it happens, it is among a certain category of women that the spirit of the sixties has been most lovingly nurtured and faithfully preserved. Of course the female penchant for dressing up does not explain the perpetuation of sixties radicalism in the feminist movement. But there may be a partial explanation in the background: Dressing up is much more accepted in women than in men.

The different strands in that political and cultural maelstrom called the sixties certainly have fared quite differently in the ensuing decades. For the most part the rebellious youth of the sixties grew up and went to work in the seventies. By now warnings against "selling out to the system" are long forgotten, as aging baby boomers worry over mortgages, stock plans, and investment retirement accounts. Few now talk about "social welfare," for which we were called upon in the sixties to "reorient our priorities." Everyone is now focused on budget deficits and burdens on the taxpayer. The Cold War has finally ended, but no one now sings about "peace." Only feminism still inspires the same spirit of shrill denunciation and nonnegotiable "demands." Only feminism still sets itself up for endless battle against "oppressive social structures."

So the Clinton administration, celebrating itself as the

generation of the sixties finally come to power, turned out to have no idea what direction to pursue in foreign policy, no clear message about civil rights, no remedy to suggest for the plight of the inner cities. But it was determined to have a female attorney general—even if it took three tries to get one. Aircraft carriers and marines are now regularly dispatched to the shores of wretched tropical countries, sometimes inflicting serious destruction, sometimes taking casualties of their own. No one in the Pentagon seems to have the slightest concern about what peace protesters or radical critics may say of these missions. But the admirals still tremble at accusations that navy fliers engaged in sexual harassment during the course of a drunken party in 1991. Feminism lives.

Feminism alone has maintained the fire of sixties radicalism thirty years later. Part of the reason may be that feminism did not seem quite so threatening to the larger society as other aspects of the sixties. It was not "taken seriously," in many ways. But even in this respect feminism was not so removed from the general character of the youth rebellion of the sixties.

The most striking thing about the sixties was that so much defiance and rebellion could emerge amid so much prosperity and security. The sixties were above all a revolt of the privileged and the overprivileged. That is why it was so much a matter of fantasy and escapism—of dressing up. Adolescents rebelled against their parents by refusing to cut their hair. Student radicals directed most of their rebellious animus against university administrators—for the most part mere bureaucrats with archaic titles ("provost," "dean") who turned out to be the most spineless "authority" figures in the whole country. A few steadfast administrators, like President Edward Levi at the University of Chicago, actually called in municipal police against students who were occupying and "trashing" administration buildings. Everyone was then shocked to discover that student radicalism might, after all, prove dangerous to the students involved. The shootings at Kent State in the spring of 1970 were altogether traumatic. Students had been chanting about "revolution" for some years by then; many students even cherished posters on their walls featuring the saying of Mao Zedong "Power comes from the barrel of a gun." But none of this prepared the student left for the possibility that people might actually get killed in their own "revolution."

Feminism has taken on the sixties' attitude of angry defiance underwritten by the confidence that no serious consequence will follow from this defiance. Feminists protest endlessly about oppression. They do not fear that their protest will bring retaliation and repression. Not really. The daddies of feminist daughters will still pay their college tuition; their boyfriends and husbands will still help support them; the government will never use force to stop them. It is all a kind of dress-up. It rests on the absurd notion that "the battle of the sexes" could actually be conceived as a serious war—as if men would do battle on behalf of the male people (or the male class? the male race?) against their own mothers, wives, and daughters.

Feminism, by its own terms, proposes an unrelenting struggle against an opponent that can't really fight back. Even strong men quail at the prospect of facing down angry women. Men are not actually supposed to fight women, not even supposed to call them names. The men are not intimidated so much as disoriented and humiliated at the prospect of confronting angry women, which is perhaps only to say that they are intimidated without quite having to admit to themselves that they are.[1]

Feminism may finally have become too sectarian and silly, too permanently mired in the fantasy world of the sixties to endure as a potent political force. For the past three decades, though, it has been a showcase for the least attractive impulses in the radicalism of the sixties.

Marxian Modes

There were, of course, feminists in America long before the 1960s. There were political radicals long before the 1960s too.

For that matter, there was abuse of narcotics in America many decades before the 1960s. Part of what was distinctive about the sixties was simply a matter of scale. What had once been confined to marginal sects or secluded elites became mass phenomena, broadcast to the whole nation by attentive (or wide-eyed) news media.

But it was not just numbers or scale that made the trends and movements of the sixties so distinctive. Above all, there was a different political atmosphere. There was, after all, a women's movement in nineteenth-century America. It waged successful campaigns for legal reforms, such as allowing married women to own property in their own names. In the early part of this century women's organizations played a central role in the political struggle that culminated in the Nineteenth Amendment (1920), guaranteeing women the right to vote.

The women who led these earlier movements were, however, highly respectable Republicans on most issues, preaching self-reliance and abstemiousness, along with equality.[2] Many of the same women who assumed prominent roles in the suffragist movement were equally prominent in the temperance "crusade" (against the sensual dissolution of alcohol consumption). The two movements indeed triumphed at almost the same time: the Eighteenth Amendment, establishing national Prohibition, was ratified only a few months before the women's suffrage amendment was adopted. For decades thereafter the tone of the older women's movement was echoed in the high-minded (and curiously nonpolitical) admonitions of the League of Women Voters.[3]

The feminist movement that was born in the 1960s had, from the outset, a very different tone. It flaunted its radicalism with a new slogan: "Women's Liberation!" It was meant to evoke comparison with the struggles of third world "liberation movements" and with the revolutionary spirit of the People's Liberation Army in Maoist China. To put the point succinctly, the old women's movement appealed to American traditions of individualism and self-reliance; the new "women's liberation" movement drew on the Marxist rhetoric of the New Left.

Of course few student radicals of the 1960s were very serious about Marxism. Then again, their heroes—whether celebrated in posters, like Che Guevara, or in paperback reprints like C. Wright Mills—did not much trouble themselves over the second and third volumes of *Das Kapital* either. The truth is that the New Left changed almost from year to year in the course of the 1960s, as it shifted its focus to new issues and rode the tide of a tumultuous decade. But from the founding of the Students for a Democratic Society (SDS) in 1962, one of the defining novelties of the *New* Left was its disdain for the anti-Communist "rigidity" of the older generation of democratic socialist.[4] Whatever else it was, the New Left was "open" to the arguments and analyses of the Marxist left. By the late 1960s national conventions of the SDS were clearly much influenced by self-avowed Marxist-Leninists, including the very bizarre Maoist faction originally organized as the Progressive Labor party.[5]

The women's liberation movement, growing out of the student left, appropriated Marxian formulations or the Marxian style of analysis from the outset. There was a certain logic to this, since Marx and Engels had openly mocked the "bourgeois family" and promised that the abolition of private property would also put an end to the subjection of women to male possessiveness. As late as the mid-1920s, when Ludwig von Mises first published his great critical study *Socialism,* he thought it necessary to include a whole chapter on feminism as one of the modern outgrowths of socialist fulmination.[6] But by the late 1960s Marxist analysis was less a learned discipline for student radicals than a rhetorical style that could be picked up on the run. Women's liberation picked it up and kept running.

Marxists taught that all conflict was ultimately reducible to, or derived from, the one master conflict between the possessing and the disposed classes; class conflict became the matrix of all conflict. Theorists of women's liberation adopted this same model, all conflict reduced, in their view, to the conflict between MEN (as a distinct "class") and WOMEN (as an equally distinct "class"). They dismissed as secondary or unimportant the particular marital disputes or lovers' quarrels that might arise over differing religious commitments, over differing tastes, even over divergent views about money or child rearing. It was not even worth distinguishing gentle and sympathetic men from bullies and wife beaters. As Shulamith Firestone and Ellen Willis put it in a 1969 "Manifesto," "Women are oppressed as a class. Our oppression is total, affecting every facet of our lives. . . . *All men* [original emphasis] receive economic, sexual and psychological benefits from male supremacy. *All men* [original emphasis] have oppressed women."[7]

Naturally, then, women's liberation also took up the Marxian teaching that tensions are not to be eased by compromise or finessed by indirection. Seeing "power" and "domination" at the bottom of all conflict, the theorists of women's liberation insisted that sexual conflict could be "overcome" only by means of struggle, struggle, and struggle. The need of the hour was "consciousness raising," a derivation from the Marxist term for agitation to instill "class consciousness" as the prelude to revolutionary activity. In the words of the Firestone-Willis "Manifesto," "Our chief task at present is to develop female class consciousness. . . . We call on our sisters to unite with us in struggle."

Some women adopted "political lesbianism" to demonstrate their independence of men. Others proceeded to champion the "clitoral orgasm" and other demands that would have made a true Leninist blush.[8] The whole argument reached its logical culmination in the brilliant and utterly demented tirades of Andrea Dworkin, purporting to demonstrate that all heterosexual intercourse is essentially rape: "The measure of women's oppression is that we do not take intercourse—entry, occupation, penetration—and . . . say what it means to us as a dominated group. . . ."[9]

Not even many feminists were prepared to take their doctrines of inherent male oppression quite *this* seriously (if "serious" is the right word for such thinking). It has become common practice, therefore, to dismiss the wilder aspects of women's lib as pardonable hyperbole and then generously to credit the movement—"for all its excesses"—with having placed important issues on the public agenda. But this soothing approach misses the point. Contemporary feminism is not so much about calling attention to problems faced by women as it is about *defining* "women's issues." And the women's liberation movement of the sixties defined those "issues" in ways that have left a permanent mark on public policy and public debate on "women's issues."

To cite the most obvious example, feminists have relentlessly hammered at the fact that "women make only 59 cents for every dollar earned by men" (or 49 cents or 71 cents or whatever the "fact" may be for the publicist of the moment).[10] But most couples pool their earnings to support themselves and their dependents. How does the income available to families with dependent children (or dependent elderly parents) compare with the income of individuals or of couples without dependents? This question is rarely pursued because modern feminism is not interested in the well-being of families. It is obsessively focused on comparisons between women as an abstract class as against the equally abstract class of men, abstracting, most of all, from the fact that the majority of women still live in families, where the overall family income is presumably more important than particular male-female earnings comparisons.

Public policy has tended to follow the vision charted by radical feminists. So, for example, Congress changed the tax laws in the 1970s to allow child care expenditures as a deductible expense. Meanwhile, despite the high inflation of that decade, Congress made no effort to readjust the value of the fixed general deduction for dependents. Families in which the mothers stayed at home to care for the children were in effect made to subsidize families with working mothers, though the latter families (in most cases) were already benefiting from a second income. The cause of "women" simply trumped the needs of families without any serious debate on the conflicting claims involved.

The claims of families were easily lost as feminists gained more and more sway over public policy in the 1970s. The continuing feminist penchant for class analysis—discussing all "women" as a class—was only part of the reason, however. Another was the feminist penchant for utopian thinking, which encouraged a view of social concerns in which the stability of family life was not of much importance.

In Flight from Reality

The notion of a "class struggle" between the sexes was one appeal of Marxian rhetoric. Another was the scientific pedigree it seemed to provide for utopian expectations of "social revolution." It would be more accurate, however, to say that talk of "revolution" spread through the student left in the late 1960s because utopian expectations were already in the air.

Young people did not remember the hardships of the Great Depression or the sacrifices of World War II. What they saw was technological progress and economic growth, seemingly advancing with inevitable, almost effortless momentum. What they saw in the mid-1960s was a federal civil rights effort that seemed to have put an end to decades of brutal segregation and black disenfranchisement in the space of a few short years. What they saw was a whole series of ambitious initiatives from mainstream politicians, promising to put an end to poverty within a generation, to revitalize decaying cities with "urban renewal," to ensure security and peace of mind to the elderly with guaranteed medical care. It was a decade in which the federal government pledged to take Americans to the moon—and actually did it.

Sad realities have doused most of the visionary hopes of the sixties. It has been a long time since anyone bothered to ask the question, so popular in the early 1970s, If we can put a man on the moon, why can't we . . . end poverty, revitalize our cities, satisfy our social ambitions? The answers now seem obvious: Social realities are not so easily redrawn as rocket designs. But the women's liberation movement was launched amid the boundless confidence of the sixties: "This was a movement without limits."[11]

Indeed, the remarkable thing about the women's liberation movement was that it took off at the very moment—the first years of the Nixon administration—when the original student left was collapsing into confusion and despair. "While men . . . were miserable with the crumbling of their onetime movement, women were riding high . . . faith remained [among women's advocacy groups] that history was beginning afresh, that the Revolution (now in its feminist incarnation) would work out the 'correct' answers and resolve all 'contradictions.' "[12] To a remarkable degree, feminists kept this faith alive in the ensuing decades.

The two most remarkably visionary projects of women's liberation were the complete emancipation of sexuality, on the one hand, and the dismissal of family obligations, on the other. Earlier generations had thought women required exactly the opposite. Suffragists at the turn of the century, for example, argued that women should be given the vote because "only a female electorate would see to it that laws were passed for the protection of the family." They urged "establishing an equality between the sexes by bringing both under the sway of Victorian morality," urging men "to treat all women with respect . . . to maintain the law of purity as equally binding for men and women."[13]

Women's liberation began with the opposite vision, one of liberation from all restraint. The vision was most unshrinkingly expressed in Shulamith Firestone's crackpot classic of 1970 *The Dialectic of Sex: The Case for Feminist Revolution,* which demanded "the defusion of the child-bearing and childrearing role to the society as a whole." Firestone enthused over the sexually liberating consequences: "[I]f the male/female and the adult/child cultural distinctions are destroyed, we will no longer need the sexual repression that maintains these unequal classes. . . . In our new society, humanity could finally revert to its natural 'polymorphously perverse' sexuality—all forms of sexuality would be allowed and indulged. . . ."[14]

Not many went quite this far. Yet the vision of liberating women from sexual constraint remained a cherished one. Partly it was an inheritance of sixties radicalism: "In the mid-Sixties, the sexual revolution surged through the New Left as everywhere else. . . . to women as to men, easy sex felt like freedom. . . ."[15] Sexual liberation was seen as a rejection of hypocritical "bourgeois conventions." Yet it was also embraced as a demonstration of women's independence, a demonstration that women could behave as wantonly as men, if they chose.

Within a decade feminism began to display what some observers described as a "new Puritanism" about sex.[16] Feminists began attacking pornography as a promoter of violent and degrading attitudes toward women. They began to focus on the problem of "date rape," by which women were forced or pressured into sex by their overinsistent boyfriends. Feminists demanded and often won campus codes under which "rape" was defined to encompass almost any sexual act that did not receive full, sympathetic endorsement from the woman—even in retrospect.

Yet feminists have insisted on making the whole issue turn on consent so that virtually no sexual conduct can be condemned if it does receive "consent."[17] Men (including teenage boys) are told in effect that sex is perfectly all right if the woman (or the teenage girl) is willing, but the woman must have the absolute right to call a halt at any time. But how do women say no if their refusal rests on nothing more than their whim at the moment? Not surprisingly, then, even in the 1990s—after decades of feminist rhetoric about "empowerment"—sex educators report that the question most often asked by teenage girls is how to say no to their boyfriends without hurting their feelings.[18]

The women's liberation movement began with a brutally simple answer to the problem of unwanted consequences from sexual liberation: It demanded the lifting of all restrictions on abortion. In 1973 the Supreme Court was persuaded to impose abortion on demand as the law of the land.[19] The number of abortions rose dramatically. But so did the number of births to unwed women. Feminists refused to acknowledge this as a problem, though it became increasingly apparent that female-headed households were often disastrous for the children.[20] As late as 1991 feminists reacted with indignation when Vice President Dan Quayle gave a speech warning of the dangers of trying to raise children without two parents. He was denounced for trying to impose morality on women who chose a different lifestyle—as if choice were the only issue or as if it were in the power of women to choose anything they might like.

The readiness to waive away the problem of child care— by "restructuring the family"—was another utopian aspect of the women's liberation movement from the outset. The SDS Women's Liberation Workshop of 1967 wanted to liberate children along with their mothers: "We call for . . . creation of communal child care centers which would be . . . controlled by the staff and children [!] involved in each center."[21]

Even the "Statement of Purpose" adopted at the founding of the National Organization for Women in 1967, while eschewing the most radical rhetoric of the era, still called for "a different concept of marriage."[22] NOW claimed to "reject the current assumption that . . . a woman is automatically entitled to lifelong support by a man upon her marriage. . . ." It looked for "new social institutions which will enable women to enjoy true equality of opportunity and responsibility in society, without conflict with their responsibilities as mothers and homemakers." How was this "conflict" to be avoided? By a "nationwide network of child-care centers. . . ."

In fact the NOW statement, which was drafted by some actual mothers, shrank from the full implications of its own rhetoric. It could not quite bring itself to urge that mothers take no time off and make no concessions regarding career ambitions when their children were very young. But its rhetoric about "true equality of opportunity" and its complaint that women were earning "on the average only 60 per cent of what men earn" invited just this conclusion. And this has now become the norm among a large segment of career women.

As Mary Eberstadt has recently documented,[23] parental advice books now feel obliged to pretend that there is no real harm in having both parents pursue their careers at full tilt because "quality" time can be scheduled at odd moments (or bedtime stories read into tape recorders for self-playback by the lonely child), and anyway, it is good for children to learn independence. These soothing assurances are unlikely to be true. And they are not quite believed, even by career women themselves, who spend much time worrying over whether their children are not, after all, being cheated or abused.[24] There was a wave of hysterical accusations about supposed sexual abuse in child care centers in the mid-1980s, almost all of which turned out to be unfounded.[25] Like most incidents of mass panic, however, this one was probably an indication of underlying anxieties.

Back in the 1920s even advocates of women's equality acknowledged that women ought to stay at home when their children were very young. A recent history notes that even the most "equalitarian feminists" in the National Woman's party of that era "never attempted to develop an ideology which would help women integrate work outside the home with marriage and children. . . . NWP members' 'solution' to this problem was available only to middle and upper middle class women who could afford to pay for household help."[26]

As President Clinton's difficulties in finding a female attorney general revealed, "household help"—now imported from Central America and paid for without the bother and expense of covering Social Security contributions—still remains the choice "solution" for the most affluent career women. For the rest there now is an "ideology" to help soothe guilty consciences. But the power of "ideology" seems not quite sufficient to answer the stress of balancing child rearing and full-time employment.

Women who train for ambitious careers before marriage

do often face very awkward choices if they try to take time off for child rearing. But feminism was imbued from the outset with the sixties' conviction that life need not involve any awkward choices. Society can be "restructured" to do away with awkward choices. Implicit in this from the outset was the notion that the family was an institution ripe for restructuring. As the implications of this have become more apparent, they have naturally provoked more resistance on the part of people who don't want to be restructured. The feminist response, in the manner of the sixties, has been to respond to resistance with more and more coercion.

MILITANCY TRIUMPHANT—OR OBLIVIOUS

The Marxist rhetoric of sixties radicals may have been no more than a pose. For most student radicals, celebrations of totalitarian figures like Mao and Fidel were perhaps just another party mask in the carnival atmosphere of the time. But no one can deny that student radicals became addicted to bullying and intimidation as a mode of "politics." Whether taking over buildings or hounding professors of opposing views, campus radicals came to see almost any tactic as justified to get their way. In the end only a small minority continued into bombings and mass violence. But the whole atmosphere of the late sixties encouraged a highly uncivil outlook, combining the arrogance of ideologues with the swagger of youth.

Feminism has never quite broken from the spell of the sixties. Certainly feminism has retained the conceit of sixties radicalism to having a privileged insight into truth. For the youth of the sixties the slogan was "Don't trust anyone over thirty"— as if young people alone possessed the unblinded vision to recognize the world's ills and the unquestionable right to make the world over again. For feminists, there is a comparable slogan: "They just don't get it"—as if disagreement could have no basis other than obtuseness. Feminists have struggled since the late sixties to force their understanding on the obtuse many who still "don't get it."

And feminists now claim to have a special understanding about almost everything. Women's studies programs have proliferated an entire set of new disciplines. There is feminist anthropology, feminist political theory, even feminist international relations. These are not simply "disciplines" that seek to focus more attention on trends or factors that particularly affect women. They claim to be a whole new approach to understanding the world. So of course there is a new discipline of feminist epistemology, stressing the "connected" thinking and "shared understandings" supposedly unique to the female half of humanity. A recent critical study of these programs—by two female professors who are in effect academic refugees from women's studies—sums up the underlying ambition:[27]

> Feminism . . . bids to be a totalizing scheme resting on a grand theory, one that is as all-inclusive as Marxism, as assured of its ability to unmask hidden meanings as Freudian psychology, and as fervent in its condemnation of apostates as evangelical fundamentalism. . . . It regards the male's (usually: the white male's) insistence on maintaining his own power as the passkey that unlocks the mysteries of individual actions and institutional behavior. And it offers a prescription for radical change that is as simple as it is drastic: Reject whatever is tainted with patriarchy and replace it with something embodying gynecentric [sic] values.

The relentless insistence on the uniqueness of the feminist understanding is, as the authors of this study note, "graphically illustrated by the widespread exclusion of male authors from course syllabi, assigned reading lists and citations in scholarly papers."[28] Not only do women's studies programs exclude men, but they try to limit faculty participation to feminists of approved views.[29] Others are hounded and shunned and treated as enemies. Women's studies programs make few pretenses of concern with academic rigor, openly insisting on their political aims,[30] as if all scholarship were simply politics by other means—as it was, of course, in totalitarian societies like the old Soviet Union.

This is not simply the outlook of jargon-ridden pedants in the isolated world of academe. Feminists have in fact been remarkably successful in imposing their ideological vision even in elementary and secondary schools. In California the state Education Department demands in its Education Code, "Whenever an instructional material presents developments in history or current events, or achievements in arts, science or any other field, the contributions of women and men should be represented in approximately equal numbers."[31] So, under the pressure of such feminist demands, textbooks now devote extensive space to utterly obscure and marginal figures because they happen to be women (one widely used history text devotes more attention to sixteen-year-old Sybil Ludding-ton, who tried to alert colonial soldiers to a British raiding party, than to Paul Revere, more attention to nineteenth-century female astronomer Maria Mitchell than to Albert Einstein, and so on).[32] History is rewritten to satisfy feminist sensibilities: Women *should* have been central to science, art, and politics, so texts must present them as if they were.

Almost as striking as the attempt to rewrite history has been the attempt to reconstitute language, another hallmark of totalitarian societies. Even without the resources of a totalitarian state, feminists have been remarkably successful in forcing the switch from traditional usage to politically approved terminology. The very term "sex" has been displaced to a large extent by "gender," a term suggesting that differences between the sexes are as arbitrary as rules of grammar. The term is virtually required in universities. Also, to a large extent, in government. The federal Equal Employment Opportunity Commission issued guidelines not long ago, quoting the agency's own organic statute—the Civil Rights Act of 1964—

as if it prohibited "gender discrimination" rather than "sex discrimination."[33] Law reviews now routinely employ the generic "she"—as in "The judge may instruct *her* clerks to . . ." or "The governor may exercise *her* pardon power." Not all legal scholars choose to express themselves in this way, but student staffs will rewrite the author's text to ensure a politically correct style. Even business correspondence routinely addresses women with the feminist coinage Ms. Though many women prefer to be called Mrs. (or even Miss), the assumption is that feminists will be offended by the use of traditional terms and more traditional women will just accept the new etiquette.

With so many easy victories, feminists seemed genuinely shocked to discover by the mid-1970s that they could still be successfully opposed. The feminist Equal Rights Amendment to the federal Constitution, endorsed by Congress in 1972, amid a welter of feminist self-congratulation, failed to gather the necessary approval of enough state legislatures. Despite increasingly intense efforts from feminist organizations, no states at all ratified the ERA after 1977, and several states that had earlier voted to ratify voted thereafter to rescind their acts of ratification. While feminists tried to blame the political opposition on male conspiracies, the "obvious if unpleasant fact" was that the opposition drew almost all its strength from the efforts of vocal and determined women.[34]

That large numbers of women opposed the feminist venture is hardly surprising. With all its talk about "sisterhood" and "female solidarity," feminism was always contemptuous of the sacrifices and priorities of more traditional women. What else did it mean to purge elementary school texts of images of women as housewives and mothers? What else did it mean to insist on rewriting high school history texts to inflate the role of obscure women scientists, artists, or publicists? What else did it mean—except that feminists thought traditional women's roles to be humiliating and contemptible ("poor role models")?

A recent study of the opposition to the ERA highlights just this reaction: "[M]any opponent women distrusted change sponsored by feminists who seemed to think marriage, love, babies and families restrictive and burdensome. . . . Feminism seemed to demean what women traditionally had valued. . . . The images, behaviors and goals that had helped traditionalist women understand what being female meant were proscribed."[35] Feminists, who had spent years demanding (and winning) changes in language, culture, and etiquette, to ensure a more favorable atmosphere for career women, now insisted that the ERA was simply about preserving choice and would not force any woman to do anything she did not want to do. They seemed genuinely surprised that opponents did not want to accept this sort of "choice"—with the larger cultural signals all controlled by feminists disparaging such choice.

Yet even when the strength and depth of opposition had been revealed by the ERA debate, feminists could not restrain themselves from pushing ahead, virtually rubbing their opponents' noses into the ground. One of the most potent issues of anti-ERA forces was the question of whether women would be drafted into the military and then forced into combat roles if all "discrimination on the basis of sex" were prohibited. Whatever their views about "equality of opportunity" in the abstract, very few women wanted this sort of "equality," with all its relentless obliteration of "gender roles." Feminist leaders refused to allow amendments or understandings to the ERA that would have made an exception for the military.[36] Indeed, feminist lawyers pressed the argument to the Supreme Court that the equal protection clause of the Fourteenth Amendment should already have been seen as a prohibition against an all-male draft; the Supreme Court rejected the argument in 1980—but by only one vote.[37] Feminist lawyers similarly urged the Court to strike down a California law imposing penalties for "statutory rape" involving female minors (under age sixteen) but not males.[38] Again they failed (by one vote) but in the meantime displayed their determination to defy the views of the overwhelming majority of Americans.

The most painful and destructive episodes of feminist arrogance, however, emerged in the debate over abortion.

From the outset of the women's liberation movement its advocates demanded ready access to abortion. When the Supreme Court acceded to this demand in 1973, it naturally provoked an intense opposition. Feminists were not content to defend the Supreme Court's ruling in *Roe v. Wade,* which in itself imposed the most extreme abortion policy in the Western world. They then demanded government funding for abortion as a constitutional right, an argument that failed in the Supreme Court by one vote.[39] As opponents of abortion won state and local measures to discourage the practice, feminists resisted every such measure. They would not tolerate any hint, no matter how indirect, that recourse to abortion was an extremely serious matter that ought at least to be surrounded with safeguards against impulsive decisions. A one-day waiting period was successfully challenged, along with a requirement that women be informed of alternatives to abortion or that husbands or parents of minors be informed before an abortion was performed.[40]

The opponents of abortion believe it is the taking of human life, as indeed, the majority of Americans continue to believe. Here again, while feminists denounce sexism and patriarchy as the source of abortion restrictions, the depth and energy of the right-to-life movement actually come from other women. Of course they are different kinds of women, as Kristin Luker documented in her attentive sociological study of the abortion debate in the mid-1980s. She found, from survey research, that pro-choice women tend to be "educated, affluent, liberal professionals whose lack of religious affiliation suggests a secular 'modern' . . . outlook on life. Similarly the income, education, marital patterns and religious devotion of pro-life people suggests [*sic*] they are traditional, hard-working people ('polyester types' to their opponents) who hold conservative views on life." While "pro-life women have *always* [original emphasis] valued family roles highly and arranged their lives accordingly . . . pro-choice women postponed (or avoided) marriage and family roles because they chose to acquire the skills they needed to be successful in the larger world, having concluded that the role of wife and mother was too limited for them."[41] Luker thus concluded that "the abortion debate has become a debate about women's contrasting obligations to themselves and others . . . it is a referendum on the place and meaning of motherhood."[42]

With all their talk of "sisterhood" and "solidarity," the feminist movement has been utterly unable and unwilling to make even minimal gestures toward the women on the other side. Thus, while the Supreme Court in recent years has begun to accommodate some regulation of abortions, feminists have continued to denounce even the slightest concessions to opposing views. Feminists have demanded that Congress enact a federal statute to overturn every new state or local restriction on abortion now permitted by the Supreme Court.[43]

Having won so much so quickly, feminists have not been overly concerned about the discipline of constructing a viable long-term movement. They have done so well from extremism that they have not had to temper their rhetoric or reconsider their aims. In truth they have not been forced to be very serious and have not shown much inclination to be so.[44] That is another thing feminism has in common with the spirit of the sixties.

SERVING THE FEMALE SELF

"Feminism," noted one academic observer, is "the most legitimate heir to the Sixties idea that the personal is political. . . ."[45] The observation is entirely valid, though not entirely flattering to feminism.

Student activists in the sixties treated their personal concerns as if they were a matter of inherent political importance. As even sympathetic chroniclers of the sixties have admitted, the posture of student radicals was partly a matter of "narcissism."[46] Student radicals did not conceive themselves to be training for a lifetime involvement in leftist political causes;

they imagined that their own student demonstrations *were* the cause.

Narcissism both reflected and reinforced an underlying lack of seriousness. Students were unalterably, passionately, furiously against the war in Vietnam by the late sixties. If a hundred thousand students had demonstrated the depth of their opposition by going to prison rather than submit to conscription, such a protest would have staggered the country and placed an impossible strain on the administrative machinery of the draft. But few actually went to prison. Fewer still submitted to induction (though they might have rallied a very destabilizing degree of opposition from within the ranks of the military if they had). The war was left to be fought by working-class boys who did not have the privilege of a college deferment from the draft. Indeed, antiwar fervor among students (who could become eligible for the draft on graduation) actually subsided markedly when the government shifted to an all-volunteer force in the early 1970s.

Radical students liked to see themselves as victims—and gave themselves a lot of license to protect themselves on this theory. When campuses erupted into protest in the late sixties, the first call (almost invariably granted) was for amnesty of those breaking university regulations by occupying buildings. The second call was for suspension of final exams since the commotion of protest would make it too difficult to study (or to recover from study time lost to protest activities).[47] This demand too was frequently granted.

The women's liberation movement picked up where student radicalism left off and pursued the game to hysterical extremes. In fact Betty Friedan had trumped all bids even before the opening of the real game in the late 1960s. Her 1963 best seller *The Feminine Mystique* protested "the problem that has no name." She then described the plight of suburban housewives as analogous to the horrors experienced by the inmates of Nazi concentration camps (the home of "the American suburban housewife" may be "a comfortable concentration camp"), seeming to suggest that "genocide" might, after all, be appropriated to answer the "name" problem.[48]

The angriest "libber" of the late sixties could not expect to top this rhetoric. But radical feminists tried to stay in the same league itself. They regularly compared the plight of women with that of blacks in the segregated South, oppressed colonial peoples, starving masses in the Third World. Despite their penchant for Marxist-style analysis, they did not often compare the plight of women with the plight of workers. Men are workers too. The point was to establish that women had it worse, vastly worse, than male factory workers or manual laborers or other sweating males of the proletariat.

The rhetoric of women's liberation was akin to a rhetorical tantrum by its privileged practitioners (almost invariably white, educated, and of affluent background). "Stop belittling our problems!" they said. "Don't keep looking at the problems of the hungry or the wretched or the oppressed masses somewhere else. Look at us! Look at me! We're suffering right here! I'm suffering!" It was never pretty. But it was remarkably effective.

Even the ostensibly "moderate" National Organization for Women protested in its founding "Statement of Purpose" that "There is no civil rights movement to speak for women, as there has been for Negroes and other victims of discrimination." NOW was not organized, however, to protect women against police dogs and firebombings in southern towns. Its statement began with the call to "bring women into full participation in the mainstream of American society." A bit farther along it zeroed in on "the *decision-making* mainstream of American political, economic, and social life." Finally it demanded, in the same statement, not merely access to the highest levels of authority but guaranteed quotas: "[W]omen . . . must demand representation according to their numbers in the regularly constituted [political] party committees—at local, state, and national levels—and in the informal power structure. . . ." Women "must have the chance to develop their fullest human potential."[49]

In other words, women were entitled to special preferences. Which women would be likely to receive them? How
many working-class women—or working-class men—could
hope to "develop their fullest human potential" amid the immediate pressures of keeping their children fed? If "women" had
to be given reserved spaces in party organizations, would they
likely be uneducated, working-class women or educated,
affluent women? If the latter, would they "represent" the concerns even of women from lower economic strata or from different ethnic groups—more so than men from these lower
strata or these marginalized groups?

NOW was, in fact, attacked by more radical groups for
being hopelessly white and middle-class. Nonetheless the
Democratic party bowed to NOW's demands in the early
1970s, instituting a 50 percent quota for female delegates at
presidential nominating conventions (with much smaller quotas for various ethnic minorities). And it was of course white
middle-class women who ended up having the largest impact
on public policy. After all, they were often married to (or living
with) white middle-class men and almost always the daughters
and sisters of such men.

So too a large part of the energy of federal civil rights
enforcement shifted in the 1970s from the concerns of blacks
and other ethnic minorities to the concerns of women. When
the federal government began to experiment with affirmative
action requirements in the late 1960s, it reasonably focused
attention on the problems of black workers kept out of construction trades by close-knit unions. Construction jobs were
paying high wages but did not require extensive training. It
was a plausible way to help a shut-out group gain a foothold in
economic security. Feminist groups almost immediately protested the failure of the federal government to pursue affirmative action against universities, where, it was said, women
were shut out. Faculty jobs at universities were not a promising path of upward mobility for struggling racial minorities.
They nonetheless received a remarkable priority in government enforcement efforts.[50]

It soon became clear that women were kicking on an open door, not only in universities. Women raised in affluent suburbs, women who had received every educational advantage, still qualified for "affirmative action." Universities and other employers could boast of their commitment to affirmative action at rather low risk by hiring women. The beneficiaries, at least at universities, have overwhelmingly been women.

In their determination to see themselves as oppressed, feminists bludgeoned a range of institutions into establishing special standards for women. Only prejudice, it was said, prevented women from entering the military academies. In due course, during the 1970s, Congress bowed to feminist pressure by opening the academies to women. Very few had the physical strength to perform drill requirements imposed on men, so the standards were simply lowered for women.

At the same time feminist groups began to protest sexual harassment. Women, we were told, are quite able to participate in combat. It was only outdated patriarchal prejudice to think otherwise. But women exposed to locker room talk were presented as humiliated and degraded and intolerably oppressed, so special protective machinery had to be geared up across the nation to protect them.

The women's movement protested the exclusionary "old boys network" that prevented women from breaking into high positions. But it was utterly silent—or else applauded "advances for women"—when men used their "network" connections to get fancy jobs for their wives. Call it the Hillary Clinton syndrome. It has become an accepted pattern in Washington: A senator is simply expected to get a fancy administrative or staff job for his wife. It has spread to universities, where academic stars bargain with prospective employers to hire their wives (or in some cases, their husbands) in "package deals."

Most astounding is the proliferation of women's studies programs. They have become totally autonomous precincts. As the most self-conscious manifestation of contemporary feminism they might be expected to be the most thoroughgoing and serious. But of course they are the very most silly and self-indulgent aspects of contemporary feminism. Women with actual careers in the real world must temper their ideological nostrums to the demands of reality. Women's studies programs have created an alternate universe, exempting themselves from the demands of academic scrutiny (such as they are), even from the most elementary standards of logic, evidence, or the principle of noncontradiction.[51] It is a world of nonstop whining, self-promotion, and agitprop in which critics are dismissed as "hostile" and contrary facts can be made to disappear by ideological airbrushing.

The extraordinary self-indulgence of contemporary feminism does not, however, represent a degeneration of a movement that once held high ideals and made tough demands on itself. It should have been expected from the tone of the original women's liberation movement of the sixties. Starting from the premise of women as a class oppressed by men as a class, feminism was launched amid self-dramatizing narcissism. It was the most natural thing for women of this character to throw tantrums, not to notice how selfish they were being, to aggrandize more and more. Succeeding in aggrandizement, they indulged totalitarian or coercive impulses. They have come to think they deserve to have it every which way. And why not? Often enough they have succeeded in having it every which way.

The only remaining mystery is, Why are they so angry?

PATHOS OF PATRIARCHY

The anger of the women's movement is perhaps not quite so mystifying after all. Feminists have not gotten everything they sought in the last twenty years. Most notoriously they failed to get the requisite number of states to ratify the Equal Rights Amendment. They have finally begun to lose ground in the debate over abortion rights. Both the anti-ERA and the anti-abortion forces largely reflected the efforts of other women, who mobilized against the stances of the feminists. Most women have been leery of identifying themselves with the angriest and most crazed of the feminists. Reason enough for professional feminists to throw new tantrums and denounce a sinister "backlash" (sponsored, as they see it, by "men"—who else?).[52] And, of course, anger serves the interest of assertive groups; it is a good mobilizing tactic.

But there remains a core of rage among feminist activists, an insistence on seeing the world through the wrong end of a broken scope, which is hard to understand. In this too there is an ultimate, ironic link to the spirit of the sixties.

The sixties erupted after two decades of peace and prosperity. In retrospect, it seems to have been too much comfort and security for the rising generation of Americans to digest. Hard times do not produce ecstatic, escapist movements. Dadaism and free love had some appeal amid the prosperity of the Roaring Twenties but vanished quite abruptly amid the mass unemployment of the Great Depression.

The young rebels of the sixties proclaimed themselves in revolt against the smug complacency of the previous decade. They surely underrated the effort it took their parents to build the secure, affluent world in which they grew up. But they were no doubt sincere in their frequent protestations against the vapid cheeriness of suburban family life. In a world preoccupied with deodorants and hair sprays, the young people of the sixties cultivated torn jeans and ragged looks. In a world preoccupied with tidiness and politeness, they relished wild gatherings and foul language.

In the 1830s Tocqueville had already noted, with a hint of aristocratic disdain, the American obsession with what came to be called creature comforts: "Everyone is preoccupied caring for the slightest needs of the body and the trivial conveniences of life."[53] While he observed that "the desire to acquire the good things of this world is the dominant passion among Americans," Tocqueville also marveled at the contrary phenomenon, the willingness of Americans to travel vast distances, through much hardship, to hear revivalist preachers and sometimes to attend to "strange sects": "Religious madness is very common there." Tocqueville thought this paradox illustrated a larger truth: "The soul has needs which must be satisfied. Whatever pains are taken to distract it from itself, it soon grows bored, restless and anxious amid the pleasures of the senses." Americans were just not well situated to deal with this problem: ". . . their social condition, circumstances and laws . . . so closely confine the American mind to the search for physical comfort" that when Americans have once "broken through these limits, their minds do not know where to settle down, and they often rush, without stopping, far beyond the bounds of common sense."[54]

One need not be especially romantic or inclined to mystical reflection to see in the spirit of the sixties a sort of misplaced spiritual quest: The student activists wanted life to offer more than an endless accumulation of comforts. But they lashed out with so little thought or focus that they ended up being swallowed by the culture they sought to challenge. The sixties began with a rebellion against commercialism and ended by making commerce of rebelliousness. As clothing fashions shifted to tie-dyed shirts and worn jeans, department stores soon accommodated with "homemade" tie dyes (which were mass-manufactured) and with new jeans having a worn, faded ("stone-washed") look, also produced by machines. Rock music and drugs were an expression of defiance against the established culture; they ended as big businesses, funding ever more lavish lifestyles for the profit makers. One need not chalk this all up to the frivolousness of the sixties. The most serious of the young people were up against forces quite a bit stronger than adolescent idealism.

Feminism has had a similar trajectory. It was born amid a feverish protest against contemporary society—indeed, against almost all known societies through all recorded history. Women's liberation was supposed to put an end to the possessiveness, acquisitiveness, and selfishness of male-dominated society. It has ended by encouraging women to be as acquisitive and selfish as men. ("It's my body and I can do what I like with it!") It started with the Marxian rhetoric of class but has been heard as the irresistible demand of individualism in a country already gasping from the excesses of individualism.[55]

Nothing perhaps better illustrates the strange misguided quest of feminism than its constant tirades against "patriarchy." As it happens, the most famous patriarchs in history—Abraham, Isaac, and Jacob—were not overbearing tyrants to their wives, at least according to the biblical account. If anything, it is the matriarchs who seem to make the decisive interventions in the central story.[56] The story of the patriarchs is not about the power of men over women but about the preoccupation of parents with their children and their descendants—and the power of God to confirm inheritance and rebuke its betrayal.

It is particularly strange that American feminists should rage against patriarchy as America has had so little patriarchy. Tocqueville noticed this in the 1830s. "In America family, if one takes the word in its Roman and aristocratic sense, no longer exists. . . . [A]s soon as the young American begins to approach man's estate, the reins of filial obedience are daily slackened. . . . At the close of boyhood, he is a man and begins to trace out his own path."[57] Tocqueville attributed much of this loss of paternal authority to the fact that young men in America expected to strike out on their own and make their own fortunes, rather than depend on the land or wealth of their fathers. But he also pointed to the whole changed outlook of a modern, democratic culture:

> When men are more concerned with memories of what has been than with what is, and when they are much more anxious to know what their ancestors thought than to think for themselves, the father is the natural and necessary link between the past and the present, the link where these two chains meet and join. In aristocracies, therefore, the father is not only

the political head of the family but also the instrument of tradition, the interpreter of custom, and the arbiter of mores. He is heard with deference, he is addressed always with respect, and the affection for him is ever mingled with fear. When the state of society turns to democracy and men adopt the general principle that it is good and right to judge everything for oneself . . . paternal opinions come to have less power over sons.
. . . [A]mong democratic nations every word a son addresses to his father has a tang of freedom, familiarity and tenderness all at once. . . .[58]

In a country with so little sense of continuity, deference, or respect, feminism railed against straw men. And blew them down. Universities, guardians of the intellectual traditions of the West, turned themselves upside down to provide pampered havens for "Gynecentric Thought." Courts, entrusted to uphold the majesty of law and the principles of constitutional government, threw all caution to the winds, overturning the abortion laws of fifty states, in their eagerness to satisfy feminist demands. Legislators and administrators, vested with the moral authority of "the people," could hear only the feminists, on one issue after another. And still feminists were angry. Might they have been less angry if men with more self-confidence had stood up to them earlier?

It is only fair to notice that American leaders have rarely been very self-confident or very good at standing up to sudden new currents in public opinion. That was also one of Tocqueville's themes, more than 150 years ago. Given the relentless individualism of American life—and the relentless democratic skepticism about romance and ideals—Tocqueville thought it remarkable that American family life remained so orderly. He attributed this admirable stability almost entirely to the heroic qualities of American women, praising them as exceptionally clear-headed, self-sacrificing, and far-seeing in their comportment and conduct. If "anyone asks me what I think the chief cause of the extraordinary prosperity and growing power" of America, "I should answer that it is due to the superiority of their women."[59]

It may be that such qualities are not to be expected of any large group of Americans in the last part of the fevered twentieth century, not even women. But even when Americans were more accustomed to the praise of heroic virtue, they retained a respect for homely truths—in other words, a sense of humor. It may have made Americans less open to the appeal of grandeur. It still left them some grip on reality. Even amid the genuine heroic sacrifice of the Civil War, Lincoln's favorite humorist Artemus Ward observed: "There's a good deal of human nature in man." He phrased his salute to women a bit differently from Tocqueville: "The female woman is one of the greatest institutions of which this land can boast."

Like much else about the sixties, feminism has been notoriously lacking in humor. ("Q: How many feminists does it take to screw in a light bulb? A: That's not funny.") It is hard to spare a breath for laughter when huffing with self-importance. "Patriarchy" in America did not even have the strength to face down the most relentless and destructive aspects of feminism. It has hardly dared to complain of the most silly and self-serving aspects of feminism. The main battles against feminism have been fought by women.[60]

But feminism finally seems to have carried on for too long to be treated with the awe and respect it received for more than decades. It still faces no solemn patriarchs in its path. But it is having great difficulty responding to the mirthful mockery of Rush Limbaugh (who is no one's idea of a "patriarch"), the sizzling satires of P. J. O'Rourke, and a growing list of un-PC comics. The worst excesses of feminism may now be ridiculed into oblivion as other pretensions of the sixties were long ago. It would be funny if this proved to be the deathblow to the political power of feminism. Almost a dirty joke. But lots of things about sex really are funny. Dirty jokes certainly have a more secure future than feminism.

"Lighten up! Chill out! Get a life!" Sometimes this is good

advice. It is certainly advice that follows in a long tradition of American democratic impulses. But these particular expressions seem to have entered popular usage only *after* the sixties.

NOTES

1. Christina Hoff Sommers, *Who Stole Feminism?: How Women Have Betrayed Women* (1994), p. 135, reports the opinion of "competent women academics" she consulted on "the failure of men—especially male deans— to stand up to feminist ideologues and their projects. . . ." Their explanation: The men "wished to avoid unpleasantness." These are women who know men (especially the "nice" sort who administer universities).
2. For example, Elizabeth Cady Stanton, in her last great speech to the National Woman Suffrage Association in January 1892, argued that the "strongest reason why we ask for woman a voice in the government under which she lives . . . is because of her birthright to self-sovereignty; because, as an individual she must rely on herself." Emphasizing the need for full education to provide women with self-confidence, she invoked the plight of the "girl of sixteen, thrown on the world to support herself, to make her place in society" who must rely on "native force or superior education . . . to resist the temptations that surround her and maintain a spotless integrity. . . ." She then proceeded to elaborate the argument by appealing to the challenges faced by the "young wife and mother" expected "to manage a household, have a desirable influence in society, keep her friends and the affections of her husband, train her children and servants well. . . . An uneducated woman, trained to dependence, with no resources in herself, must make a failure of any position in life." "The Solitude of Self," reprinted in *Man Cannot Speak for Her: Key Texts of the Early Feminists,* ed. Karlyn Kohrs Campbell (1989), vol. II, pp. 373– 74, 377–78.
3. See the somewhat despairing "social feminist" analysis of the LWV in Naomi Black, *Social Feminism* (1989).
4. Martin Sklar and James Weinstein, "Socialism and the New Left," *Studies on the Left* (March–April 1966) complained that the Communist party U.S.A. had simply "mimicked American liberalism" since the initiation of the Popular Front strategy in the 1930s but then explained: "Anti-communist socialists fare no better with the new Left, despite (maybe because of) their tireless reiteration that they are the 'democratic Left.' This is in part because they lack any convincing intention of transforming American society, a condition which flows from their gradual acceptance of American democratic capitalism as preferable to Communism as it has developed in

Russia." Reprinted in Loren Baritz, ed., *The American Left: Radical Political Thought in the 20th Century* (1971), p. 420.

5. In fact, the lurch to the left started in the mid-1960s, well before the "traumas" of 1968 and the most intense period of American involvement in Vietnam that supposedly drove student radicals over the edge. The social democratic League for Industrial Democracy, which had helped launch SDS in the early 1960s (arranging, for example, to make the UAW's Port Huron campground available for the student activists who drafted the ensuing "Port Huron Statement"), severed all ties with SDS at the beginning of 1966 to protest the organization's refusal to exclude self-avowed Communists from membership and its insistence on "cooperating with Communists in anti-Vietnam war protests." By August 1966, SDS had voted down a proposal at its national convention to require Communist party and Progressive Labor party leaders to disclose their dual party affiliations when running for offices in SDS, even after "the blatant fear was expressed that members of PL and CP would try in the coming year to take over SDS or use it as a recruiting ground. . . ." Edward Bacciocco, Jr., *The New Left in America, from Reform to Revolution* (1974), pp. 175, 182.

6. Ludwig von Mises, *Socialism,* tr. J. Kahane (1981), ch. 4, "The Social Order and the Family."

7. "Redstockings Manifesto," reprinted in Miriam Schneir, *Feminism in Our Time: The Essential Writings, World War II to the Present* (1994), pp. 127–29.

8. In fact Lenin himself did blush. In 1920 he told the German Communist agitator Clara Zetkin, "In the sphere of sexual relations and marriage, a revolution is approaching. . . . Nothing could be falser than to preach monastic self-denial and the sanctity of the filthy bourgeois morals to young people. However, it is hardly a good thing that sex, already strongly felt in the physical sense, should at such a time assume so much prominence in the psychology of young people. . . . I am an old man and I do not like it. I may be a morose ascetic, but quite often this so-called 'new sex life' of young people—and frequently adults, too—seems to me purely bourgeois and simply an extension of the good old bourgeois brothel. . . . The revolution . . . does not tolerate orgiastic conditions. . . . Promiscuity in sexual matters is . . . a sign of degeneration." Zetkin, "My Recollections of Lenin," in Miriam Schneir, ed. *Feminism: The Essential Historical Writings* (1992), pp. 339–40.

9. Andrea Dworkin, *Intercourse* (1987), p. 133.

10. As Hoff Sommers notes (*Who Stole Feminism?,* pp. 238–241), the figure is constantly revised and in any case "highly misleading," since it compares aggregates of people with very different levels of training, experience and career commitment; for young people with comparable training and experience, male-female earnings ratios differ by less than 10 percent, according to a recent economic study (241).

11. Sara Evans, *Personal Politics: The Roots of Women's Liberation in the Civil Rights Movement and the New Left* (1980), p. 206.

12. Todd Gitlin, *The Sixties: Years of Hope, Days of Rage* (1987), p. 374.

Feminism: Where the Spirit of the Sixties Lives On 77

13. Barbara Leslie Epstein, *The Politics of Domesticity* (1983), pp. 129, 127. The latter phrases ("to treat women with respect . . . maintain the law of purity . . . for men") are taken from a pamphlet issued in the 1890s by the Social Purity Department of the Woman's Christian Temperance Union, which was already urging women's suffrage in that era as a means to advance its broader goals.
14. Shulamith Firestone, *The Dialectic of Sex: The Case for Feminist Revolution* (1970), pp. 236–37.
15. Gitlin, p. 371.
16. The charge has been most insistently made by Camille Paglia (see, e.g., "Rape and Modern Sex War" in *Sex, Art and American Culture* [1992]): "The women of my Sixties generation . . . sought total sexual freedom and equality. . . . Today's young women . . . see that feminism has not brought sexual happiness. The theatrics of public rage over date rape are their way of restoring the old sexual rules that were shattered by my generation" (51–52). But as Paglia points out, contemporary feminism still refuses to acknowledge that this is what it is doing because it is so committed to the idea of freedom—and the idea that sex can be "sanitized" of its wilder passions.
17. So, for example, my own campus, which has a draconian system for policing sexual harassment, has no rule against sexual relations per se between professors and students. Our senior sexual harassment counselor, a well-known feminist scholar, reported to a faculty meeting that she had been contacted by anxious faculty members on this point and had assured them that professor-student sexual relations are not prohibited so long as there is no abusive "power relation" involved.
18. Barbara Dafoe Whitehead, "The Failure of Sex Education," *Atlantic Monthly* (October 1994).
19. As Mary Anne Glendon, *Abortion and Divorce in Western Law* (1987) has demonstrated, this gave the United States the most extreme abortion law in the Western world.
20. For a review of the evidence, see Barbara Dafoe Whitehead, "Dan Quayle Was Right," *Atlantic Monthly* (April 1993).
21. The SDS women also thought homemaking would soon take care of itself: "Ultimately technology and automation will eliminate work which is now necessary for the maintenance of the home." "An SDS Statement on Women's Liberation," *New Left Notes* (July 10, 1967), p. 4; reprinted in Schneir, *Feminism in Our Time*, p. 105.
22. Reprinted in Schneir, *Feminism in Our Time*, pp. 96–102.
23. Mary Eberstadt, "Putting Children Last," *Commentary* (May 1995).
24. The contrary evidence has been marshaled by psychologist Selma Fraiberg, *Every Child's Birthright: In Defense of Motherhood* (1977). Betty Friedan in *The Second Stage* (1981) was sufficiently rattled by the book to cite it by name and then complain that it did not answer the problem of women who were forced to work by economic necessity (259–60). She then proceeded to inflate the argument to a parody of Marxist economic determinism: "As capitalism itself created the conditions that could overthrow it, by creating the vast armies of exploited individual workers . . .

so capitalism in its advanced stage has created the new, irrepressible armies of feminism" (299). There is some truth in the argument insofar as housing prices, private school tuitions, and other middle-class amenities increasingly came to be adjusted to demand levels created by two-earner families. But Friedan herself had originally urged the need for women to work, as a matter not of economic necessity but of "self-realization" or "self-actualization": ". . . even if a woman does not have to work to eat, she can find identity only in work that is of real value to society—work for which, usually our society pays." *The Feminine Mystique* (1963), p. 334. The 1981 version of the argument reflected an evident defensiveness about the costs to others in having mothers of young children pursue full-time careers.

25. For the most recent retrospective on this episode of mass panic, which does not hesitate to describe it as hysteria, see Ruth Shalit, "Witch Hunt," *New Republic* (June 19, 1995), pp. 14–16.

26. Susan D. Becker, *The Origins of the Equal Rights Amendment: Feminism between the Wars* (1981), p. 264.

27. Daphne Patai and Noretta Doertge, *Professing Feminism: Cautionary Tales from the Strange World of Women's Studies* (1994), pp. 183–84.

28. Ibid., p. 5.

29. Both Sommers and Patai-Doertge complain at length of this tendency and provide numerous examples from personal experience.

30. The preamble to the constitution of the National Women's Studies Association (the professional organization for the discipline) openly proclaims its political aims: "Women's Studies owes its existence to the movement for the liberation of women; the feminist movement exists because women are oppressed. . . . Women's Studies, then, is equipping women . . . to transform the world to one that will be free of all oppression."

31. Cited in Sommers, p. 62. Similarly, a study of new high school texts in literature and social studies in the mid-1980s found "certain themes just do not occur. . . . Hardly a story celebrates motherhood or marriage as a positive goal or as a rich and meaningful way of life." Paul Vitz, *Censorship: Evidence of Bias in Our Children's Textbooks* (1986), p. 73.

32. Sommers, p. 58.

33. "EEOC Guidelines on Discrimination because of Sex," 29 CFR 1604.11 (1992).

34. Donald G. Mathews and Jane Sherron Hart, *Sex, Gender and the Politics of ERA* (1990), p. 153.

35. Ibid., pp. 152–53.

36. Jane J. Mansbridge, *Why We Lost the ERA* (1986), pp. 84–86. Mansbridge reports a similar pattern with respect to abortion: Pro-ERA advocates condemned opponents for claiming that the ERA would force federal funding of abortions, while feminists proceeded to argue at the same time that even the existing Constitution should be read to do so, thus strengthening the warnings of ERA opponents (122–27).

37. Rostker v. Goldberg, 453 U.S. 57 (1981).

38. Michael M. v. Sonoma County Superior Court, 450 U.S. 464 (1981). This was a particularly telling challenge since the law does not restrict any

woman's opportunity to do anything (unless it is the "opportunity" of sexually active teenage girls to become involved with older men without risking any legal sanctions on the men). Feminists attacked the law not on the basis of "choice" but solely on the ground that differential treatment of males and females should not be tolerated in the law.

39. Maher v. Roe, 432 U.S. 464 (1977); Harris v. McRae, 448 U.S. 297 (1980).
40. Planned Parenthood of Central Missouri v. Danforth, 428 U.S. 52 (1976); Akron v. Akron Center for Reproductive Health, 462 U.S. 416 (1983); Thornburgh v. American College of Obstetricians, 476 U.S. 747 (1986).
41. Kristin Luker, *Abortion and the Politics of Motherhood* (1984), p. 199.
42. Ibid., pp. 192–93.
43. The Court signaled its more accommodating approach in Webster v. Reproductive Health Services, 109 S.Ct. 3040 (1989). The proposed Freedom of Choice Act to overturn *Webster* was first proposed in 1990.
44. Friedan's *The Second Stage* is virtually the exception that proves the rule: She deplored the divisive emphasis on abortion rights in feminist politics, but her cautions seem to have made no difference at all to feminist political priorities in the 1980s.
45. Morris Dickstein, "After Utopia, the Sixties Today," in *Sight on the Sixties*, ed. Barbara L. Tischler (1992), p. 17.
46. For example, Gitlin, p. 5, notes: ". . . the New Left resolved to be a student movement and a left at the same time. Twenty-two year olds set out to change the world. Starting from such ambition, the movement oscillated between narcissism (imaging itself to be the instrument of change) and self-disparagement (searching for the *real* instrument of change). . . ."
47. In the spring of 1971, during my freshman year in college, I was puzzled by the fretfulness of older students as our final exams drew near. It turned out that most had never taken final exams in the spring semester, as campus convulsions had brought their cancellation in the previous two years. Our exams took place as scheduled that spring. The sixties were finally over.
48. Friedan offers an entire chapter (12) on "Progressive Dehumanization: The Comfortable Concentration Camp." Later she writes: "If we continue to produce millions of young mothers who stop their growth and education short of identity, we are committing quite simply genocide [!], starting with the mass burial of American women and ending with the progressive dehumanization of their sons and daughters."
49. Schneir, *Feminism in Our Time,* pp. 96, 97, 102.
50. On the initial deflection of affirmative action enforcement to women's concerns regarding universities, see Hugh Davis Graham, *The Civil Rights Era: Origins and Development of National Policy* (1990), pp. 408–19; on the deflection of enforcement efforts to feminist concerns, see Rabkin, *Judicial Compulsions* (1989), ch. 5.
51. A recent study, purporting to defend "feminist international relations theory," thus concludes: "I have argued that to have meaningful identities and to query them too situates us as appreciators of the many ways we stand in a space or a moment of identity and look at other identity allegiances within ourselves and our context of knowledge with an empathetic-critical

gaze. This gaze keeps us somewhat unsurefooted by defying the fixed 'I.' It also dispels fears about those who would colonize us by providing the resource of mobility that enables us to be many things at once, to be elephants and el(l)ephants. The empathetic cooperative gaze can divest IR's nostalgic gender settlements of power by infusing them with the knowledges that come from listening to and engaging canon-excluding and canon-including subjectivities." Christine Sylvester, *Feminist Theory and International Relations in a Postmodern Era* (1994), p. 213. Alas, the passage is by no means taken out of context. Nor is this book unusual in its genre, which has become terrifyingly vast: Our campus bookstore now offers twice as many books on "women's studies" as on European history.

52. The most famous purveyor of the "backlash" doctrine is Susan Faludi, *Backlash: The Undeclared War against American Women* (1991). Its numerous factual misrepresentations are challenged in Sommers, ch. 11, "The Backlash Myth."

53. *Democracy in America*, ed. J. P. Mayer (1969), vol. II, part ii, ch. 10, "The Taste for Physical Comfort in America," p. 530.

54. Ibid., ch. 12, "Why Some Americans Display Enthusiastic Forms of Spirituality," pp. 534, 535.

55. In fact antifeminist women viewed feminists as trying to impose male norms. Opponents of the ERA, according to one study, "believed that being a woman demanded female solidarity lest males and their values threaten, punish or corrupt women within their own world. . . . Women who endangered this sisterhood and behaved like men were strike breakers of the worst sort. . . . To their opponents, they were angry, foul mouthed, lesbian (masculine), mean, arrogant, elitist, self-centered or aggressive— to select a few recurring adjectives. These personal characteristics could also be read as competence, self-confidence and dedication to a goal, that is, things valued by feminists. Such qualities could also be read as characteristics commonly identified with the masculine ideal and that is the way many women read them. . . . Feminists could deny that equality is sameness, but, when identified with work as self-fulfillment or as economic independence, it seemed to make demands on women that many thought masculine." Mathews and Hart, pp. 168–69.

56. It is Sarah who persuades Abraham to send away Ishmael to secure the inheritance of Isaac (Genesis 21:9–14); it is Rebecca who arranges the deception by which Isaac is induced to give his main blessing to second-born Jacob, securing Jacob's inheritance (Genesis 27:5–18); it is Leah and Rachel who fortify Jacob's decision to leave their father, Laban, and return to Canaan, and Rachel who underscores the meaning of this return by snatching away her father's household idols (Genesis 31:14–17, 19, 34–35).

57. Vol. II, part iii, ch. 10, "Influence of Democracy on the Family," p. 585.

58. Ibid., pp. 587–88.

59. Vol. II, part iii, ch. 12, "How Americans View the Equality of the Sexes," p. 603.

60. Which is not to say these battles were lacking in resolution and courage. In the mid-1970s, when Presidents Nixon and Ford and virtually all other

leading Republicans (as well as Democrats) endorsed the ERA, successful opposition was rallied by Phyllis Schlafly, mother of six, who calls her political activity "a hobby." Having already participated in a wide range of Republican political campaigns and written two books about arms control and foreign policy, Mrs. Schafly was the first and most important conservative leader to recognize that the ERA might have destructive consequences—and that it still could be defeated. Few men in politics have ever displayed so much forceful, energetic leadership to such impressive effect. She certainly had no equal among conservative political leaders in the United States during the 1970s.

Women in the Sixties

MARTHA C. NUSSBAUM

In my high school class in 1964—a private girls' school in Bryn Mawr, Pennsylvania—there was just one working mother. Her work was understood by the gossip of the day to be a sign of economic distress. It was seen as a black mark against her husband since it was well understood that good men were good breadwinners whose wives did not need to leave the home. Because the family was weird in other ways as well (they had a lawn that looked like a jungle, and they were the only people I knew who drove a foreign car), they were socially rejected. It was no surprise when their daughter, my best friend, did not receive invitations to the formal predebutante dances known as the Junior Dance Assembly, to which I went with no pleasure at all. Nor was it any surprise when Sara ended up going to Oberlin College, a "pink" school, to which my father did not even permit me to apply. After all, they dressed very strangely, those Matheson women, wearing thick black stockings and shapeless tweeds and hair that hung shapelessly straight down their backs, as they drove through Bryn Mawr laughing a little too loudly, in their bright yellow VW Beetle.

There was a great deal of female misery in Bryn Mawr in those days, but it was on the whole unacknowledged silent misery. The immaculate lawns and elegant Georgian houses, the dresses from Bergdorf Goodman, the Italian shoes with three-inch heels, the carefully sprayed hairstyles, the long, sleek high-finned cars concealed from public view much depression and self-contempt, much aimless sadness, much diffuse and unfocused anger, much heavy idleness, much alcoholism—along with, and frequently subverting, much love and intelligence and hope. Sometimes, I am sure, this misery was conscious, and the women themselves could have said that they preferred and would choose another life. More often, aspirations having been blunted over the years, they could not have pictured to themselves a possible life that would be both theirs and more flourishing than the one they knew. They had been brought up to believe that fulfillment for a woman consisted in the sort of life they had, and so they felt that they should be happy. To the extent that a married woman was uncertain whether she was happy, she tended to sense that there was something wrong with her, for certainly the message of the times was there was nothing wrong with her world. She usually tried to conceal this unspecified flaw from others, frequently to some extent also from herself. This limited her capacity to imagine other ways of life.

The happiest women I knew in those days, besides the socially deviant Mathesons, were my teachers at the Baldwin School, who were also considered by my parents to be odd and ill dressed and politically suspect. They had a gleam in their eye and an energy in their step that I rarely saw in my classmates' mothers or in my own. When I went to work at the local Republican headquarters—for I was a Republican and a libertarian in 1964 and a staunch campaign worker for Goldwater—I took note of the fact that most of the registered Democrats on the voting rolls of Bryn Mawr were teachers at my school, and this made them seem to me very strange. But I was happy in their company in a way that I was not happy in the company of most other women, and my libertarianism, which was at times perhaps a bid for the energy of their outraged attention, also involved an attempt to capture and to praise something about human liberty that I sensed in their presence. Above all, there was Mme. Melchior, who for four years taught me French literature and history and political thought. She was under five feet tall, and when she denounced us for a stray word of English, the room trembled. *"Un sou pour le petit chien,"* she would thunder, and the offending Anglophone would immediately produce a penny for deposit in the slit of the smiling Dalmatian on the front of her desk. Under her direction we wrote and produced a five-act play about Robespierre, who was then my great hero (you see that my politics were very confused). Since Baldwin's drama department encouraged cross-dressing as well as other forms of deviant thought and speech, I proudly assumed the lead role. Mme. Melchior celebrated her ninetieth birthday in 1993, and she had changed remarkably little. As she attacked the arguments of Simon Schama with withering scorn and merciless command of fact, she chortled, *"Vous voyez, Martha, je suis encore jacobine."*

When I arrived at Wellesley College, I was greeted by a speech from the president of the college, Margaret Clapp. It set out the differences between the Wellesley Girl and her rival the Radcliffe Girl. The Wellesley Girl was a highly educated woman who devoted her life to her husband, children, and community and sought no career for herself. By the time she graduated from Wellesley she had marriage plans, and she dressed with unobtrusive elegance. The Radcliffe girl dressed weirdly, with unwashed long hair and black stockings. She had radical views of unspecified content. She did not identify herself primarily as mother and wife. Her sexual behavior would not bear close scrutiny. In short, the Wellesley Girl was the mother of my classmates; the Radcliffe Girl was the Mathesons and my high school teachers. By that time many of us in the audience knew which sort of woman we wanted to be; we connected this with freedom, with flourishing, with a strong sense of happiness. Many of us took increasing pleasure in dressing weirdly. As the emphasis of fashion shifted from Marilyn Monroe to Jane Fonda as the norm of female bodily perfection, women felt, even with respect to their clothes, a new sense of mobility and freedom. My father told me that if a woman wore short skirts in the cold, she would develop an extra layer of insulating fat on her legs, but this argument, like so many parental arguments, no longer had the power to sway me.

Like so many women in America, I was "radicalized" in the sixties. I have tried to tell you something of "where I am coming from" so that you will see how typical my social and political formation was in some ways, how atypical in others. And I can also tell you that I was not as radical, even later on, as this story might have led you to conjecture. I was married when I was graduated in 1969; by the time Harvey Mansfield first taught me in 1972 I was pregnant. As Harvey may be able partly to confirm, having been in my presence at some parties, I am that rara avis of my generation, a person who has never used marijuana, even without inhaling, and I was a health and exercise addict even in the sixties and early seventies, long before it was fashionable to be so. Yet in the most fundamental way—in my aspirations for myself and my sense of what constituted a flourishing life—I was, like so many other women, changed by the sixties, by the new possibilities for aspiration that were beginning to open up. When I went to my dean at NYU (from which, having left Wellesley, I eventually graduated) to prepare for the final rounds of interviews for a Danforth Graduate Fellowship, he said, "That's fine, but don't smile so much; they will think you are being ingratiating and are not serious." My interviewer turned out to be the distinguished Harvard primatologist Irven DeVore, and I greeted him with not one gesture of primate submission.

Women's lives changed in the sixties in America; they changed radically in a very short period of time. The basic change was, I think, a change in thought. Certain patterns in women's lives and relationships that had been uncritically accepted for years, that had formed women's expectations and desires at a very deep level were now subjected to critical scrutiny and recognized to be nonnecessary social formations. So too the preferences and desires based on them. As my story of my teachers reveals, in some ways this was not so much a revolution as a return to an older generation of feminist aspiration that had been only partially blotted out by the fifties' images of Doris Day and her sisters. There were always Radcliffe girls around; there was always the image of Katharine Hepburn to remind us of what the fifties had suppressed. Nonetheless the change was so sweeping that it deserves to be called a revolution. For the first time women in large numbers, women all over the country, looked critically at where they were. And if they recognized frustration or depression in themselves, they refused to accept that the fault lay in their own deficiencies. They decided that it might possibly lie with the world that did not recognize them as fully equal human beings. Preferences that had been formed under the assumption that one's life was defined relatively to the life of a man were now revised under the new demand for full agency, subjecthood, and freedom.

When women looked at where they were, their central demand was a demand for full equality as persons and citizens. This meant real equality of opportunity in education and in the workplace; it meant patterns of male-female relationship that supported, rather than impeded, those demands; it meant a recognition that a woman, like a man, is an autonomous being with a plan of life to make and well-being to sustain, economically and spiritually. It meant the recognition that many alleged differences between males and females have not been shown to be basic or natural differences by any good scientific argument; many are best explained as caused by inequalities that are socially shaped. It meant too the recognition that such differences as undoubtedly are present, such as the ability of females to become pregnant, become disabilities only in the context of laws and institutions that treat them in certain ways.

And this went with a host of related more concrete demands: demands for access to contraception and for the legalization of abortion; demands for greater understanding of women's sexual responses and greater concern for women's sexual pleasure; demands for an end to the sexual double standard that had enjoined playful experimentation for young men, chastity for young women; demands for an end to male networks of informal job placement and for the institution of public procedures open to all; demands for blind hiring in institutions such as symphony orchestras (responsible for a huge increase in the number of female players[1]) and for blind refereeing in academic journals; demands for the recognition of sexual harassment as a serious offense in the workplace and of domestic violence and marital rape as criminal offenses in the home. (These last two items rose to the surface later than the sixties, but their recognition had its roots in sixties thinking.) A list like this could and should go on and on, for it is hard to realize without making such lists how unequal things really were, all through and indeed well beyond the sixties, how deeply assumptions about women's proper role and about the public-private distinction had shaped every aspect of American civic life.

Why were these demands so deeply felt in American life? For two reasons, I believe. First, because they brought to light some facts that could hardly be denied to be facts, once they were looked at head-on: women's capacities for development; their frustration and misery; the inequality of the treatment their capacities were receiving.

Second, because these demands brought to the surface a deep inconsistency between general American aspirations and America's particular history, an inconsistency that can be traced right back to this nation's founding, when the founders defended basic human rights but refused to extend them to women, whom they could hardly in all consistency have denied to be human beings, with the basic capacities for living and flourishing that all human beings share. To the founding, when Thomas Jefferson wrote, "Were our state a pure democracy there would still be excluded from our deliberations women, who, to prevent depravation of morals and ambiguity of issue, should not mix promiscuously in gatherings of men."[2]

In fact we might say that the lives of women in America had since the founding been characterized by a tension. On the one hand, women were brought up to subscribe to certain ideals of liberty and equality, and these ideals were presented as human rights—not simply ideals to which every human being as such could aspire but also items of worth to which, just by virtue of being human, any human being had a claim. On the other hand, they were also brought up to acquiesce in, and even to defend, a normative conception of women's "nature" that held that full citizenship and autonomy were not for women, that women were made for domestic life and for the support of husband and family, not for political participation or for work or for economic independence and self-determination. In the process the idea of "nature" was used here, as it so frequently is, in a slippery and multiple way. Differences between the sexes that were old and habitual were described as "natural," and this was taken to imply both that they could not be changed and that it was right and proper for them to remain, even though, as Mary Wollstonecraft and John Stuart Mill had long since pointed out, neither implication followed. In other contexts, the common existence of a disability—for example, illiteracy—was not taken as evidence that this disability was unchangeable or that it would be right and proper for it to remain as it was. Yet the fact that women were less accustomed than men to some aspects of public and political life, to professional careers in science, and so forth was repeatedly taken as evidence of both the unchangeability and the goodness of the old divided state of affairs.[3] Feminists of the sixties and seventies rightly understood one of their major tasks to be the criticism of this logically sloppy and injurious rhetoric of "nature."[4]

This critical move led naturally to a critical reexamination of old conceptions of the gender-divided family. For if one called into question the idea that women are "made for" domesticity and child rearing rather than for citizenship, and if one noticed that the undivided burden of domesticity and child rearing frequently made it very difficult for women to aspire to careers and to full political participation, then it became natural either to reject the nuclear family altogether, as a small group of radical feminists did, or, as was far more common, to imagine its transformation in the direction of greater justice. It has been a fundamental point in the feminism of the sixties and later[5] to point out that domestic labor and child care can be far more equally divided than it usually has been and that a more equal division would have advantages both for women, who would be more able to pursue careers and to achieve economic self-sufficiency, and for men, who would have more contact with their growing children. Both parties, furthermore, would have the advantage of participating in a just rather than an unjust institution, and feminists saw no reason why justice and love should be taken to be incompatible. It seemed, and seems, very reasonable to suppose that love can flourish better in a family characterized by justice—all the more since it is in the family that young children are supposed to be learning their moral ideals, including those of justice.[6]

In short, the women's movement of the sixties was in one sense, and very deeply, a liberal revolution: It was about realizing in women's lives the ideals of liberty and equality that are at some level definitive of the American tradition. I believe that this is a central fact about it that feminists should not be quick to scorn. If one does not have equality and autonomy as moral ideals, the fact that women are being unequally thwarted makes no difference. If one does not have liberty as a moral ideal, the fact that women are not free to plan their own lives makes no difference. Thus it is to the great credit of the American liberal democratic tradition that this argument can be made within it, in the straightforward way it is now being made. It is altogether a different and harder matter to argue for women's equality in a tradition that has no commitment to human equality at all, no tradition of holding that persons should not be deprived of basic rights in an arbitrary way. Thus it is no surprise to me that in my work in international development ethics, it is frequently my colleagues from the non-Western world—for example, Roop Rekha Verma from India, Xiaorong Li from China[7]—who most vigorously defend the Enlightenment concepts of rights, liberty, and equality, while the Western feminists hold more skeptically back, believing that these concepts may be tainted by the history of imperialism, slavery, and sex inequality with which they are associated. The feminist revolution is everywhere in the world, I believe, a liberal revolution, in the sense that it is based upon a radical demand for equal personhood and autonomy, equal rights, liberties, and opportunities. One can be most hopeful about such a revolution if one is already living in a liberal polity in which general ideas about equal human development and empowerment are honored in speech, if not always in practice.

Indeed, one can make one further specific claim about the liberal antecedents of the feminism of the sixties and seventies. A central charge against men in feminist literature is that they treat women as objects, or "objectify" them. This notion has by now become familiar in the feminist analysis of sex relations, of the workplace, of rape and harassment and pornography. As has been stated explicitly by its proponents, the idea of "objectification" is at its root a Kantian idea, the idea that it is always wrong to treat a human being as a tool or means, rather than as an end in him or herself.[8] When women complain about the "thinglike" treatment of women, they are alluding to this profound moral ideal, which is at the root of the Enlightenment traditions deriving from Kantian liberalism: the idea that one should always treat humanity, whether in oneself or in another, as an end rather than as a means and that both individuals and political institutions should be criticized for their failure to accord such treatment to women, insofar as they do.

On the other hand, in one very fundamental way the feminist revolution was not a liberal revolution, if that means one that accepts the distinctive type of liberalism dominant in the British utilitarian tradition and its heir, neoclassical economics. For that liberal tradition believes that the ends of both personal and public life should be a function of the preferences that individuals, as things currently are, happen to have. And the feminist revolution of the sixties revealed graphically the extent to which the existing preferences of women were an artifact of oppression and constraint. If happiness in the sense of satisfaction was not altogether irrelevant to the difference between my teachers and the women I saw around me, and it clearly was not, it was not the whole story either. For as I have insisted, one cannot characterize what was wrong with women's lives at that time without mentioning the deformation in aspiration and desire, in the very sense of what satisfactions were possible and achievable, that was the product of years and years of subordination.

If this was true of the women of Bryn Mawr, who were adequately nourished, sheltered, and clothed and, for the most part, college-educated, it was and is all the more true of the millions of women in the world who are deprived of equal nutrition, health care, and education. For it is difficult to aspire if one has no information about the lives that people lead elsewhere; it is difficult to know how it feels to be healthy if one has never had enough to eat. Economic liberalism is ill equipped to diagnose the ills of women, and the "consciousness raising" of the sixties, which both seemed and was radical in the sense that it asked us not to accept that our happiness was a function of current preferences, was, I believe, a necessary precondition of any adequate realization of female liberty and equality. In that sense it was not as strange as I first thought that the teachers who seemed to me to exemplify liberty should have been on the voting rolls on what I took to be the antilibertarian side, for laws and institutions are required to produce genuine liberty, and simply to defer to existing preferences was at that time a recipe for continued constraint. It always was a mistake, for example, to suppose that the family is "personal" if this means "nonpolitical," for the shape of that institution is influenced in countless ways by laws and political arrangements. So too, obviously, are the desires and choices of its members.

This brings me to a fundamental theoretical point. The idea that desires and preferences should be scrutinized as (at least in part) social artifacts has recently been represented as an idea that feminists cannot accept without ceasing to be supporters of liberal democracy. For example, in *Who Stole Feminism?: How Women Have Betrayed Women* (1994), Christina

Hoff Sommers arrives at the conclusion that any feminism that criticizes the existing preferences and desires of women as irrational, or deformed by hierarchy or depression or resentment, is in and of itself undemocratic and, indeed, dangerous to democracy. This is the central route by which Hoff Sommers arrives at the conclusion that the feminism of the sixties was not just silly or mistaken but a profound threat to cherished American ways of life. Hoff Sommers's argument is not idiosyncratic; it is typical of a backlash against feminist argument that by now has wide currency. I have suggested that the central claims of this feminism are both true and a realization of what is best in the American and Kantian liberal traditions. Analyzing and criticizing Hoff Sommers's argument will help me clarify these claims.

The Hoff Sommers argument reports the views of a mixed group of feminist writers who describe ways in which women are led by upbringing and other social forces to internalize and endorse images of themselves that impose hardship and deform self-expression. This idea that social norms can deform preferences, creating internal forces that militate against one's own happiness, Hoff Sommers then associates with an idea that she ascribes to the writings of Michel Foucault—namely, the idea that we all live in something like an authoritarian police state that tells us what to do and who to be. She concludes: "It would be a mistake to think that the idea of a tenacious internalized power that is keeping women subjugated is on the fringe of the New Feminism and not at its center." Conclusion: The New Feminism is committed to ignoring the difference between liberal democracy and a police state and to a rejection of individual liberty that is both implausible and dangerous. Anyone who holds that women's preferences may be distorted by lack of opportunity or lack of information is "prepared to dismiss popular preferences in an illiberal way," and "anyone, liberal or conservative, who believes in democracy will sense danger in" such ideas. Such views might have had some plausibility at the time when John Stuart Mill uttered them, she concedes, for then women did not have the

vote. Now, however, they do have the vote, and "their preferences are being taken into account." So we must reject the
idea that any criticism of their preferences is required or even
admissible. "Since women today can no longer be regarded as
the victims of an undemocratic indoctrination, we must regard
their preferences as 'authentic.' Any other attitude to American women is unacceptably patronizing and profoundly
illiberal."

The conclusion of Hoff Sommers's argument is interesting
for the way in which it casts some doubt on what preceded, for
she now admits that the feminist ideas she criticizes are to be
found in John Stuart Mill, among the greatest of the liberal
political philosophers, and are not the private property of a
radical thinker such as Foucault. And of course Mill did not
hold that women's preferences were deformed merely by the
denial of the right to vote or that the suffrage alone would correct women's perception that their second-class status was fitting and "natural." The denial of suffrage explained why their
preferences were not duly recorded. But Mill's account of why
these preferences were in any case *distorted* is a different matter altogether. Here he speaks of a multitude of factors: the
absence of equal education; the absence of accurate information about women's potentialities and abilities; the hierarchical
behavior of men, who treat women with condescension and
cast aspersions on their achievements; the pervasive social
teaching that women are fit only or primarily for domestic and
nonintellectual functions; women's own justified fear of questioning authority, which leads them to shy away from new
choices and pursuits; their equally justified fear of moving
from a position of comfortable inequality to a position that
would be both unprotected and still unequal. Men's preferences too were corrupt, he argued, for to be taught that without any personal distinction, just by virtue of being male, one
is superior to the most talented woman is the source of a view
of oneself and one's conduct that is diseased and that leads
men to endorse diseased social choices. In short, Mill argued
that a liberal democracy—even one with women's suffrage—

could contain preferences deformed by a legacy of social hier-archy and inequality. Because of the priority he attached to liberty, he did not conclude that people with diseased prefer-ences should suffer political disabilities. But he did hold that insofar as possible, social policy should not be based upon these diseased preferences. How was this to be accomplished without illiberal restrictions on liberty? By intensive attention to education of the young and by the force of public persuasion and public argument.

Mill, then, makes the very argument that I outlined through my narrative examples, the very argument that is, I have held, at the core of sixties feminist thinking. The views about desire and its social formation on which such arguments rest have a long philosophical pedigree. In one or another form they go back to the thought of Aristotle and of the ancient Greek Stoics, all of whom held that their society contained many preferences and desires that were distorted by social conditioning and that should therefore be discouraged by edu-cation and public discourse, and discounted, where possible, in the formation of social policy. (Prominent examples of such deformed desires were the desire to accumulate wealth with-out limit, the desire to achieve honor and status for their own sake, the desire to get the better of others.) As I have sug-gested, such ideas are fully at home in the tradition of Kantian liberalism, with its insistence that it is always wrong to treat humanity as a tool or a means and its strong condemnation of human desires, including prominently sexual desires, that prompt such treatment. What we now see as well is that such ideas, far from being alien to the Anglo-American tradition of liberalism, with its strong defense of individual liberty, are fully at home inside this tradition and are in fact thought by Mill to be crucial to the adequate realization of liberty in indi-viduals and in the society as a whole. In short, the feminist critique of male and female desire and preference that I have traced to the sixties actually has a far longer and more compli-cated ancestry.

I have said that such criticisms of existing preferences are alien to recent economic utilitarianism. But even this by now is not altogether true, as work on preference formation has made the facts recognized by Mill uncontrovertibly clear. A representative, and especially clear, formulation of the problem of diseased preferences, within the economic utilitarian tradition, is given by Nobel Prize-winning economist John Harsanyi, in an article entitled "Morality and the Theory of Rational Behaviour."[9] Harsanyi begins by taking the characteristic economic-utilitarian position that "in deciding what is good and what is bad for a given individual, the ultimate criterion can only be his own wants and his own preferences" (55). So far he agrees with Hoff Sommers. But, he immediately continues, "Any sensible ethical theory must make a distinction between rational wants and irrational wants, or between rational preferences and irrational preferences. It would be absurd to assert that we have the same moral obligation to help other people in satisfying their utterly unreasonable wants as we have to help them in satisfying their very reasonable desires." It might seem that a preference-based theory such as utilitarianism will have difficulty making this distinction. Not so, according to Harsanyi:

> In actual fact, there is no difficulty in maintaining this distinction even without an appeal to any other standard than an individual's own personal preferences. All we have to do is to distinguish between a person's manifest preferences and his true preferences. His manifest preferences are his actual preferences as manifested by his observed behaviour, including preferences possibly based on erroneous factual beliefs, or on careless logical analysis, or on strong emotions that at the moment greatly hinder rational choice. In contrast, a person's true preferences are the preferences he *would* have if he had all the relevant factual information, always reasoned with the greatest possible care, and were in a state of mind most conducive to rational choice. [55]

Social policy, Harsanyi continues, should be based, insofar as possible, on the true preferences of individuals. And not on all of these, for some true preferences are "antisocial," deformed by "sadism, envy, resentment, and malice" (56). These, he concludes, "must be altogether excluded from our social-utility function" (56). This, in a nutshell, is the personal and political proposal made by the feminists of the sixties. Its logical political expression is a certain form of democratic choice, democratic choice understood not as the aggregation of all actual preferences, but democratic choice understood as public deliberation in search of the common good.[10]

Harsanyi does not connect his ideas to feminism, but their implications for feminist analysis are clear and very much in the spirit of the sixties' feminist critique. The implications of related ideas for the analysis of sex inequality have been taken up in quite a few parts of the economic literature. Economist Amartya Sen, for example, has for some years emphasized the many ways in which women's unequal situation and lack of access to opportunities produces "adaptive preferences," in which women themselves come to validate their unequal status. The existence of such "adaptive preferences," Sen argues, gives us reason to be highly mistrustful of existing preferences in our choice of social policies.[11] Sen uses this insight to support feminist demands for institutional reform, even where existing preferences do not clearly support such changes.[12]

More recently a related idea has been endorsed in the Nobel Prize address of Gary Becker, whom even Roger Kimball would presumably not call a "tenured radical."[13] Becker argues that prejudices of various sorts, especially "the *beliefs* of employers, teachers, and other influential groups that minority members are less productive," can be self-fulfilling, causing the members of the disadvantaged group to "underinvest in education, training, and work skills," and this underinvestment does subsequently make them less productive. In short, disadvantaged groups (among which Becker includes "blacks, women, religious groups, immigrants, and others") internalize their second-class status in ways that cause them to make choices that perpetuate that second-class status. Any theory of social rationality, Becker holds, implicitly agreeing here with Sen, should be alert to and critical of these facts, which certainly do imply that it can be risky for a democracy to build policy on all those preferences that happen to be around in the society, especially where that society contains traditional hierarchies of race or gender.

I conclude that the core ideas of the sixties' feminism I have described are both radical and in the best sense liberal: radical, because they ask us to look searchingly at the formation of preference and desire in our own selves and our own democracy; liberal because they embody the deepest insights of the Kantian liberal tradition about personhood and freedom, as well as the best ideas about preference formation to be found in the Millian, and now even in the economic, version of the utilitarian tradition. Sommers and other critics of feminism are wrong to think that it is dangerous for democracy to consider these ideas. Instead it is dangerous not to consider them as we strive to build a society that is both rational and just.

There was much in the feminism of the sixties that I would criticize. There was frequently a vindictive character to many proposals and a failure to be just to the complexities of individual lives. There was frequently a hasty acceptance, on the part of women, of norms that turned out on further examination to be all too close to the traditional preferences and wishes of males and not terribly well suited to realize the equal aspirations of women. Among these I would include the acceptance of norms of ambitious work without flexible time and parental leave. Among these I would also include the acceptance of sex without love and commitment; in this sense, I think, the sexual revolution was very ambiguous for women.

There was frequently a lack of forethought too in the rejection of traditional family roles without the careful creation of a more adequate alternative. The nostalgic talk one frequently hears today about "family values" does not win my sympathy, for it is all too plain (here I am in full agreement

with Susan Okin) that the traditional nuclear family has all too
often been a home of injustice and constraint for its female
members. Indeed, if one looks around the world, one soon dis-
covers that it has all too often been a home of unequal nutrition, of the denial of equal health care, of contempt and neglect
for its women, especially its girls. So I am far from saying that
the love and care of the traditional nuclear family (or its many
variants around the world) should have been cherished. But
there should have been more constructive thought given to
what children need in order to flourish, physically and psycho-
logically, and more thought to the redesigning of family-type
institutions and relationships with those ends in view.

This is happening now in many places—not least in the
many worldwide discussions that have taken place in connection with the United Nations International Year of the Family,
1994. The basic Interagency document defining the goals of
this project has reaffirmed the commitment of the nations
involved to families as "primary agents of socialization" and
even "an essential mechanism for promoting respect for
human rights of all individuals." It also, and consequently,
insists: "A partnership between men and women on the basis
of equal rights and responsibilities is the challenge for the modern family. Basic to this challenge is gender equality in the
household, equal sharing of family responsibilities between
men and women as well as participation of women in employment." These issues of family structure, and the human challenge they present, were confronted too rarely in the rhetoric
of the sixties.

But the greatest defect of sixties feminism is one that may
already be apparent from the direction of my argument. It was,
I think, the frequent insularity of American feminism, its
neglect of the lives of women in the rest of the world. Women
were so busy becoming conscious of the fabric of their own
lives that they had little time for other women whose lives
were different and possibly much worse. One heard a great
deal about sex roles, child care, equality in hiring. One heard
little of inequalities in access to literacy and basic education,

nothing of inequalities in the very right to go outside one's home to seek employment, in the right to see a doctor when one is ill, in the right to get fed. Yet these inequalities are a prominent fact of women's lives in many parts of the world. According to the 1993 UN *Human Development Report,* there is no country in the world in which women's quality of life is equal to that of men, according to a complex measure that includes longevity, educational opportunities, and other variables. But one heard no comparative discussion of those data. One heard nothing of inequalities in nutrition and basic medical care, inequalities that cause the deaths of women and girls every day. A recent calculation by economist Amartya Sen concludes that one hundred million women in the world are dead who would have been alive had they received equal nutrition and health care. One heard nothing of such deaths. Sexual pleasure, the right to affirm a lesbian identity are, if important matters of individual freedom, still not the first items on the agenda of international feminism, which is focused on these basic matters of survival and elementary human rights. To this extent sixties feminism was myopic, and it also led us to direct all our critical attention against a tradition—our own—that is in many important respects relatively benign to women, however much it deserves criticism in others.

Let me therefore conclude this paper by suggesting a feminist agenda for the early years of the next millennium. I suggest that while not forgetting the many important issues already on the American agenda, we turn much of our political attention to these international questions, working for a world situation in which female infants will not be killed or allowed to die, in which the same amount of food will be put on the plates of girls and of boys, in which girls and boys will be taken to the doctor equally often when they are ill, in which all citizens of all nations in the world will be literate, in which all will have the right to go out and look for work without intimidation and without discrimination, in which all will have the right to vote and to compete for political office, in which all will have the right to claim support from the law against domestic violence, in which none will face intimidation or sexual harassment in the workplace, in which sex-selective abortions will not take place. This means, I think, putting pressure on the developed countries to link foreign policy and foreign aid to these aspects of a nation's life—so that, to give just one example, we do not find ourselves, as we did in Afghanistan, assailing the specter of world communism while ignoring the fact that we were supporting one of the most brutally repressive regimes toward women in all the world. It means, on the other hand, recognizing that many parts of the world that we have unreflectively seen as "primitive"—for example, much of sub-Saharan Africa—have traditions of leadership for women in productive economic activity from which we can learn, which can help us enrich our understanding of our own goals of liberty and flourishing. I would suggest that every course in feminism in the nineties begin with the study of many facts about the lives of women, as presented, for example, in the *Human Development Report,* and that instead of merely looking at our own lives in the mirror of feminist theory, which was an essential stage but one that can breed narcissism if too long continued, we focus on what is actually happening to women other than ourselves, in partnership with them and learning from their insights; that we work with them to support social changes that will bring the world closer to a general realization of the feminist goals of liberty, personhood, and full human equality.

N O T E S

1. One need only compare the sex balance of leading symphony orchestras in the United States and in Europe, where there is still no blind auditioning, to see the power of this simple change. It is sobering to ask oneself what changes that have not been made might have been made if that same procedure had been available in other careers and professions. The belief that a woman cannot play the bassoon, the bass—all this colored players'

and conductors' perceptions of the sound they heard. So too, one may conjecture, related beliefs about the capacities of women in science, mathematics, and other "male" fields.

2. See the discussion of Jefferson's views in Susan Moller Okin, *Women in Western Political Thought* (1980).

3. For examples of the use of this rhetoric in barring women from the professions and public life, see Okin.

4. Mill's dissection of this idea in *The Subjection of Women* (1869) remains of fundamental importance.

5. Most eloquently articulated in Susan Moller Okin's *Justice, Gender, and the Family* (1989), but the roots of Okin's critique go back to sixties feminist thinking.

6. This is among Okin's central arguments, but once again, its roots can be found in sixties thinking.

7. See their essays in *Women, Culture, and Development*, ed. M. Nussbaum and J. Glover (1995).

8. See the discussion of this connection in Barbara Herman, "Could It Be Worth Thinking with Kant about Sex and Marriage?" in *A Mind of One's Own: Feminist Essays on Reason and Objectivity*, ed. L. Antony and C. Witt (1992), referring to the discussion of objectification in Andrea Dworkin's *Intercourse* (1987). See also Catharine MacKinnon, *Toward a Feminist Theory of the State* (1989); MacKinnon does not consider her view to be a "liberal" view as she understands this term, largely on account of her commitment to a criticism of the social formation of desires and preferences; but she stresses her affiliations with Kantianism, and of course Kantian liberalism is profoundly critical of existing desires and preferences.

9. In *Utilitarianism and Beyond*, ed. Amartya Sen and Bernard Williams (1982), pp. 39–62.

10. The idea of "deliberative democracy" has been connected with feminism by Cass Sunstein in, for example, *The Partial Constitution* (1993).

11. See the essays in Sen, *Choice, Welfare, and Measurement* (1982), and see Sen's "Gender Equality and Theories of Justice," in *Women, Culture, and Development*.

12. He gives evidence of cases in which perceptions even of so apparently obvious a matter as one's own basic health and nutritional status can be deformed by lack of experience and relevant information.

13. Gary Becker, "The Economic Way of Looking at Life," the Nobel Foundation 1992; also printed as Law and Economics Working Paper No. 12, the Law School, the University of Chicago.

Whatever Happened to Children's Rights?

MARTHA MINOW[1]

I was a child in the 1960s. Born in 1954, I entered school in 1960. I learned of John F. Kennedy's assassination over the school's public address system as I sat with my fourth-grade classmates. Before long we also heard of the assassinations of Martin Luther King, Jr., Medgar Evers, and Robert Kennedy; I wrote my adolescent poems about assassinations and my student newspaper columns about political protests. When my older sister turned thirteen, I envied the cake she had with the ceramic figure of a teenaged girl talking on the telephone. But when I turned thirteen, I joined protests of the war in Vietnam and seemed to live in a more serious and political world than the one evoked by the ceramic telephone teen. In high school I participated in the first Earth Day events as well as continuing protests of the war. I also joined classmates in seeking reforms of school rules requiring hall passes, dress codes, and a set curriculum. By the time I was graduated we had succeeded in establishing within the large high school an alternative school, which my younger sister later attended.

Perhaps this all explains my interest in children's rights. I was a child in the 1960s. It was a time of high political consciousness, hopes for institutional change, and, in fact, some dramatic shifts in cultural mores. But I am also an amateur student of history, and I wonder how the waves of reform in this country have treated differently the issues involving race, gender, and age distinctions. In the 1860s, after the abolitionists had pressed to end slavery, a movement for women's legal rights grew and culminated in the constitutional amendment assuring women the vote. This movement overlapped with reforms protecting children with the creation of new institutions like juvenile courts and new laws establishing compulsory education and restricting child labor. The next civil rights movement that ultimately produced *Brown v. Board of Education* and the 1964 Civil Rights Act also helped inspire a movement for women's rights. And a diverse group of people urged an agenda for children's rights in this country during the 1960s and 1970s.

Whatever happened to this movement for children's rights? After briefly describing it, I will situate that movement in the older history of advocacy for children and in a subsequently troubled history of child advocacy through the early 1990s. I will close by assessing what the historical analysis could or should mean for a political and legal agenda for children, for rights, and for all of us as we head into the next century.

I. THE SIXTIES AND CHILDREN'S RIGHTS

During the 1992 presidential campaign some Republicans attacked Hillary Rodham Clinton, who had written several articles during the 1970s advocating rights for children. Those articles stimulated opponents to satirize the claim for children's rights as a claim that children should be able to divorce their parents.[2] Hillary Rodham was a law student when she wrote her now-famous *Harvard Education Review* article entitled "Children under the Law" in 1973.[3] There, and in two subsequent pieces, she reviewed the emerging children's rights movement and argued that courts should stop assuming that all children are legally incompetent until they reach the age of majority. Instead, she argued, the question of competence should be decided on a case-by-case basis. She also observed that children's rights seemed "a slogan in search of a definition" and recommended careful study of both the psychological and legal issues implicated by the idea of rights for children.[4]

Republican campaigners who dug up these articles during the 1992 campaign assaulted her views as radical. Some charged that Hillary Clinton "believes kids should be able to sue their parents rather than helping with the chores that they were asked to do."[5] Other less partisan observers have commented that Clinton's views were "comparatively mild versions of what the children's rights movement wanted at the time."[6] Indeed, in books such as John Holt's *Escape from Childhood* and Richard Farson's *Birthrights,* some child liberationists in the early 1970s viewed children as the next group entitled, like blacks and women, to a civil rights revolution.[7]

Bearing the imprint of the optimistic and at times revolutionary rhetoric of the 1960s, child liberationists like Holt and Larson drew on works by Rousseau and John Dewey[8] to argue that children deserve rights to participate fully in society,[9] that perceptions of children as dependent reflected their experiences of subjugation,[10] and that experiments such as the open school at Summerhill showed children's capacities to participate in self-governance.[11] A publication of the radical caucus at that school at one point quoted Huey Newton of the Black Panthers as saying, "An unarmed people are slaves," and then stated, "[W]e are asking for a human standard to arm kids with, within which we as adults can deal with our own problems and uptightedness while kids are free to determine their own lives."[12] Many liberationists argued that children's voices were wrongly absent even from public discussions of children's rights.[13]

John Holt, for example, urged equal legal treatment so that children would be like adults before the law. He specifically promoted children's rights to vote, to work for money, to sign contracts, to manage their own educations, to travel, and to form their own families.[14] Richard Farson's agenda called for the creation of alternative home environments. He also urged children's rights to information, self-education, freedom from physical punishment, sexual freedom, and economic and political participation and the full extension of legal protections to young people charged with violating the law. Others challenged schools as repressive and authoritarian and urged schools to adopt "open classrooms" allowing students to select their own activities and pursue their own interests.[15]

Yet alongside those who urged children's rights to liberate young people from a constraining status worked others who also advocated for children but sought new protections, services, or care.[16] Advocates in this vein worked to protect children through judicial rulings, legislation, changes in existing programs, and a public rhetoric about children.

The child protectionists included presidential leadership advocating special programs and services for children. President Lyndon Johnson sent the first congressional message devoted exclusively to children in 1967 and called for a range of medical, social service, summer employment, and compensatory education programs for children.[17] Perhaps even more notably, President Richard Nixon followed up within a month of his inauguration in 1969 by calling for a "national commitment to providing all American children with an opportunity for healthful and stimulating development during the first five years of life."[18] Nixon took pains to express along with the commitment to child welfare his respect for "the sacred right of parents to rear their children according to their own values and own understandings."[19]

Whether liberationists or protectionists—or something in between—growing numbers of advocates for children in the 1960s and 1970s used the language of rights. That language offered a way to argue for both more protection and more independence for different children or for the same children in different circumstances.[20]

The rights-based model of legal advocacy for blacks informed the most effective national organization for children. When Marion Wright Edelman founded the Children's Defense Fund (CDF) in 1973, she drew on her experiences as a civil rights attorney and her involvement with Head Start and child development programs focusing on poor and minority children.[21] CDF also from the start advocated due process protections prior to school suspension and a right to privacy for children regarding their school and juvenile court records. CDF pursued as well the same kind of sustained advocacy for children that the NAACP Legal Defense and Education Fund instigated for people of color.[22]

Yet Edelman's initial agenda for CDF included challenging the exclusion of children from school, the labeling and treatment of children with special needs, the use of children in medical experimentation, and the quality of day care—all comfortably within the tradition of child protection. Edelman said explicitly in 1974 that "we are not a children's liberation operation. . . . Children are not simply another oppressed minority group who could function independently if allowed to do so. . . . We don't yet have a sound enough conceptual framework to approach children's rights."[23]

Nonetheless Edelman drew on the rhetoric of rights in helping to draft the Comprehensive Child Development Act of 1971. The preamble to the act, in her words, "put the nation on record as saying that children have certain rights: to basic nutrition, health care, education, and child developmental care in their early years" regardless of each family's ability to pay. President Nixon accompanied his veto of the act with a message warning that federal support for child care would lead to communal child rearing, contrary to American family values; Edelman defended the act as one mandating parental control.[24] This example illustrates both the dominant association of government programs with communism and the political and practical difficulties in articulating rights for children without seeming to undermine parental authority.

This same set of difficulties marked litigation over children's rights in the 1960s and 1970s. Advocates for children used rhetorics of rights to place children in the same legal position as adults but also to seek special protections. Courts sometimes accepted one or both of these formulations but also often responded with concerns about governmental power or about threats to parental authority. It is tempting to treat the late 1960s and early 1970s as the high-water mark of children's rights, but a closer look suggests the better description of an intense period of debate over children's rights.

Consider litigation in the U.S. Supreme Court; it is a small and selective sample but nonetheless a body of especially influential decisions. The impact of the civil rights and student rights movements of the 1960s—which included the early 1970s—is unmistakable in this sample. The Supreme Court decided in 1967 that the Constitution protects a child who faces commitment to a state institution; accordingly the juvenile court must assure a right to counsel, a right against self-incrimination, a right to notice of charges, and a right to confront and cross-examine her accusers.[25] In 1969 the Court assured public school students some degree of First Amendment rights in a case involving students disciplined for wearing black armbands to protest the Vietnam War.[26] And in 1975 the Court ruled that the due process clause of the Fourteenth Amendment requires notice of charges, reasons, and an opportunity to present his case prior to the suspension of a student from public school.[27] These cases reflected social science criticisms of the juvenile court, national turmoil over the Vietnam War and racial tensions, and widespread legal challenges to unfettered authority.[28] They also reflected shifting views of the legal and political status of children and young people.

Prompted in part by successful test case litigation in the lower courts, some notable legislative developments articulated rights of children with disabilities to education and related services.[29] Growing from medical studies of battered children, another legislative initiative provided federal aid to stimulate improvement of state responses to child abuse, neglect, and adoption issues.[30] These developments combined conceptions of children's procedural rights restricting the discretion of public decision makers with notions of children's needs that the larger society should meet. Most basically these decisions departed from the traditional view of children as properly subjected to parental and institutional authority beyond state review because such authorities no longer seemed entirely trustworthy. The Supreme Court, and thus the law of the land, began to recognize children as distinct individuals deserving a direct relationship with the state under a legal regime protecting liberties against both public and private authorities.

Halting the report of legal developments here would be misleading, however. In 1971 a Supreme Court decision refused to extend the constitutional right to a jury to juvenile court proceedings.[31] In 1972 the Court permitted Amish parents to keep their children out of high school without calling for any consideration of the children's views on the matter,[32] and in 1977 it ruled that a teacher's use of corporal punishment—a beating with a wooden paddle—required no prior due process hearing but only the possibility of a subsequent tort action.[33]

The Court's decisions in these cases indicate legal ambivalence in the face of repeated efforts by advocates to extend constitutional rights to children. Ambivalence here should not be misconstrued as a kind of wishy-washy balancing act. Ambivalence is that wonderful word for our simultaneous commitments and attractions to inconsistent things. The Court's ambivalence swings between two starkly contrasting alternatives. One would extend adult rights to children. The other would treat children as importantly subject to different authorities, institutions, and relationships from adults.[34]

Advocates for children's rights sometimes resolved the tension between protection and liberation through a conception of children as potential adults, deserving rights but needing care on the way to adulthood. For example, Peter Edelman, the husband of Marion Wright Edelman and a longstanding child advocate himself, served as director of the New York State Division for Youth in the 1970s.[35] In 1977 he described a position that favored some rights for children but searched for a program responsive to children's needs. He explicitly resisted the goal of "total parity of rights for children" and instead argued that the proper goal would "extend some adult rights and improve government programs so that children will be assured protection and dignity and the chance to develop their maximum potential."[36] Unclear about which additional adult rights should be extended and which modified, Edelman lauded children's freedom of religion, racial equality, freedom of expression, procedural due process, and the right to privacy—adult-type rights—along with a right to education that would be unique to children.[37]

Where in this vision should entitlement programs—for day care, for medical services—fit? When should children be given second chances and protections against criminal punishments, civil liabilities, or other obligations placed on adults? The advocates' own uncertainty about the scope of children's rights produced no clear answers to these questions and left them largely open to political and institutional pressures.

II. THE LEGACY OF AN EARLIER CHILD-SAVING MOVEMENT

Some ambivalence in the courts about children's rights thus may have reflected disagreements among advocates for children. Perhaps ironically some of the most vivid issues cast as claims of rights for children arose in response to the institutions created by a prior generation of child advocates. Between 1880 and 1930 reformers around the country identified the special needs of children as an appropriate subject for public responses.[38] Some of the reformers participated in the settlement house movement to assist recent immigrants; others specifically drew on emerging social and psychological sciences to shift from moral to treatment approaches to social programs. Initiatives to address child welfare ranged from efforts to improve the quality of milk to laws requiring school attendance and restricting child labor. These Progressive Era reformers launched a "child-saving" movement with a focus on children's welfare, confidence in experts, and acceptance of the government as a paternal presence in children's lives.[39]

The juvenile court under challenge in *In re Gault* itself was a product of Progressive Era reforms, notably fueled by Jane Addams, Florence Kelley, and other settlement house workers in the late 1890s. Imbued with the turn-of-the-century belief in scientific expertise and in a malleable human nature, the original design of juvenile courts counted on the benevolence of judges and the possibilities of therapeutic treatment to address misbehavior by both children and their parents. Removing young people from adult courts and bringing them to a special institution connected with social and psychological experts, the juvenile courts rejected the use of procedural safeguards in favor of a model of therapeutic paternalism. Yet within a decade of the origin of the first juvenile court in 1899, critics claimed this therapeutic approach proved too lenient for juvenile offenders and too intrusive for young people who had broken no laws. Social workers, probation officers, and other experts seemed unable to deliver the promised improvement in children's behavior and lives. Placement facilities for juvenile offenders became overcrowded. Social scientists documented abuses by juvenile court judges and in juvenile correction facilities. Law reformers used that documentation in the challenges that ultimately produced *In re Gault*.[40]

Similarly, restrictions on child labor and compulsory education—both products of Progressive-Era reforms—occasioned critiques at least by the liberationists in the 1960s and 1970s. (Coming from a different quarter, the Reagan administration in the 1980s sought to loosen restrictions on child labor not in the name of children's rights but as part of a deregulation move.)[41] The special protections fought for by an earlier generation became the fetters attacked by sixties-era reformers. At the same time some advocates for children in the sixties and seventies sought to continue or extend the earlier era's efforts to meet children's special needs through governmental and private programs. Both liberationists and protectionists harkened back to the turn-of-the-century reformers, but with opposite goals.

III. REACTIONS TO CHILDREN'S RIGHTS

Considerable opposition could be found to both versions of rights for children. Whether cast as adult rights or instead as special protections, rights for children troubled judges, scholars, and traditionalists who sometimes also opposed women's liberation.

Justices on the Supreme Court—sometimes in majority opinions, sometimes as dissents—expressed a third position responding to both the arguments for state protections for children's welfare and for extending adult-style rights to children. This third position stressed traditional authority and warnings against the conflicts and disorder that rights for children could engender. Whether respecting and protecting the authority of parents,[42] teachers,[43] or doctors,[44] this view rejects rights for children as either unnecessary or harmful given the relationships of authority and responsibility held by adults in children's lives.[45]

For example, Justice Powell's 1975 dissent in *Goss v. Lopez* argued against due process protections surrounding school suspensions as unwise and unnecessary intrusions on the schools, which must maintain authority and discipline.[46] Justice Powell two years later wrote the majority opinion in *Ingraham v. Wright,* finding no constitutional problem with an act of corporal punishment by a teacher, which after all was a traditional form of discipline.[47]

Arguments resisting children's rights claims as inconsistent with traditional authority bear a strong resemblance to some reactions to the women's rights movement in the 1960s and 1970s. Then, too, some observers worried that extending rights beyond their traditional reach would undermine the smooth operation of the traditional family that should be trusted to fulfill its duties to children.[48] In addition, many of the arguments raised in opposition to women's rights argued that children would suffer if women were "liberated" from conventional roles as wives and mothers.[49]

These observers were not wrong to predict an impact on children if women altered traditional family roles. Leaders in the women's movement specifically and intentionally wanted to remake the way society raises children. Inspired by popular works like Betty Friedan's 1963 *The Feminine Mystique,* they challenged the assumption that women's destiny is to be mothers, that wives should be subordinate to husbands, and that the care of children should fall entirely to their mothers. Friedan and other feminists wrote about motherhood as enslaving women and preventing their equality with men. Opponents of the women's movement joined others to oppose national child care legislation advanced by both women's rights and children's rights advocates.[50]

Is it fair to blame the women's movement for neglecting children? Many in the movement specifically attended to children's needs but argued that they should be met by fathers as well as by mothers or by new societal arrangements, such as affordable, quality child care. Failures to secure rights for children could have reflected fears of women's liberation independent of fears that women would no longer care for children; one way to keep women in conventional family roles is to appeal to their desires to protect children. Moreover, societal neglect of children's needs—indeed, the degradation and social unimportance of children—may stem from the degradation of traditional women's work.[51] In this light, rather than blame the women's movement, advocates for children should have joined them in challenging the low status accorded to women and to the work of caring for children.

But did the feminist movement itself fail to fight hard enough for child care in contrast with its strong commitments to reproductive freedom and the Equal Rights Amendment?[52] Sylvia Ann Hewitt particularly takes the American feminists to task in contrast with women's movements in Europe that focused energy on family policies and joined labor coalitions to support maternity leave, child care, and other family support programs.[53] In their defense, feminists did support child care[54] and also advocated welfare rights in general without framing

them as children's rights.[55] Perhaps American women's organizations declined to pursue a more expansive social welfare
agenda, including child care, human services, family allowances, and medical care for children because of a political cli-
mate hostile to such ideas. Yet Betty Friedan herself wrote a
popular book looking back in 1981 on the women's movement
that she helped launch and calling for a new focus on meeting
the needs of children and families.[56] Friedan called for a "second stage" for the women's movement to advocate family-
friendly policies, such as child care, flex time for workers, and
other reforms responding to the influx of women in the paid
labor force. These recommendations had something in common with the century-long child welfare tradition launched by
the Progressives, although they show a distinctively late-twentieth-century focus on women's equality.

Critics who blame the women's movement for children's
unmet needs too often think that massive numbers of women,
including mothers of young children, entered the paid labor
force in the 1970s and 1980s as a political statement. Evidence
suggests that most women joined the paid labor force because
of economic need as men's salaries failed to meet the needs of
families.[57] Rising divorce rates and growing numbers of single-
parent households also made women's paid labor a necessity.

By the start of the 1980s the movement for children's
rights had failed to secure a coherent political or intellectual
foundation, not to mention a viable constituency with political
clout. It triggered defenses of traditional authority, yet it also
continued to inspire a small but forceful set of advocates for
children in the courts and in the legislatures. The patchwork of
judicial decisions governing children's legal status placed only
the barest cover for continuing ambivalence. It remained possible to argue that young people deserve the same legal treatment as adults, that young people deserve special legal
protections differing from the law for adults, and that law
should refrain from intruding on the ordinary practices of
adults responsible for children.[58]

The absence of a consistent conception permitted people

to blame parents for failures of state responsibility, to blame the state for failures of parental responsibility, and to view children's rights as threats to both parental and state authority. These blame games grew more into criticisms of the welfare state and even the New Deal safety net programs and helped create the insecurity of children during the Reagan years and since.

IV. BRINGING THE STORY TO THE PRESENT

The insecurity of American children in the last decades of the twentieth century became cause for some attention but also continued to reflect how many adults use the topic of "children" to serve their own political agendas.[59] A *New York Times* reporter wrote the following in 1981 while assessing the Reagan administration's plans to cut services for children: "The children's rights movement, a stepchild of the liberation struggles of the 1960's, has grown into a force affecting the battle over billions of Federal dollars, a host of Government services, and an ever-increasing number of issues involving parents and the courts."[60] In contrast, consider this statement in 1977 by Gilbert Steiner, a leading expert on the needs of children: "We have had several opportunities in recent years to develop theories of intervention and I find the most depressing single aspect of the child-development movement in this country to be that each of these opportunities has been a failure."[61] No dramatic accomplishments of a children's rights movement occurred in the intervening five years; instead observers with different perspectives make what they want of the rhetoric of children's rights in the service of their own political purposes.

From the perspective of advocates for children, legislative efforts to provide quality early-childhood education, health care for families, and universal protections against poverty went nowhere; initiatives to protect children from abuse by their parents and guardians failed to stem rising rates of reported abuse; and children seemed too often victims of a violent world indifferent to their needs. Head Start, often described as the one demonstrated success of the 1960s War on Poverty, remained underfunded and thus not available for many eligible children. From the perspective of critics, even the limited legislative achievements for children—special education for children with disabilities, expanded public expenditures for protecting children from abuse and neglect, and poverty programs benefiting children and their parents—seemed wasteful and bureaucratic burdens on schools, parents, and states.[62] Underlying divisions about the proper role of the government in private life, about race, poverty, and immigration, about gender and religion seem more at work in this discussion than an honest assessment of children's entitlements in this society.

One way to stand outside these debates is to compare the status of children during this period with the status of the elderly. Strikingly the elderly impressively moved out of poverty and strengthened public programs meeting their financial and medical needs at the same time that more children fell into poverty and federal and state governments cut public programs for children. Paul Peterson offered one comparison along these lines and concluded with the "immodest proposal" that children obtain voting powers to begin to duplicate the successes of the elderly.[63]

Perhaps because children do not vote, adults invoked the interests of children in the context of divisive social issues. In the 1980s and 1990s legislative and court battles over abortion rights spilled into the children's rights terrain as pro-choice advocates sought rights for minors and pro-life advocates lobbied for parental consent or notification procedures.[64] This may be one of many instances in which children's rights are only a superficial frame for what more fairly is a larger national controversy with little opportunity to put children's interests into the picture. Thus the abortion controversy involves religion, gender roles, and the role of federal courts in politics but has little to do with the well-being of children, once born, or teenagers, once capable of sexual activity. In a very practical way the national controversy over abortion fuels local disputes over the distribution of condoms in high schools, which also touch on the equally hot topics for public health and morality: HIV and other sexually transmitted diseases. One thing is clear: Social ambivalence about children's rights will not offer a path through this thicket. Other agendas will prevail, just as they did when the Clinton administration responded to the pharmaceutical industry and abandoned plans for a national distribution of vaccinations to assure immunization of all children.[65]

Crime control is another agenda driving treatment of children and producing incoherent results. Some new developments on the "child liberation front" would surprise and might dismay child liberationists from the 1960s because children may now receive adult treatment for purposes of criminal prosecution, sentencing, and corrections.[66] The Supreme Court has rejected a cruel and unusual punishment challenge to the death penalty for a person who committed a crime as a minor.[67] A number of academic commentators have called for the abolition of the juvenile court in order to assure children the same legal treatment accorded adults.[68] At the same time the Supreme Court has ruled that public schools do not need to apply adult-style standards for searches or for free speech in dealing with violations of school rules, suspected drug use, or school discipline.[69] What joins these decisions is a sense that the world is a dangerous place and young people both face and pose serious risks, requiring a public response. Children's rights advocates in the 1960s and 1970s may never have imagined children with AIDS, infants exposed in utero to crack, or the massive dissemination of guns to children, but these are pressing issues in the 1990s.[70] Efforts to change public policies to protect these children are enmeshed in efforts to regulate and punish "bad mothers" who are so frequently poor and black or Hispanic that again agendas unrelated to children are hard at work. Rights for children—however conceptualized— are swamped by other kinds of social dilemmas and the political reactions they elicit.

As I write, Congress considers cuts in school lunches, nutrition programs for pregnant women and infants, Social Security assistance for children with disabilities, and special education. One cartoonist depicted congressional leaders noting, "We tried a war on poverty; we tried war on drugs; let's try a war on children."[71] In response at least some people will use mass media during this political season to focus attention on the situation of children in poverty. The Children's Defense Fund along with others documents the increasing percentage of American children in poverty.[72] By 1990 families with children under three became the single largest group living in poverty in this country; 25 percent of all such families fall below the poverty line.[73] Another way to put the point: A fifth of all children are poor, and children are 40 percent of the poor in this country.[74] Again, the success in fighting poverty among the elderly during the same decades raises real questions about the equity in public policy.[75] The racial disparities in the circumstances of children are also striking; 50 percent of African American and 40 percent of Latino children under the age of six live in poverty.[76] A focus on children in poverty may seem like yet another agenda using children; it is the basis for a fourth position on children's rights: social resource distribution.

Some child protectionists have long sought redistribution of resources to help children; some redistribution of resources to help children; some redistributionists throughout the past century have often focused on children as an appealing group for making the case. A 1980s-style campaign for investment in children is still under way in some parts of the corporate community, but it seems to have had little effect on the congressional debate. For better or for worse, redistribution questions will in this country be legislative ones, requiring electoral coalitions.[77] And this is precisely the method that has proved unsuccessful in varied efforts organized around children who have no ability to vote themselves.[78]

I have no plan or even hope for mobilizing public support for children, especially poor children, at this point in American history. Each of the four rhetorics—child protection, children's liberation, children's rights as potential adults, and redistribution—has failed to find a strong constituency. Instead political figures win strong support by invoking conventional authority structures, family privacy, and self-reliance and by attacking a social welfare state. It is tempting to look at other Western industrialized countries and to wonder why state-subsidized health care, day care, child allowances, and other programs are well established elsewhere and politically infeasible here. The failure of the varied rhetorics for children here can be only a symptom of, not an explanation for, the failure of initiatives for children here.

What, then, might be explanations? The history suggests four. First, children do not vote, and no lobby has appeared on their behalf.[79] Second, we have seen cycles of reform and disillusionment, epitomized by changes in juvenile court. The reforms of one generation become the problems to be reformed by a later generation and cautions against further reform. Third, children's needs are connected to larger, intractable issues, such as the economy's failure to provide good jobs for many people, the presence of women in the paid labor force without reallocation of some child care from mothers to fathers and others, negative views of poor parents, misallocated health care expenditures, failures of public education, and divisive conflicts over abortion and crime control. Finally, cultural and ideological sources produce great resistance to state intervention in families, resistance articulated by both the left and the right in American politics. Conceptions of personal responsibility and privacy, government bungling and individual freedom, cultural diversity and mutual distrust fuel this resistance. As a result, we treat other people's children as beyond public concern. Perhaps because of our troubled heterogeneity, with historic racism and intergroup distrust, we do not view other people's children as *ours* in many important ways.[80]

Given these reasons, rhetoric alone will not alter the situation of children. Yet it is tempting to seek yet another rhetoric, and an emerging one is the human rights rhetoric with which I began. It has much appeal to those who have believed in any prior version of rights for children. More practically an occasion for political mobilization has arisen now that the president has directed the U.S. ambassador to the United Nations to sign the Convention on the Rights of the Child. Because of the international framework, this could also become an occasion to look beyond the parochial and idiosyncratic views that undermine children's legal protections in this country and to consider the standards for treating children developed elsewhere.

So, in closing, I will explore the argument for international human rights for children—but also consider the limitations of any existing rights framework for this group of human beings. The argument is to treat children as candidates not for "children's rights," "child protections," or "adult rights" but instead for "human rights."[81] As human beings children deserve the kind of dignity, respect, and freedom from arbitrary treatment signaled by rights.[82] This dignity, respect, and freedom do not displace or undermine parents but instead remind parents—and other adults—of their fundamental responsibilities toward children.

Unlike children's liberation, the human rights formulation rejects the pretense that children are just like adults in all respects relevant to the law. Thus the convention calls for development rights—rights to education, cultural activities, play and leisure, freedom of thought—to meet the needs of children in reaching their full potential.[83] More comprehensive than child protection, the human rights formulation underscores that the absence of rights exposes children to risks of abuse by both their parents and government employees, including teachers, social workers, and judges. Unlike social resource redistribution, this formulation does focus on children specifically and affords a point for evaluating the entire range of legal treatments of children, not only those dealing with access to resources. Thus as human beings children deserve economic and social benefits appropriate to their needs.[84]

Human rights in the international sphere depend upon the development of a community that believes in them rather than an authority—court or legislature—that will enforce them. Organizing to influence and shape such a community may line up means and ends in precisely the way most important for children. Without adults who believe in the importance and entitlements of children, no phrase, judicial order, or legislative statement will alter their conditions.

The vulnerability of international human rights for children to the willingness and commitments of adults seems like a weakness, a failure to secure something with force. This vulnerability in another sense is a strength because it reveals how dependent and interdependent children are upon adults. In a basic sense, all rights—for adults as well as for children— require a commitment by others to recognize the claims of others and to behave accordingly. Liberal freedoms of association and religion, rights to marry and to procreate, and rights to maintain relationships with family members presuppose and enable relationships.[85] Rights should be understood as community commitments to include the rights bearers in the group deserving respect and attention.

Rights rhetorics in the past have tended too often to imply only freedom from: freedom from state control; freedom from interference by others. Children may need some forms of such freedoms, but they also need guidance, involvement, support, and even control to protect them from harms against which they cannot protect themselves. I suggest that nothing inherent in rights rhetorics prevents acknowledging these needs of children, and at the same time the rhetoric of rights is the coin of the realm in national, and increasingly international, law and politics. Not only does invoking this language put children on the map of public concern, but it also crucially implies "a respect which places one in the referential range of self and others, which elevates one's status from human body to social being."[86]

Many may ask whether it is practical to press for human rights on behalf of children.[87] A negative answer gains support from the history of children's rights movements throughout this century. Children's rights, as a phrase in search of a program, by the 1980s encompassed many contrasting and even conflicting commitments to children without notable improvement of the circumstances for many, many children. Whether styled as children's liberation or child protection or as social welfare redistribution programs, each effort found powerful opponents poised against it. Moreover, the conventional conception of rights as implying an autonomous person who needs freedom from interference seems ill suited to meeting the needs of most children.

Yet I am still a child of the 1960s. I think the past does not determine our future but instead offers a set of lessons about the relationship between ideals and contingent realities. I think that powerful concepts, like rights, are amenable to new interpretations and applications that may in turn make good on their earlier promise and deeper meanings. So I suggest we roll up our sleeves and work on every front—our workplaces, schools, communities, and states, our Congress, our medical care, our world—to explore what it would mean to view children as human beings entitled to human rights, or else we must find a better way to summon attention and resources on their behalf.

NOTES

1. Professor of law, Harvard University. A longer version of this chapter was presented as the Lockart Lecture, University of Minnesota, March 16, 1995. Thanks for the superb research assistance of Liz Tobin, additional help by Laurie Corzett, Jane Park, Justin Weiss, Liz Yap, and Terry Swanlund, and useful comments by Anita Allen and Stephen Macedo.
2. Thomas C. Palmer, Jr., "How Much Power Should a Child Wield, Anyway?," *Boston Globe,* August 16, 1992, p. 57; Eleanor Clift with Pat Wingert, "Hillary Clinton's Not-So-Hidden Agenda," *Newsweek* (September

21, 1992), p. 90; Mimi Hall, "GOP Attacks Hillary Clinton on Children's Rights," *USA Today,* August 13, 1992, p. 7A.

3. Hillary Rodham, "Children under the Law," *Harvard Education Review* 743 (1973), p. 487. She later published "Children's Policies: Abandon and Neglect," *Yale Law Journal* (1977), p. 1522 (book review), and "Children's Rights: A Legal Perspective," in *Children's Rights: Contemporary Perspectives,* ed. Alicia A. Vardin and Ilene M. Brody (1979). Clinton had worked as a student on a project at the Yale-New Haven Hospital; her task was to define the standards for defining and judging child abuse. See Clift, p. 20. See also Garry Wills, "H. R. Clinton's Case," *New York Review of Books* 39 (March 1992), p. 39.

4. Rodham (1973).

5. Reynolds Holding, "Children Are Losing, Not Gaining Rights," *Houston Chronicle,* September 27, 1992, p. A1, quoting GOP Chairman Rich Bond.

6. John Leo, "Who's Right on Children's Rights?," *San Francisco Chronicle,* (September 6, 1992), p. 5121. See also Holding, arguing that Republican critics of Clinton wrongly assumed children were gaining rights when "children are losing ground in the American legal system."

7. See Richard Farson, *Birthrights* (1974); John Holt, *Escape from Childhood* (1974). See also Beatrice Gross and Ronald Gross, "Introduction," *The Children's Rights' Movement: Overcoming the Oppression of Young People* (1977), pp. 1, 11. Hillary Clinton and Peter Edelman both explicitly drew analogies comparing children with blacks and women—all as people treated in the past as chattel and deserving rights. Clinton; and Edelman, "The Children's Rights Movement," in *Gross and Gross,* p. 203.

8. Farson, p. 9.

9. Ibid., p. 3.

10. Ibid.

11. Ibid., p. 52.

12. This passage is quoted in Paul Goodman, "Reflections on Children's Rights," in Gross and Gross, pp. 141–42.

13. See, e.g., Helen Baker, "Growing Up Unheard," in Gross and Gross, pp. 187, 189, and Youth Liberation of Ann Arbor, "We Do Not Recognize Their Right to Control Us," in Gross and Gross, pp. 125–34.

14. John Holt, "Why Not a Bill of Rights for Children?" in Gross and Gross, pp. 317, 324–25.

15. See Charles Silberman, *Crisis in the Classroom* (1970); James Rothenberg, "The Open Classroom Reconsidered," *Elementary School Journal* 90 (September 1989), p. 69.

16. See Henry H. Foster, Jr., *A "Bill of Rights" for Children* (1974); Gross and Gross, p. 12; Rosalind Ekman Ladd, *Children's Rights Re-Visioned: Philosophical Readings* (1995), p. 2.

17. Gilbert Steiner, *The Children's Cause* (1976), pp. 10–11.

18. Ibid., p. 11.

19. Ibid.

20. It is true that some people used the language of rights in an earlier period; see Michael Grossberg, "Children's Legal Rights? A Historical Look at a Legal Paradox," in *Children at Risk,* ed. Roberta Wollans (1993), pp. 111,

114–26. As secretary of commerce Herbert Hoover presented Congress with a proposal for a Children's Bill of Rights, *The Memoirs of Herbert Hoover*, vol. 2, *The Cabinet and the Presidency, 1920–1933* (1952), pp. 99–100, 261–64. But the earlier uses of "rights" language referred specifically either to efforts to achieve earlier emancipation—and adult legal status—or else to legitimate paternalism and enlarged use of state power to protect children. pp. 115, 121.

21. "An Interview with Marian Wright Edelman," 44 *Harvard Education Review*, (February 1994), p. 53.

22. Ibid., pp. 53–57.

23. Ibid., pp. 66–67.

24. "An Interview with Marion Wright Edelman," p. 70. See also Rothman, pp. 275–76. Joseph M. Hawes cites the defeat of the child development bill in 1971 as the beginning of the downhill slope of the children's rights movement. Hawes, *The Children's Rights Movement: A History of Advocacy and Protection* (1991), p. 119.

25. In re Gault, 383 U.S. 1 (1967).

26. Tinker v. Des Moines Independent School District, 393 U.S. 503 (1969).

27. Goss v. Lopez, 419 U.S. 555 (1975).

28. On the racial dimensions of *Goss v. Lopez*, see Franklin E. Zimring and Rayman L. Solomon, *Goss v. Lopez: The Principle of the Thing, in In the Interests of Children*, ed. Robert Mnookin (1985), pp. 459–72.

29. Education for All Handicapped Children's Act, PL 94-142 (1975), amended and renamed; reflecting success in cases like Pennsylvania Association for Retarded Children (PARC) v. Pennsylvania, 343 F.Supp. 279 (E.D.Pa. 1972) and New York State Association for Retarded Children, Inc. v. Rockefellar, 357 F.Supp. 752 (E.D.N.Y. 1973); 393 F.Supp. 715 (E.D.N.Y. 1975) (Willowbrook Case). See generally Martha Minow, *Making All the Difference: Inclusion, Exclusion, and American Law* (1990).

30. Child Abuse Prevention and Treatment Act of 1973 (requiring states to meet federal standards for custody, including empowering state child welfare agencies to remove a child from a family for three days if the agency believes the child is in danger); Adoption Assistance and Child Welfare Act of 1980.

31. McKeiver v. Pennsylvania, 403 U.S. 528 (1971).

32. Wisconsin v. Yoder, 406 U.S. 205 (1972).

33. Ingraham v. Wright, 430 U.S. 651 (1977).

34. See Minow, "Rights for the Next Generation: A Feminist Approach to Children's Rights," *Harvard Women's Law Journal* 9 (1986), p. 1.

35. He later became a law professor, and then counsel to secretary of the Department of Health and Human Services.

36. Peter Edelman, pp. 203–04.

37. Ibid., pp. 204–06.

38. See, e.g., Hamilton Cravens, "Child Saving in Modern America 1870s–1990s," in *Children at Risk in America*, p. 3; Margo Horn, "Inventing the Problem Child: 'At-Risk' Children in the Child Guidance Movement of the 1920s and 1930s," in *Children at Risk in America*, p. 141.

39. See Michael Grossberg, "Children's Legal Rights? A Historical Look at a Legal Paradox," pp. 111, 119–126.
40. See Martha Minow and Richard Weissbourd, "Social Movements for Children," *Daedalus* 122 (1993), pp. 1, 7–8; Ellen Ryerson, *The Best-Laid Plans* (1976).
41. The Reagan administration also adopted regulations cutting back on the nutritional quality of federally funded school lunches, including a rule treating ketchup as a vegetable substitute. After ensuing public criticism, the administration withdrew the rule. Helen Thomas, "Proposed School Lunch Rules Scrapped," September 26, 1991 (UPI, P.M. cycle).
42. Wisconsin v. Yoder, 406 U.S. 205 (1972); Parham v. J. R. 422 U.S. 584 (1979).
43. Ingraham v. Wright, 430 U.S. 651 (1977).
44. Parham v. J. R., 422 U.S. 584 (1979). See generally Robert Burt, "Developing Constitutional Rights of, in, and for Children," *Law and Contemporary Problems* 39 (1975), p. 118.
45. Bruce Hafen, "Children's Liberation and the New Egalitarianism: Some Reservations about Abandoning Children to Their 'Rights,' " *Brigham Young University Law Review* (1976), p. 607.
46. 419 U.S., 580.
47. Ingraham v. Wright, 430 U.S. 651 (1977).
48. See Deborah Rhode, *Justice and Gender* (1989), pp. 70–77.
49. See Sylvia A. Hewitt, *A Lesser Life* (1986), pp. 183–90; Hawes, p. 98; Rothman, pp. 246–47.
50. Edward Zigler and Susan Muenchow, "How to Influence Social Policy Affecting Families and Children," *American Psychologist* 39 (April 1984), pp. 415–16.
51. See Susan Faludi, *Backlash* (1991).
52. Hewitt, p. 190. See also Steiner, pp. 155–57.
53. Hewitt, ch. 6. See also Sheila B. Kamerman, *Starting Right: How America Neglects Its Youngest Children and What We Can Do about It* (1995).
54. See, e.g., Karen DeCrow, "Universal Child Care Is a NOW Priority," *National NOW Times* (April 1989), p. 4; *National NOW Times* (January 1979), quoting *Meet the Press,* November 20, 1977.
55. See Katha Pollitt, "Welfare Reform: Many Feminist Voices Lead to Almost as Many Messages," *Chicago Tribune,* July 17, 1994, p. 6.
56. Betty Friedan, *The Second Stage* (1981). In her own best-selling *Backlash,* Susan Faludi charges Friedan with revisionism in writing *The Second Stage* and contributing to a backlash against feminism.
57. David Ellwood, *Poor Support* (1988); William Julius Wilson and Kathryn M. Neckerman, "Poverty and Family Structure: The Widening Gap between Evidence and Public Policy Issues," in *Fighting Poverty: What Works and What Doesn't,* ed. Sheldon Danziger and Daniel Weinberg (1986), pp. 232–59.
58. See Jane Knitzer, "Children's Rights in the Family and Society," *American Journal of Orthopsychiatry* 52 (July 1982), p. 481.
59. See generally David A. Hamburg, *Today's Children* (1994), examining

threats to children's physical and emotional well-being along with failures of public responses.

60. Glenn Collins, "Debate over Rights of Children Is Intensifying," *New York Times,* July 21, 1981, p. 1.

61. Gilbert Steiner, in Milton J. E. Senn, *Speaking Out for America's Children* (1977), p. 193.

62. Ibid., Douglas Besharov, "How Child Abuse Programs Hurt Poor Children: The Misuse of Foster Care," *Clearinghouse Review* 22 (July 1988), p. 219.

63. Paul Peterson, "An Immodest Proposal," *Daedalus* 121 (1992), pp. 151–74.

64. See, e.g., City of Akron v. Akron Center for Reproductive Health, 462 U.S. 416 (1983); Bellotti v. Baird, 443 U.S. 622 (1979).

65. Robert Pear, "The Health Care Debate: Immunizations," *New York Times,* August 23, 1994. Immigration policy is another in which children's rights become a superficial topic caught in the midst of a larger debate. See, e.g., Reena Shah Stamets, "Like It or Not, Immigration Debate Is Coming Your Way," *St. Petersburg Times,* May 7, 1995, p. 99A, discussing California's Proposition 187, and Flores v. Meese, 942 F.2d 1352 (CA 9 1991), striking down as a violation of children's due process rights the Immigration and Naturalization Service regulation requiring that undocumented children be released only to the custody of certain relatives.

66. Michael J. Dale, "The Burger Court and Children's Rights—A Trend toward Retribution?," *Children's Rights Journal* 8 (Winter 1987), pp. 7, 8. See also Gregory J. Skibinski and Ann M. Koszuth, "Getting Tough with Juvenile Offenders: Ignoring the Best Interests of the Child, *Juvenile & Family Court Journal* 37 (Winter 1986), p. 43. Perhaps the liberationist rhetoric of the sixties reflected a kind of romanticism about especially privileged children; if so, it is especially ironic that poor and minority children are the "beneficiaries" of policies treating minors as adults for criminal justice purposes.

67. Stanford v. Kentucky, 492 U.S. 361 (1989).

68. E.g., Janet E. Ainsworth, "Re-Imagining Childhood and Reconstructing the Legal Order: The Case for Abolishing the Juvenile Court," *North Carolina Law Review* 69 (1991), p. 1083; Barry C. Feld, "The Transformation of the Juvenile Court," *Minnesota Law Review,* 75 (1991), p. 691.

69. Dale, p. 11, discussing New Jersey v. T. L. O., 469 U.S. 724 (1985); Bethel School District v. Fraser, 478 U.S. 675 (1986).

70. For an overview of issues, see Gary B. Melton, "Children, Families, and the Courts in the Twenty-first Century," *Southern California Law Review* 66 (1994), p. 1993.

71. Dan Wasserman, *Boston Globe,* November 29, 1994, editorial page.

72. James D. Weill, "Child Poverty in America," *1991* Clearinghouse Review (1991), p. 336 adapted from Children's Defense Fund, *Child Poverty in America* (June 1991); Marian Wright Edelman, Investing in Our Young—or Else, *Human Rights* 16 (Summer 1989), p. 19.

73. Carnegie Corporation, *Starting Points: Meeting the Needs of Our Youngest Children* (April 1994), p. 17.

74. Ray Marshall, *The State of Families: Losing Direction* (1991), p. 29.

75. See Peterson.
76. American Bar Association Presidential Working Group on the Unmet Legal Needs of Children and Their Families, *America's Children at Risk: A National Agenda for Legal Action* (1993), p. 10.
77. The Supreme Court has refused to view wealth as a suspect classification. San Antonio School District v. Rodriguez, 441 U.S. 1 (1973).
78. Steiner; Zigler and Muenchow. Peterson suggests granting parents the ability to exercise extra votes as trustees for their children. Peterson, p. 151.
79. See Peterson, proposing votes for children after comparing reductions in poverty among seniors during the same period of increased poverty among children.
80. For a fuller discussion of these four factors, see Minow and Weissbourd, "Social Movements for Children."
81. This brings us back to the UN Convention, and the history of viewing children as eligible for human rights. See generally Cynthia Price Cohen, "The Developing Jurisprudence of the Rights of the Child," *St. Thomas Law Review* 6 (1993), p. 1.
82. The UN convention explicitly recognizes children's individual personality rights for this reason. Ibid., p. 7.
83. Susan Fountain, *It's Only Right! A Practical Guide to Learning about the Convention on the Rights of the Child* (n.d.), p. 2.
84. Ibid., p. 8 and n. 31. Some describe these as survival rights that include provision for an adequate living standard, shelter, nutrition, and access to medical services.
85. This is a theme I have tried to develop elsewhere. See Minow, *Making All the Difference,* pp. 267–311; Minow, "Rights for the Next Generation," pp. 1, 16.
86. Patricia Williams, *The Alchemy of Race and Rights* (1991), p. 416.
87. Some U.S. advocates for human rights worry about efforts to place the convention on children's rights as so high a priority as to defeat other human rights efforts currently under way. This is a real worry given the history of the response to the convention on genocide and the targeting of the children's rights convention currently by right-wing interest groups. One need not place the convention on children's rights ahead of others. The worry really raises the political calculus and priority of purposes: Should one abandon the convention on children's rights because it is controversial or should one support it to weigh in on the controversy?

PART TWO

——

THE
UNIVERSITIES
AND
EDUCATION

The Destructive Sixties
and Postmodern Conservatism

SHELDON WOLIN

There are profound things that went wrong starting
with the Great Society and the counterculture. . . .
We simply need to erase the slate and start over. . . .
I am a genuine revolutionary. They are the genuine
reactionaries. We are going to change the world. They
will do anything to stop us."

—Speaker Newt Gingrich[1]

An Unlikely Legacy of the 60's: The Violent Right.
The Radical Right Has an Unlikely Soulmate in the
Leftist Politics of the 60's, Historians Say."

—*New York Times* (in the aftermath
of the Oklahoma City bombing)[2]

I

About a half century ago conservatism was little more than a
crotchety defense of what used to be called vested interests,
or a distaste for New Deal "leveling," or a fondness for taste-
less jokes about Franklin and Eleanor, or the affectation of
English cultural ways. A short time ago any suggestion that
associated conservatism with a dynamic politics would have
been dismissed as a contradiction in terms. No longer a curiosity or an anachronism, conservatism has been made over into

the opposite of its former stodgy self. It is in the process of becoming transformed from a status quo, resolutely antimodernist ideology—typified by William Buckley's jejune *God and Man at Yale*—to a futuristic one—Newt Gingrich canonizing the author of *Future Shock*—that is strikingly postmodernist in some of its elements.[3] Old-style conservatism longed to be Burkean; new style has more than a touch of Nietzsche.[4]

There is a certain paradoxical quality to recent conservative attacks upon the sixties and their simultaneous claim that it is contemporary conservatives who are the real radicals with truly revolutionary ideas. Such boasting might have seemed plausible had it emanated from the far side of the left, but coming from the political establishment of the right and at the very moment when the alumni(ae) of the Berkeley free speech movement were gathering for the thirtieth anniversary of events that marked the beginning of the student "movements" of the decade, it seemed more like a tactic for stealing the thunder of the opposition—except that in this case the thunder of the sixties is scarcely audible. Attempting a response, the aging representatives of FSM, in vintage style, detected a whiff of neofascism in the air and insisted that the principles of 1964 were as relevant as ever.

Before we dismiss the attack upon the sixties as the prelude to political repression, or the claim to radicalism by conservatives as so much political hot air, it might be worthwhile exploring a different possibility. The rhetorical formulations of both the defenders of the sixties and the critics may be indicative of a historical transformation occurring in both conservatism and radicalism. At its center is a reversal of historical roles and of historical consciousness and, along with it, of the political identities formed around conceptions of past and future that once distinguished radicalism from conservatism. The complexity of a reversal that finds conservatives professing to be revolutionaries, while in actuality they are more accurately described as counterrevolutionary, may be a product of the strict taboos imposed by the American political tradition on discussion of the idea of counterrevolution. Consequently conservatives are nudged toward a language that encodes that idea while seeming to contradict it. Although "revolutionary conservatism" may in reality be counterrevolutionary, one effect of that rhetoric is to deprive radicals of their distinctive claim. The effect of having revolution snatched from them may leave exposed an important strand of counterrevolution in contemporary radicalism.

One way perhaps to unravel the complexity is to recognize that the conservative fixation upon the sixties is, in large part, driven by *revanchisme,* specifically by the memory of certain searing defeats that have left their marks on conservative psyches and in the long run contributed to the election of conservative presidents during the eighties and a deeply conservative Congress in 1994. During the sixties there were three substantial victories that the left considered emblematic and about which the right remains unforgiving. Those victories constitute an important part of what defines the counterrevolutionary substance of the "revolutionary" right and the democratic substance of the sixties. They are: the civil rights movement and the drive toward equality, the antiwar movement and the rejection of the whole expansionist mentality of the political and corporate establishment, and the politicalization of a substantial number of students and a smaller number of faculty at many major institutions of higher learning.

Conservatives have believed that these victories were tainted by illegitimacy, concessions extracted by pressure and force emanating from outside the usual political processes. It was a short step from the notion of illegitimacy and a narrow conception of the political to constructing a violent, destructive sixties. There were, of course, actions and rhetoric that could be used to illustrate that construction. Yet the charge is, unintentionally, ironic given the general atmosphere of the sixties. The years from, say, 1964–1974 fairly reeked of violence, most of it officially inspired, sanctioned, or encouraged. The Vietnam War, the murders and beatings that were the normal response to the nonviolent tactics of the civil rights movement, the suppression of the Watts uprisings and the urban ghetto riots, the murders of the Kennedy brothers and Martin Luther King, the police action at the Democratic National Convention of 1968, the tear gas sprayed by helicopters upon campuses, the murder of students by police and National Guard at Berkeley, Kent State, Jackson State, and Orangeburg provided a seemingly endless succession of shocks, a shattering firsthand experience in the delegitimizing of the authority of the state for a whole generation of young Americans.

To its defenders the sixties were a time when Americans, especially younger ones and especially students, began a quest to expand the meaning and practice of freedom. It was a time for seeing the world and themselves with fresh eyes, for believing that it was possible to begin things anew. Criticism and protest—in words, actions, song, and dress—were the means for clearing a space by focusing the revulsion of the young against "the system." That term encompassed not only political and corporate power structures but also conventional moral and sexual norms and the work-and-success ethic. The system was condemned roundly, for being racist and repressive at home and imperialist and bellicose abroad. With the deepening of the war what began as a yearning for liberation quickly became an attack upon modern forms of power and their scales: of a state that was grotesquely overextended, of a corporate system that was heedless of the environment, and of technologies that recognized no limits. To their conservative detractors, however, the sixties were a case of subjectivity run amok, of expressions of personal feelings, no matter how bizarre, being treated as deep truths while any plea for common sense or moderation that issued from some authority could expect only hoots of derision. In conservative eyes the sixties were lawlessness bordering on anarchy, antipatriotism courting treason, and drug abuse masquerading as innocent hedonism.

The incommensurability of the two versions of the sixties extends even to disagreements about when they began, when, or if, they ended, and what their defining moments were.

Defenders stretch the decade to include the expansion of the Vietnam War into Cambodia (spring 1970), the shootings at Kent State, and, not least, the disgrace of President Nixon. Detractors prefer to mention the deadly bomb planted at the University of Wisconsin, the battles between police and Black Panthers, and the occupation of campus administration buildings by armed students.

In what follows I shall refer to the conservative version of the sixties as the Myth of the Sixties and the conservative version of its own identity as the Countermyth. And I shall call the response by the defenders of the sixties the Myth Manqué and attempt to explain that designation by recounting some personal experiences of Berkeley during that decade. Naming the myths as I have is preliminary to showing that the identities of the Countermyth and the Myth Manqué are bound together not simply as opposites but in an exchange relation that reveals some of the profound changes taking place in American political life.

By employing the idea of myth with reference to contemporary beliefs and commitments, I do not mean to belittle the serious efforts at description and analysis by those who have criticized and / or defended the Sixties.[5] Nor do I want to assimilate my formulations to the usages of cultural anthropologists and students of comparative religion or, worse, dismiss them as false or crude ideologies. The concern is with political myths—that is, with myths that are contesting for the true identity of society by means of a narrative heavy with *fatefulness* and constructed to attract support for the political project of those whom the mythmakers represent. Political myths tend to portray peoples, events, and ideas in language that verges on the preternatural. This is because myths are meant to heighten tension; they are fraught with foreboding and promise. The peculiarity of contemporary myths is that they are meant for an age for which, as we shall see, the preternatural has been normalized.

II

Although myths are made, they are not totally made up. Their persuasiveness to late-twentieth-century information-conditioned audiences requires that mythmakers pay some heed to facts. The content of myths tends toward a compound of the factual and the factitious while their structure comes to resemble that of docudramas: There is a "real basis" for the drama, but "liberties" have been taken.

As a political intervention myths do depict not impersonal forces but actors who represent actual or potential forces. Myths present dramatic personifications, charged narratives rather than formal arguments. These are intended to evoke responses by literally characterizing events or states of affairs. The idea of myth is appropriate precisely because of a crucial change taking place in advanced industrial societies, an evolution from a social form in which science was primary, and technology derivative, to one in which technology is the driving force. The primacy of technology is owing to a direct and virtually immediate relationship between the introduction of new technology and the production of supporting cultures. Technology invents its own cultures almost instantaneously; consider the several cultures, from computer hackers to cyberpunks, brought in by the latest electronic revolutions, or the cultures ushered in by changing technologies involving the reproduction of contemporary music. In contrast, modern science required nearly three centuries before it enjoyed broad support, and even then the culture of science could not be described, as technological culture can, as mass-based. Today new cultural forms are technologically driven and postscientific. The culture of a society that once looked to science as exemplifying the highest ideals of truth telling and seeking but that now has, if not dethroned, at least demoted science can truly be described as postmodern. A society that shapes its life to accord with the pace and competitive requirements of a market economy founded upon technological innovation will, as a matter of course, ceaselessly destroy and re-create values or, more precisely, beliefs. It is ripe for myths. For as Schumpeter recognized when likening capitalism to "creative destruction," the market is as nihilistic as any full-blooded Nietzschean could desire, and because of its destructiveness, that same society yearns to believe. Its publicists elevate the market into a dogma and urge submission to its "forces" and faith in the priesthood of advertisers and in the speculative strategies of junk bond dealers.

This is not to suggest that science has by any means disappeared, any more than the "triumph of science" led to the disappearance of religion. Nor is it to assert that science will cease to play the main role in the production of knowledge. What is being suggested is that the cultural context over which neoconservatives are seeking to establish hegemony has undergone a significant shift. Certain ascetic ideals that had formed important elements in the culture of science—rigorous demonstration, parsimonious explanation, empirical proof, verification procedures, and a community of practitioners—have lost their aura of authority, and as a result, the urge to emulate scientists has perceptibly weakened.

Dialogue, which for centuries has been regarded as a method distinctive to philosophy and the humanities, seems pointless at a moment when truth claims are regarded either as a matter of discursive conventions that happen to be in place or as the expression of a will to power. Discourse becomes performance rather than persuasion. The content of the materials is a secondary consideration. What is all-important is that discourse has an inexhaustible supply of materials to process by interpretation, and this technology can supply endlessly. "Culture" is to the eighties and nineties what science was from 1930 to 1960. The difference is that between endless interpretation and cumulative knowledge.

Belief is the operational correlate of poststructuralism and perhaps *the* necessary condition of a postmodern society. Contrary to the faith of earlier theorists of modernization, it appears that as societies modernize, there is a resurgence of religion. In the United States commentators are continually surprised at the vitality of organized religions and at the high percentage of citizens who claim to "believe" in God. That phenomenon is not, I would suggest, a matter of the credulous many resisting the sophisticated few and the blandishments of secular humanism. It reflects instead an interplay going on *within* a large number of individuals in this high tech society. Consider the parallelism between, on the one hand, a dynamic system of technological innovation that is continuously pushing past previous limits of achievement and, on the other, the extent to which *transgression* has been popularized. Recall the recent news story about the young man who participated in a talk show that explored the "problem" of how he might go about losing his virginity. Five young women hidden behind screens egged him on by graphically describing how they would assist and facilitate. One was his sister. The program was sponsored by some of the country's largest corporations, which are, by most reckonings, among the principal agencies of change. This suggests that transgression—the deliciousness of risk symbolically acted out—is a way of legitimating change, of asserting that it is normal to challenge established limits. The talk show mystifies power (corporate sponsorship) into legitimating authority *(vox populi),* We the People, the undisputed sovereign, that fill the media every day with our opinions, unaware that culture is ephemera, its demos a construction of an electronic market and a ghostly impersonation of a lost political sovereignty.

Hence the puzzle: The audiences for talk shows are widely acknowledged to be conservative, religious, and staunchly in favor of "family values," yet significant numbers of that population are apparently avid fans of cultural performances in which those same norms are publicly flouted. Transgression is, however, far from signifying the absence of belief or atheism. Transgression is initially defiance, even a death wish inciting retribution. The symbolic transgressor, however, does not want to die but to change. Transgression thus generates a need for belief that is parasitic off the radical element in transgression but simultaneously contains it and then endlessly recycles it. The transgressor can sin yet be saved in order to sin and be saved, etc. ("Jesus loves sinners.") Contrary to what sophisticated neoconservatives sometimes suggest, the Religious Right, Moral Majority, fundamentalists, and anti-abortionists are not an embarrassment to the new change-oriented conservatism but a necessary mythic element in its Countermyth. If rapid technological change means anything, it means social disruption, uprooted populations, and an anxious work force, all the elements that serve to justify increasing the means of social control. Many liberals, it might be noted in passing, could enthusiastically welcome technological change but were unable to face its implications, preferring to euphemize social control as welfare.

Transgression was a cliché in the sixties, but then it signified individual choice. Its inspiration was likely to be Camus, not Rush Limbaugh, and it was typically a protest against the powers and dominations. Today transgression is a form of complicity with the powers. It has become a permanent practice for the new conservativism because the two crucial forms of power with which that ideology identifies most closely, the market and technological innovation, are viewed as beyond control. As denizens of a market society endlessly exposed to fresh "waves" of change, we are fated to transgress just as surely as any heir of Calvin's Adam was fated to sin.

The Myth and Countermyth of our inquiry, then, are post-, not prescientific; hence the premodern responses to myth, such as awe, wonder, and mystery, are inappropriate or, more accurately, impossible. Postmodern myths are *fabricated,* in the double meaning of the word. They are constructed, and they are, like stories, made up. Premodern mythmaking sought to contemporize the past. The self-conscious project of postmodern conservative mythmaking is to futurize the present, whose meaning it wants to determine and whose direction it hopes to control. Premodern myths were created anonymously, invisibly, and atemporally. Their authors were unknown, while the processes by which they were assembled and the moments when they first appeared remain vague, "lost in the mists of time," in the older formula. Contemporary myths, in contrast, are objects of calculation and forethought; hence their origins and modes of production are, for the most part, transparent. This is especially true of the Myth and Countermyth; they are indebted to conservative foundations, certain publishing houses, and business corporations. The highest expression of the process of fabrication is the think tank where everyone seems to think pretty much alike, the lowest being the talk show host who talks back to everyone but brooks no backtalk from anyone.

The persistence of myth in advanced industrial, scientific societies is related to the second or pejorative meaning of fabrication, the manufacture of untruth. Broadly stated, ancient myths were believed because they were thought to have been *revealed*. Revelation was the guarantee that grounded belief in truth. Today's myths are constructed for an era when truth is embarrassed by its name and subverted by the quotation marks that usually accompany most references to it. They are believed because they are believable to an era in which distraction is ubiquitous and belief is transitory. "Credibility" is accordingly a popular item in the current political vocabulary. That it is rarely embarrassed by quotation marks is testimony to both the kinship of *what* is made credible with *who* is being rendered credulous as well as to low expectations that truth will emerge in public discourse or that it can linger without inducing boredom. A similar skepticism surrounds concepts of "reality" that a short time ago had been assumed to be truth's necessary presupposition. Credibility / credulity is a sign of the displacement of reality, first by the normalizing of the fantastic and the fantasizing of the normal. It includes everything from the latest "world" concocted by computer technology for the few to the latest television commercial that dazzles the many by images of magical transformations of familiar objects, such as an automobile that suddenly soars into space or beer bottles that play football. Second, fantasy and reality become interchangeable, as when a television actress who regularly plays the deceived wife in a soap opera thereby acquires credentials to appear as an expert dispensing counsel about "real" love and marriage on a program for teenagers.[6]

This is not to suggest that contemporary myths are the work of confirmed liars. Rather they are the expression of an age in which the will-to-truth, though not the will-to-believe, has been overwhelmed by perspectivism, the belief that no view is privileged, that each view is merely one among many possible interpretations.[7] So pervasive is perspectivism that what passes as insight among political consultants, advertising executives, and academic Nietzscheans is already the stuff of clichés in less exalted quarters. Stanford's football coach recently noted, "Perception is everything." Postmodern myths are for a world where the distinction between "angle of vision" and "spin" is a matter of concern only to the next to last man.

III

The vitality of our Myth Manqué in comparison to the Countermyth provides an index to the relative power of the political and social forces represented *in* and *by* the competing myths. At the present moment conservatism is clearly in the ascendancy, so much so that it is commonplace to remark that the United States is a conservative country. The banality of that observation, however, doesn't lessen the dramatic changes taking place in contemporary conservatism and shaping its Countermyth.

The evolution of conservatism from standpatism to futurism encompasses a dramatic switch in temporal perspectives that underlies our myths. Ever since the eighteenth-century revolutions in America and France and continuing down to the Bolshevik Revolution, the identity formation of what might loosely be called left and right, as well as the dividing line between them, has importantly turned upon their different conceptions of the relationship between past, present, and future.

Historically the myths most closely associated with the modern left—progress, modernization, and revolution—have been oriented toward a conception of the future as ever more expansive and inclusive. The past in turn was condemned as being scarcity-ridden for all but the few. Discontinuity with the past and even with the present was therefore a positive value. The older right, as represented in the title of Buckley's book, affected a nostalgia for a past whose values were held to be superior to the innovations of the present. Often its cultivated tone belied a certain literalness: Conservatives were dedicated to conserving what was best in the past and present, the best invariably being created and appreciated only by the few who were pledged to defending it against change and the *vulgus*.[8]

At the present moment, however, conservative politicians feel no awkwardness in proclaiming themselves to be the "true revolutionaries," an identification no conservative politician would have dared whisper during the years of the Cold War. What enables the contemporary conservative to talk easily about revolution, about reducing the scope of government and decentralizing its powers, about sweeping alterations in social policies is the new conception of change being hatched that shares certain family resemblances with themes of the sixties. As I write these lines, Senator Dole, a traditional conservative politician desperate to seem modish, has announced that his presidential candidacy would emphasize change, and he contrasted it with the position of the liberal incumbent, saying that President Clinton was firmly opposed to all change.

The postmodern sympathies among self-styled revolutionary and radical conservatives does not prevent them from cohabiting with the primarily Protestant Christian Right. Fundamentalist and evangelical Christians have often described themselves as radicals, as movers and shakers, and associated their radicalism with individual rebirth and renewal, with personal change and vigorous patriotism.

The reversal in temporal conceptions has the consequence of exposing the paradoxical character of postmodern conservatism. It is counterrevolutionary because of its postmodernism, the same postmodernism that allows conservatives also to proclaim their radicalism in the language of anti-Enlightenment. Critiques of the Enlightenment, it will be recalled, are nowadays in fashion among the left literati. Since the Enlightenment change has typically been associated with the widest possible extension of certain fundamental values, such as education, economic opportunity, healthful conditions, leisure time, access to aesthetic objects and experience, and improvements in the technologies of daily life. Change meant improvement in the lot of the Many. During the sixties, however, radicals began attacking the idea of "technological society." Liberal assumptions concerning "growth," "development," "modernization," and technological-scientific solutions to social problems were called into question and declared destructive. At the same time, however, the left held fast to the Enlightenment agenda of extending to all the benefits of education, healthy living conditions, economic opportunity, and leisure—in other words, the benefits that modern technology alone seemed able to deliver. The left was thus accepting a vision of the future that was riven by a deep contradiction between an expansive social program and a constricted, small-is-beautiful economy designed according to "appropriate technology."

Today's conservatism has taken on that dilemma, not to resolve but to puncture it. Conservatives have done nothing less than reconceive change in exclusionist terms while embracing wholeheartedly the gospel that technological innovation is necessary to survival under the Darwinian conditions of international economic competition. In the postmodern era change is no longer as promissory as it was in the expansive and inclusive terms of the Enlightenment. Change does mean dazzling opportunities of wealth, prestige, and power for the few, but for the many it delivers widening disparities, less of most of the basic values, and obsolescence. The Enlightenment is thus turned on its head: The redefinition of change spells the paradox of technological advance in support of counterrevolution. Already the advent of the computer is driving a deeper wedge between classes and races, between those who have the resources to stay abreast of a rapidly changing technology, the educational background to grasp symbolic modes of reasoning, and the material means for joining information networks.[9] At the same time, as is well known, these new technologies offer unparalleled means for control of the contents of education and culture by governments and corporations.

IV

Paradoxically, in the right's Myth the sixties are depicted as a dynamic, dangerous force, as destructive now as it was then. While the decade is kept alive and contemporary in the rhetoric of its foes, the defenders embalm it, conserving it as a myth about origins, a Genesis recounting epical deeds in the past. It is Myth Manqué, an exhausted narrative, unable to say why its story is relevant to the present or the future and fated to shuffle off into nostalgia, a memorial service at Woodstock for pudgy yuppies. What was there about the sixties that encouraged this denouement?

While, in fact, there were several simultaneous sixties, there was also an amazing amount of carryover, especially from politics to culture, personal life to politics, education to politics, and vice versa. One powerful unifier was the self and collective dramatization centered on a myth of liberation.[10] At the time critics described it as sanctioning anarchy and the subversion of values. The notion common to both the experienced myth and the unfriendly reconstruction of it was / is revolution. To the committed, revolution functioned like a Sorelian myth, a unifying image that fortified the will to act and lent coherence to what were otherwise disconnected, heterogeneous, and random "happenings." The mass demonstrations, acts of civil disobedience, communal experiments, aesthetic innovations, Earth Day celebration, educational innovations did not spring from of a desire to "participate" but from a newly discovered passion for significant action. In later decades revolution dropped out of the myth, and with it the element that had unified the sixties in the eyes of those who were living it. What remained after the dissolution were a Myth Manqué and a heap of disaggregated events and tendencies that made it possible to select the sixties of one's choice: The sixties could be drugs, sexual revolution, or rock 'n' roll, or the civil rights movement, or the antiwar demonstrations, or the agonizing of SDS.

While the counterculture in its critical cultural forms may be said to have ended with the decade, the political sixties did not, although they narrowly missed interment in the McGovern debacle. During the Democratic primaries of 1972 and the McGovern campaign a substantial effort was made to lure the sixties' rebels into the processes of mainstream politics. The result was a Nixon landslide and a rite of passage for a new generation of mainstream cadres. It is tempting to claim the sixties were finally vindicated by Watergate and its aftermath, but that would reinforce the notion that while Nixon might eventually be rehabilitated and later generations forced to lick the backside of stamps bearing his face, the sixties have passed.

The sixties were, in fact, one of the two great political decades of this century. The New Deal thirties were the other. Both left an imprint on subsequent decades, and both made a permanent contribution to American democratic traditions. Yet in many ways the political sixties and the political thirties were antagonists. The New Deal constructed a powerful bureaucratic state and tried to use it for democratic social ends. During the forties and afterward, however, those purposes became entangled with the projection of American military and corporate power abroad and were ultimately overwhelmed by the Vietnam War.

The sixties were the first great attempt, mostly spontaneous and improvised, at a democratic revival of American political life since the Populist revolts of the last quarter of the nineteenth century. The sixties stood in a long line of protests against the monopolization of politics by the electoral system and the consequent confinement of political action to the official processes that by the mid-twentieth century were dominated by imperial presidents, global corporations, bureaucratized institutions, and big money. But where the New Deal had sought to enlarge the scope and scale of the state, the sixties sought to diminish the state and to relocate and intensify politics by reducing its scales. Protest was a way of opening space for new political forms and rhetoric, new actors and agendas, Groups that had hitherto been mostly silent and passive were galvanized: African Americans, Hispanics, Asian Americans, gays and lesbians, women, students. The sixties converted democracy from a rhetorical to a working proposition, not just about equal rights but about new models of action and access to power in workplaces, schools, neighborhoods, and local communities.

In that vein I should like to offer a brief personal memoir of those days by recalling and reflecting upon two episodes that took place on the Berkeley campus, one in 1964, the other in 1970. During that period I was a tenured member of the faculty and an active participant in the events as well as coauthor of several essays dealing with them.[11] A comparison of the two events is instructive in showing, first, the different dynamics at work even though the setting and the actors remained roughly the same and, second, how the development of the events contained a microcosm of why the sixties became a Myth Manqué instead of the starting point for the redemocratization of American politics.

V

In December 1964 the Berkeley faculty voted overwhelmingly for a series of resolutions aimed at protecting freedom of speech, assembly, and political activity on the campus and at setting down conditions meant to ensure that their exercise would not interfere with the ordinary functions of the university.

It was in the best sense of the term a liberal solution. Constitutional guarantees of free political activity were recognized, and the faculty asserted an implicit claim to being a coeval partner with the administration in determining campus policies. The controversy itself had been cast primarily in a liberal idiom as a dispute about "rules": Who had the authority to make rules—the regents who governed the whole statewide system? The local administration? Representatives of students, faculty, and administration? Who should judge violations?

The idea of rules was seized upon by all sides and argued with unflagging zeal. Proceduralism became the element that could unify most shades of opinion and prevent the fissures among the faculty from deepening further. There was virtually no discussion of topics such as educational reform or of the proper role of faculty members as consultants to corporations or to federal agencies. What made the politics of the time seem radical was that the student-faculty objectives presented a challenge to the Board of Regents. The board's authority extended over all matters on all the campuses. Its members were appointed by the governor, and the vast majority owed their positions to their wealth and influence. In the end the regents accepted the solution because of the awkwardness of arguing against constitutionally guaranteed rights. Their acceptance, however, was tacit and involved no ceding of formal authority.

The liberal-constitutionalist solution, however, only hinted at tendencies harboring a counterpolitics that had assumed two distinct forms. One was democratic, spontaneous, amorphous, suspicious of the cult of individual leadership, skeptical and humorous, and willing to take risks for ideal rather than material values The other was corporate (in the medieval sense), attentive to formalities, deliberate in action, liberal rather than populist. The first group of tendencies was most evident in the student "movement"; the second in the actions of the faculty. For the two to find common ground, each had separately to challenge the official conception of the university as a nonpolitical institution established to serve "society."[12]

For the faculty the challenge meant defending the notion that it was consistent with, and not demeaning of, the nature of a university to permit political life on campus. The official conception was that the fundamental prerequisite for a university was for it to be "outside" politics and that the role of the regents was to protect the academy from the corrupting pressures of "real life" in order that faculty would pursue truth and students learn.[13] Instead the controversy brought the "outside" in as the entire state began to focus on the Berkeley campus. The necessity for students and faculty to address a broader audience of citizens, alumni / ae, and legislators and to relate local concerns in more general terms transformed both groups. The faculty, habitually riven by departmental rivalries, budgetary disputes, and senior-junior divisions, came to recognize that what was at stake was the idea that a public university not only might stand scholarly comparison with the great private universities and reject the social, economic, and cultural snobbery that seemed an essential element of identity but could go beyond them and attempt the task of nurturing a *political* culture appropriate to a public institution supported by the citizenry.

In submitting passively to centralized system in which administrators alone had a public responsibility for the institution as a whole, the faculty had settled for the status of a special interest in a division of labor in which its responsibilities were confined to research and teaching. The administration managed the campus, dealt with the regents, and oversaw student conduct.[14] The regents were formally the final authorities in all matters, in those affecting not only the Berkeley campus but the entire statewide university structure of nine campuses.[15] They were the sole representatives of the entire system before the political authorities of the state.

In the course of the controversy the faculty evolved into a political actor claiming a share of responsibility for the order and well-being of the institution. It became the mediator between the administration and students. That new role was possible only because certain influential faculty members were trusted by the students and because in an important sense a significant number of faculty and students had become allies against the administration and regents. Although many faculty members grumbled about the research time lost to political deliberations, in the process they not only discovered a corporate identity but fashioned themselves into an academic citizenry, at least for the moment. The locus of that transformation was the Academic Senate.

From a sleepy, ill-attended assembly that took its marching orders from the administration, it became an independent, vibrant deliberative institution. Its meetings were packed; the debates were charged with the excitement of competing ideas about the future of the university, yet a decent level of civility and collegiality consistently prevailed. Outside the assembly many faculty members spontaneously organized into distinct political groupings, which divided roughly along liberal and conservative lines. The faculty soon extended its reach by electing an executive committee to represent it in negotiations with the administration and the regents.

This was, in sum, the liberal constitution favored by a majority of the faculty. It sought to establish an element of faculty power against the campus administration and the regents. It allowed politics on the campus but conceived that politics essentially as an extension of the Bill of Rights to students, not as a redefinition of the faculty vocation. It legitimated student political activity on campus, but it was not prepared to break new ground and make room for student participation in any of the areas traditionally conceived as the prerogatives of the faculty—e.g., curriculum and faculty appointments. The conservative faculty who opposed the settlement wanted to preserve the old constitution but with provision for a stronger chancellor. Theirs was a vision of a nonpolitical campus, insulated from political pressures and protected by the oligarchy of the regents. They saw nothing political in the close relationships of faculty with business corporations, agribusiness, or federal agencies (a view shared by many liberal faculty members). Their tacit assumption was that their idyllic enclave was the quid pro quo for services rendered to "society."

Although the Berkeley students were widely characterized as "radicals," their radicalism was not in their objectives but in their appetite for politics. Several of them had acquired it from a political apprenticeship served not in Moscow but in Selma and the civil rights movement. What was truly radical about the students—and the faculty—was the transformation from an apolitical to a political mode of being, from what was assumed to be a career-oriented way of life to one that was denigrated as "politicized." Over several months, without flagging, students kept pressure on the faculty and administration while inventing their own organization, tactics, ideology, and rhetoric. Although their tactics, such as sit-ins, demonstrations, and mass rallies, struck many as outrageous in the disrespect for authority, the name the students chose, the Free Speech Movement, was an accurate indicator of the limited and conventional nature of their aims: to have the right to hold political rallies on campus, solicit contributions for political causes, choose speakers for their own events, and not be subjected to academic punishment for illegal actions committed off campus (e.g., sit-ins). The rhetoric of "student power" was never raised. At no time did students deliberately disrupt teaching or research, much less damage university facilities. They did disrupt the habits of administration.

The achievement of the Berkeley students and faculty was constructive and a tribute to good sense and moderation. That critics, then and now, should have seen "radicals" at work not only is an example of the vocabulary of marginalization at work but also as testimony to much else: to the difficulties of moderate liberal-democratic reforms, to the acute sense of fragility that bureaucrats have of their own structures, and to the general incomprehension of otherwise intelligent people that politics might be seriously concerned with matters other than material self-interests or self-promotion. What was illuminating about the troubles at Berkeley in 1964 was how little it took to arouse the wrath of the leaders and dominant powers of the society. The truly dark side of the times was not the temporary victory of sixties radicalism but the active dislike of democracy—couched as a contempt for "politics"—among the powerful.

VI

The events in Berkeley of the spring of 1970 could, with only slight exaggeration, be called a failed revolution. They were generally overlooked by outsiders and, significantly, have been ignored ever since. One reason was that Berkeley was no longer an anomaly but the name for a general condition.

In that so-called Cambodian spring more than 150 campuses were in a state of revolt. The triggering events were the killings at Kent State and the decision of President Nixon to widen the war by invading Cambodia. By 1970 the war had become a national nightmare, polarizing and paralyzing and ratcheting to an excruciating turn the problem of the university's entanglement with corporate structures and its "complicity" in the war. A special element in the Berkeley context was a strong feeling of beleaguerment caused by the continuous tirades against the campus by the newly elected governor, Ronald Reagan; these culminated in 1969, when the governor ordered the occupation of Berkeley by the National Guard. That led to the shooting death of an innocent bystander, a helicopter attack that sprayed tear gas over the campus, and the encirclement of the university by armed guardsmen with fixed bayonets.

The campus responded to the expansion of the war at home as well as in Southeast Asia by holding a gigantic open-air meeting and voting to strike against the university. The moral, legal, and political implications of that decision were temporarily stayed by the individual decision of striking faculty members to continue with their classes but to hold them off campus, most often at local churches and seminaries. The faculty was deeply divided by the strike, and the divisions became more intense when the strike evolved into a movement for the "reconstitution of the university."

Although reconstitution was never spelled out in detail, the basic idea involved nothing less than the attempt to restructure and redirect the university, toward becoming an educational institution, rather than an auxiliary of government and corporations, and replacing the bureaucratic model of university membership and governance with participatory relationships intended to allow students and staff a role in matters affecting their lives and work. Far more than the settlement of 1964, it meant altering the power relationships within the university and reconstituting them around more egalitarian notions of membership. Except for the later inclusion of student representatives on some faculty committees, the movement came to naught, in part because Governor Reagan ordered the campus shut down and in part because the academic calendar decreed the end of the term, causing students and faculty to disperse for the summer. But the larger reason was that among the faculty the will to radical change never took hold.

The faculty had been willing to make considerable sacrifices for liberal principles of free speech and assembly and even to oppose the war by striking, but they had resisted most of the proposals for educational reform suggested by the special committees appointed by the Academic Senate during the years between 1964 and 1970.[16] Above all, however, the vast majority of faculty drew back from the heavy civic commitment involved, not only in rethinking the nature of the university but in reorganizing it as well. Such an involvement seemed incompatible with the idea of a "research university" that had attracted a distinguished faculty in the first place. The crucial turning point had occurred earlier, in 1969, when, acting upon a proposal initiated by conservative and disenchanted liberal faculty, the faculty ignominiously voted to emasculate its power by establishing a representative assembly (based on the election of departmental representatives) that would function as the principal organ of the faculty. The Academic Senate, which was open to all regular faculty members, would be relegated to a subordinate status, meeting at widely spaced intervals and mostly restricted to dealing with matters sent to it by the assembly. The change was designed to neutralize the most democratic faculty institution and to elevate the importance of a body that, by being closely tied to departments and reflecting their hierarchical and gerontic character, could be relied upon to reflect the interests of the more powerful departments (e.g., physics, chemistry, and engineering) and to support the administration and the authority of the regents. The faculty had clearly signaled its disfavor of the democratic tendencies of the times and its desire to return to the "real work" of research and publication.[17]

VII

It is easy to deflate the significance of the abortive "revolution" of 1970 by saying that participatory democracy was inconsistent with the requirements of a high-powered research university whose central role in the production and dissemination of knowledge made it of crucial importance to a technologically advanced society. But the same could be said of democracy's seemingly anachronistic relationship to virtually every major institution in contemporary United States: to trade unions, corporations, political parties, and governmental structures. Amid the periodic hoopla about Q-groups, worker participation, sensitivity training, and open-neck shirts at IBM, the simple fact is that all of our major institutions are hierarchical in organization and antidemocratic in spirit.

So with every major bastion of power firmly controlled by

antidemocratic practices, why the need to stomp on the sixties and to construct an elaborate myth to counter a nonexistent threat?

One obvious answer is that the sixties formed an irresistible target for those whose sensibilities had been honed by decades of subversion sniffing, loyalty mongering, and humorless politics. The sixties offered acres of nuttiness, lots of shocking behavior, impudent language, outrageous costumes, and innocent forms of spirituality competing with brazen sexuality. And of course, civil disobedience and mass opposition, which, to its undying credit, interfered with the prosecution of the war and in all likelihood helped end the killing and destruction. What went mostly unnoticed, however, was a strong undercurrent of despair, largely fed by the simple observation that the chasm between American ideals and reality was bridged by hypocrisy and, as *The Pentagon Papers* revealed, by official lies. The Countermyth hints at disloyalty where it should see idealism, even an innocent patriotism.

The less obvious answer is that the Countermyth reflects a felt need to suppress the tendencies that, when combined, are perceived as truly threatening to a society whose ever-changing economy is a breeding ground of perpetual insecurities and fears. The main question posed during the sixties was: Where amid American imperialism, its culture of war, cult of leadership, and brutal suppression of attempts to establish equal civil rights was democracy to be found? The sixties responded by saying democracy had to be reexperienced through transforming actions that would attempt to alter the ways in which Americans perceived their environments, responded to the claims of authority, considered the hype accompanying the food they ate and the clothes they wore, treated the knowledge claims of experts, and accepted the superpower categories that had defined the culture of American politics for a half century.

Unlike the "threat" of communism, which could be exploited to increase the power of the state and the legitimacy of corporate capitalism, the main ingredients of the sixties—democracy, spontaneity, rebellion, anticonsumerism, environmentalism, and antielitism—were less easily converted into power, and unlike the values of communism, some of them were the staples of public rhetoric. The animus against the sixties has been framed as an indictment of the alleged destructiveness of the sixties, but fundamentally it is directed against a conception of democracy that carries the threat of breaking out of the molds into which it has been cast by electoral politics and plutocratic democracy. The varied forms of action developed to oppose the war and to extend civil rights *were* destructive of a certain simplistic understanding of national unity, of some racist folkways, and of a mindless patriotism, and they also exposed the shallowness of consensus politics and its ideal of a depoliticized citizenry. Both the civil rights movement and the antiwar protests politicized hundreds of thousands of Americans and simultaneously contested the boundaries of the political domain, its forms, and the monopoly on action enjoyed by the elites. Thousands who had never spoken, protested, advised, or criticized in public did so. The prevailing ideal of the passive citizen, who had to be "motivated" to vote, was being challenged. While the transformation was only temporary, it would make it possible in later decades for a strange and sometimes wonderful assortment of beings to venture out of closets, kitchens, and ghettos.

The sixties, then, serve as cover for the antipolitical and antidemocratic impulses that were strikingly evident in the actions by the conservative majority following the 1994 elections. The campaign itself was remarkable for the vituperation that the victors heaped upon politics, politicians, and government. Following their electoral victory, conservatives in the House and Senate proceeded to denounce Congress and offer to surrender powers to the president and to the states. Somehow forgotten were the old conservative concerns for "authority," or possibly exposed for the sham they had always been.[18] Certainly the profligacy displayed toward cluttering the Constitution with amendments on matters over which there existed more dissensus than consensus (balanced budget, outlawing of abortion and flag burning, school prayer) was suggestive of opportunism rather than reverence toward the nation's fundamental law. That cynicism could only be deepened as Republicans gathered in astronomical amounts of money from the few while promising to relieve the rest of us of a system of governmental favors and benefits. Senator Domenici may have said more than he intended when he declared recently that if Americans wished to have certain social programs, they would have to be prepared to pay for them.

Undeniably there have been serious attempts by conservative thinkers at constructing a coherent, historically rich account and defense of authority.[19] There has also been a lot of maundering about "lost" authority. However, when placed in the context of the last four decades, the ideology of authority seems little more than a defensive maneuver, a smokescreen thrown up to conceal what no amount of Cold War triumphalism or puerile fantasies about the "end of history" can disprove: that American political elites of the postwar era are a sorry excuse for a political class. From JFK to George Bush they have left a tawdry trail of corruption, constitutional violations, incalculable death and destruction visited upon hapless populations abroad, steadily worsening racial relations, deepening class divisions, discreditation of the idea of public service (except for convicted felons) and, not least, a political system that large numbers of Americans wish to disown. That system desperately needs a countermyth to cover a shameful reality of a society in which politics, culture, and economy are merely mechanisms for exploiting resources, people, and values. The sixties may lack their myth, but its ideal of redemocratization is not dead. It forms a part of a recurrent aspiration: to find room in which people can join freely with others to take responsibility for solving their common problems and thereby sharing the modest fate that is the lot of all mortals.

NOTES

1. *New York Times,* November 10, 1994, pp. A1, B3; January 21, 1995, p. 8.
2. Headlines from story by Peter Applebome, *New York Times,* May 7, 1995, pp. A1, 18.
3. "New is always better?," plaintively asked Representative Henry Hyde, a traditional conservative Republican. "What in the world is conservative about that? Have we nothing to learn from the past? Tradition, history, institutional memory—don't they count anymore?" *New York Times,* April 11, 1995, p. C22.
4. For examples of this earlier conservatism see Russell Kirk, *The Conservative Mind* (1953); William F. Buckley, Jr., *God and Man at Yale* (1951). There were of course other conservative intellectuals, including self-consciously tough-minded theorists, such as Wilmoore Kendall and James Burnham. But note the terms used by the self-styled neo-Machiavellian Burnham in his criticism of Arthur Schlesinger Jr.'s liberalism: the "liberal emphasis on continuous change, on methods rather than results, on striving and doing rather than sitting and enjoying." Cited in John R. Diggins, *Up from Communism: Conservative Odyssey's in American Intellectual History* (1975), p. 419. For a recent thoughtful account of changing emphases in liberal and conservative thinking, see Wilson Carey McWilliams, "Ambiguities and Ironies: Conservatism and Liberalism in the American Political Tradition," in *Moral Values in Liberalism and Conservatism,* ed. W. Lawson Taitte (1995).
5. Such as Todd Gitlin, *Years of Hope, Days of Rage* (1987); Kirkpatrick Sale, *SDS* (1974).
6. Linda Gray, who played the long-suffering wife of J. R. Ewing on "Dallas," also appeared on the program described above.
7. For a discussion of the problem in Nietzsche, the modern father of perspectivism, see Alexander Nehamas, *Nietzsche: Life as Literature.* (1985) and Arthur Danto, *Nietzsche as Philosopher* (1965), p. 68ff.
8. Curiously, one bridge between the older conservatism and the new is the Nietzschean element in the Straussian persuasion. It is best represented by Harvey Mansfield, Jr., *Taming the Prince: The Ambivalence of Modfern Executive Power* (1989).
9. This is described, with malice toward many, by Richard Sennett, "Back to Class Warfare," *New York Times,* December 27, 1994, p. A15.
10. See Herbert Marcuse, *An Essay on Liberation* (1969).
11. Sheldon S. Wolin and John H. Schaar, *The Berkeley Rebellion and Beyond: Essays on Politics and Education in the Technological Society* (1970).
12. For documents illustrative of these positions in their early stages see *The Berkeley Student Rebellion,* ed. Sheldon S. Wolin and S. Martin Lipset (1965).
13. In the background were the events of the early fifties, when a loyalty oath was imposed on the faculty and several nonsigners were fired.

14. "Administration" here and elsewhere refers to the local or campus administration as distinct from the overall university-wide administration that governed all nine campuses.

15. The regents were political appointees chosen for their wealth and / or political connections. The state constitution provided that the governor, lieutenant governor, and speaker of the assembly would automatically serve as regents.

16. Muscatine Report, *Education at Berkeley*, March 1966; *The Culture of the University Governance and Education*, 1968.

17. The structure of faculty governance was altered again in the late eighties. The reforms further diminished the role of the senate and essentially converted faculty governance into an administrative function rather than a collective deliberation. See *University of California Manual, Berkeley Division of the Academic Senate*, November 1992.

18. A good example is Daniel Bell, ed., *The Radical Right* (rev. ed. *The New American Right*) (1971 [1963]).

19. For example, Robert A. Nisbet, *The Quest for Community* (1953); John H. Schaar, *Escape from Authority* (1961); Richard Sennett, *Authority* (1980).

The Assault on the Universities: Then and Now

WALTER BERNS

The assault on the university began with the student revolt at the Berkeley campus of the University of California in December 1964. Berkeley was followed by Columbia in 1968, Harvard and Cornell in 1969, and Yale and Kent State in 1970; during this same period some three hundred universities were the scenes of student sit-ins, building takeovers, strikes, riots, and other forms of rebellious behavior. In addition to its violent character, what distinguishes this assault from those of the past is that it came from within the university itself and that it met little resistance from professors and administrators.

The issue at Berkeley, initially at least, was free speech, but free speech had little or nothing to do with the subsequent campus disruptions; here the issues were, or were said to be, university involvement in neighborhood deterioration, in the draft and the Vietnam War, in racism, as well as in university governance, especially in disciplinary matters, and the alleged irrelevance of the curriculum. Except for the neighborhood issue (so prominent at Columbia), all these figured in the events at Cornell, which, under pressure from gun-bearing students, proceeded to jettison every vestige of academic integrity. In this respect the Cornell of the sixties became the prototype of the university as we know it today.

Shortly after he was installed as Cornell's president in 1963, James A. Perkins formed a Committee on Special Educational Projects charged with recruiting black students whose SAT scores were substantially below (as it turned out, 175 points below) the average of Cornell's entering class. Subsequently it was revealed that many of these students were to be recruited from the slums of the central cities, and perhaps not surprisingly, they proved incapable of being, or were unwilling to be, integrated into or assimilated by the Cornell student body; assimilation, they said, threatened their identity and needs as blacks.

In 1966 they formed an Afro-American Society, which in short order demanded separate living quarters, an Afro-American studies program—and seized a university building to house it—and ultimately an autonomous degree-granting college. To justify it, they issued a statement saying that "whites can make no contribution to Black Studies except in an advisory, non-decision making or financial capacity" and therefore that the program must be developed and taught by blacks and, as it turned out, only to black students.

This demand for an autonomous, degree-granting college took the form of an ultimatum, to which President Perkins responded by saying that he was "extremely reluctant to accept this idea of a college exclusive to one race, but [that he was] not finally opposed to it; it would involve a lot of rearranging of [his] own personality."* To head this college, or as it came to be known, this Center for Afro-American Studies, the university, without the consent of the faculty, hired a twenty-eight-year-old graduate student in sociology at Northwestern University who, despite repeated requests, failed to submit a statement explaining the center's purpose and operation. (The closest thing to a statement of purpose came from the Afro-American Society, which said that the aim of the center "would be to create the tools necessary for the formation of a black nation.") To teach the first course in the program

---

*In the event, and, as those who knew him had come to expect, his "personality" needed no rearrangement. As he said after the guns had brought him to his knees, "there is nothing I have ever said or will ever say that is forever fixed or will not be modified by changed circumstances."

(on "black ideology"), the university, over the objection of two (and only two) faculty members of the appropriate committee, hired a twenty-four-year-old SNCC (Student Nonviolent Coordinating Committee) organizer who had completed a mere two years of college.

This jettisoning of academic standards, respecting the courses to be taught and the faculty to teach them, was largely the work of various members of the administration, only one of whom (the vice provost) was honest enough to admit that it was being done under pressure from the Afro-American Society—but, he assured the few dissenting members of the faculty, "it would never be done again." To refuse to accommodate the black "moderates," he said, would only strengthen the hands of the "militants."

Within a few months these "moderates" were burning buildings; joining with the SDS (Students for a Democratic Society) to barricade Chase Manhattan bank recruiters; removing furniture from a women's dorm and placing it in a building taken over by the Afro-American Society; disrupting traffic; overturning vending machines; trashing the library; grabbing President Perkins and pulling him from a podium (and, when the head of the campus police rushed to Perkins's aid, driving him off with a two-by-four); harassing campus visitors with toy guns; and, at five or six o'clock of a cold morning, seizing the student union building, driving visiting (and shivering) parents from their bedrooms—it was Parents Weekend—out into the street. Justification for this seizure was said to be the burning of a cross on the lawn of a black women's dorm, which, the university now implicitly admits, was done by the "moderate" blacks themselves. They then brought guns—real, not toy, guns—into the student union and, two days later, at gunpoint, forced the university to rescind the mild (very mild) punishment imposed on the blacks found guilty of these various offenses by the student-faculty Committee on Student Affairs; in effect, they took control of the university. Photographs of the arms-bearing blacks, led by Thomas W. Jones, and of Vice President Steven Muller signing the surrender document appeared on the covers of the leading national newsmagazines.

All that remained to be done was to get the faculty to agree to the surrender terms, but this proved to be easy. Jones went on the radio to say that Cornell had only "three hours to live" and that the "racist" professors—by which he meant those professors who opposed the surrender—would be "dealt with." (But Cornell's most famous philosophy professor was speaking for the majority of the faculty when he said, "You don't have to intimidate us.") The final act took place at a Nuremberg-like faculty-student rally at which one famous professor after another pledged his allegiance to the new order. As Allan Bloom put it, the students "discovered that pompous teachers who catechized them about academic freedom could, with a little shove, be made into dancing bears."

No one should have been surprised by the faculty's willingness to capitulate to the armed students; the stage had been set for it a year earlier, when black students brought a charge of racism against a visiting professor of economics—he had made the mistake of employing a "Western" standard to judge the economic performance of various African countries—and, not satisfied with the professor's subsequent apology (which the administration required him to make), took possession of the Economics Department office, holding the chairman and the department secretary prisoner for some eighteen hours. The students were never punished, and much to the relief of the dean of the College of Arts and Science, the accused professor left Cornell. On the basis of the findings of a special faculty-student commission, the dean then pronounced the professor innocent of racism but went on to announce that the university and faculty were guilty of "institutional racism" and were obliged to mend their ways.

Nor should anyone have been surprised by the faculty's willingness to "reform" the curriculum, which is to say, to obliterate whatever differences there might still have been between the purposes of higher education and what were perceived to be the immediate, and pressing, concerns of the world outside. In the years immediately preceding the "crisis," one requirement after another of the old "core curriculum" had been dropped in favor of what can best be called consumer freedom or, in the jargon of the day, of allowing the students "to do their own thing." One of the university's most famous professors, Paul de Man (of whom more later), argued that nothing of value would be lost by doing away with these requirements.

Begun as an assault on university "racism," the Cornell student uprising quickly became an assault on the integrity of the academic enterprise, an assault that was bound to succeed because it was met with only nominal resistance on the part of the faculty and none at all from the administration. Although university rules were broken left and right, the dean of the law school supported the president and voted for peace (to paraphrase Shakespeare's Hamlet, "What was law to him or he to law that he should weep for it?"); at a special meeting of the Arts College (in which, for the first time in its history, students were allowed to participate), the so-called humanists confessed their sins and called upon the president to do what he was not legally entitled to do—namely, nullify all the penalties imposed on black students "since the beginning of [the] spring term"; and the natural scientists, in the spirit of "better them than us," confident that none of it would reach the doors of their laboratories, remained aloof from the battle.[1] On the whole, just as George Orwell's Winston Smith came finally to love Big Brother, so the typical Cornell professor came to admire the student radicals and sought their approval. From his perspective, theirs was the only moral game in town.

The black students, while threatening the lives of named members of the faculty, claimed to be putting "their [own] lives on the line"; others, inspired by Cornell's resident priest, Father Daniel Berrigan,[2] insisted that they had "the moral right to engage in civil disobedience" and proceeded ceremoniously to burn their draft cards; the SDS, the vanguard of the New Left, led the assault on the "irrelevant" curriculum, insisting that the university could not remain disengaged from the great moral issues, war, racism, and the rank injustice of "bourgeois society." The largely bourgeois faculty agreed, thereby demonstrating that Andy Warhol was right when he said that "nothing is more bourgeois than to be afraid to look bourgeois."

With the faculty acquiescent and the students either triumphant or confused, Perkins had only to deal with the university trustees. They had been willing to fund the black studies program with a million dollars and had remained quiet when Perkins placed the university airplane at the disposal of black students, enabling them to go to New York City to purchase, with two thousand dollars in university funds, a set of bongo drums for Malcolm X Day. The one thing they could not abide was negative publicity—could not abide and, as it turned out, could not prevent. Covering the Cornell story for the *New York Times* was a Pulitzer Prize war reporter, Homer Bigart, who had learned to distrust official press releases, in this case those issuing from Muller's public relations office. Bigart's stories provided *Times* readers with a vivid account of what was in fact going on at Cornell, and when, despite Perkins's efforts to have it suppressed, the *Times* eventually ran on its front page a particularly damaging story, summarizing the events (the *Cornell Alumni News,* a publication with forty thousand subscribers and over which Perkins and Muller had no control, hurried into print with its own damaging account), the trustees called for Perkins's resignation, or according to the story handed out, he chose to resign.

But Perkins and his friends survived, their reputations (at least in some circles) unblemished. Muller became president of Johns Hopkins University; in 1993 Thomas Jones, the erstwhile black revolutionist, having been named president of TIAA-CREF (Teachers Insurance and Annuity Association—College Retirement Equities Fund, the world's largest pension fund), was appointed to the Cornell Board of Trustees, and in 1992, by way of recognizing "his outstanding leadership and extraordinary contributions to [the] University," Cornell established the James A. Perkins Professorship of Environmental Studies. In 1995 Jones "made a large contribution to the University," enabling it to endow an annual Perkins Prize of five thousand dollars "for the student, faculty, staff member or program that has done the most during the preceding year to promote interracial understanding and harmony on campus."

To say the least, not everyone thought Perkins deserved this recognition—Bayard Rustin, the great civil rights leader, called him "a masochistic and pusillanimous university president"[3]—but even his critics would have to admit that Perkins left his mark on the university, and not only on Cornell. By surrendering to students armed with guns, he made it easier for those who came after him to surrender to students armed only with epithets ("racists," "sexists," "elitists," "homophobes"); by inaugurating a black studies program, Perkins paved the way for Latino studies programs, women's studies programs, and multicultural studies programs; by failing to support a professor's freedom to teach, he paved the way for speech codes and political correctness; and of course he pioneered the practice of affirmative action admissions and hiring. In a word, while it would exaggerate his influence to hold him responsible for subsequent developments, he did provide an example that other institutions found it convenient to follow. For evidence of this, consider these news items, culled from four months of the *Chronicle of Higher Education:*

- Bates College students protest admissions policy; student body only 8 percent minority; dean of admissions agrees with protesters (April 13, 1994).
- Cornell trustees approve a Latino Living Center and studies program after Hispanic students occupy administration building and block off sections of the campus (April 30, 1994).
- Under student pressure, University of Wisconsin (Milwaukee) is likely to approve gay and lesbian studies program (April 30, 1994).
- Howard University asks Yale Professor David Brion Davis (Pulitzer Prize, National Book Award, for his

studies of slavery) to cancel his lecture because of anti-Semitic atmosphere on campus (May 4, 1994).

- Vassar College found by U.S. district court to have discriminated by denying tenure to a woman; judge found that her scholarship record was far superior to that of three men who received tenure (June 1, 1994).
- University of Oregon requires all students to take two courses meeting the "Race, Gender, Non-European American Requirement" (June 15, 1994).
- U.S. Department of Education, Office of Civil Rights, cites eighty-six colleges for violating rights of disabled, forty-four for sexual bias, forty-four for racial and ethnic bias, and one for age bias (June 22, 1994).
- Northeastern University accords gays and lesbians preferential treatment in hiring (June 29, 1994).
- National Endowment for the Humanities funds summer institute with $320,000 to help professors and administrators think about how diversity and democracy "should be dealt with in the classroom" (June 29, 1994).
- University of Wisconsin requires all students to take course in ethnic studies (June 29, 1994).
- Under pressure from U.S. Department of Education, University of Missouri will triple black enrollment by granting scholarship aid, despite low test scores or "marginal grades," to all but handful (July 13, 1994).
- University of Michigan criticized for failure to hire sufficient number of black and Hispanic professors (July 13, 1994).
- Georgetown Law School admits, then rejects white student who, on application form, checked box marked "Black/A.A." (July 20, 1994).

When Perkins assumed the presidency of the university in 1963, there were only 25 black students at Cornell (out of a total of about 11,000). Too few to be segregated, these 25 lived in the same dormitories and received the same education as the other students. By the time of Perkins's departure in 1969, there were 250 black students on campus, but with their own self-segregated living quarters and their own studies program.

What was true then remains true today, and not merely at Cornell. Blacks are a visible presence on every campus, but on every one I know or know about, so are the racial divisions. For example, black and white students at the University of Pennsylvania "tend to live in separate dormitories, beginning with the freshman year; they eat in separate portions of the dining hall; they belong to different clubs and campus organizations."[4] The only thing they seem to have in common, beyond their status as students in the University of Pennsylvania, is the desire to live apart from each other. This is not as the university would have it. On the contrary, it would prefer (or, at least, claims to prefer) an integrated student body, one where students associate regardless of race, sex, religion, national origin, or "sexual orientation"; such differences are supposed to be irrelevant, and on most campuses probably are irrelevant.

But there is one difference that is not irrelevant and the effects of which cannot be ignored, especially in a university: a difference in aptitude (or whatever it is that is measured by the SAT). Aptitude is directly, and predictably, related to success or failure in the university (and, since birds of a feather tend to flock together, at least indirectly related to campus social relations), and because the SAT is a reasonably reliable measure of it, there is no denying that the difference between white and black students is huge. At Penn, the mean SAT score (verbal and math) of the whites is 150 points higher than that of the blacks; translated into centiles, the SAT score of the average black student is about equal to the SAT score of the tenth percentile of white students. This means that 90 percent of the whites and 50 percent of the blacks are above that point (whatever it is), and 10 percent of the whites and 50 percent of the blacks are below it. What is true at Penn is true at the other so-called elite institutions—but less so at those that are able to attract the best black students—and to judge from the data from the universities of Virginia and California, the gap between blacks and whites may be even greater in the state universities.

In effect, as was the case at Cornell in the sixties, affirmative action means admitting students from different worlds, students with different capacities, interests, and habits, students who have little in common but, if left to their own devices, might be expected to live together peaceably even if separately; like members of the general public (65 percent of whom now approve of interracial dating, for example), students have come to be tolerant of differences. Unfortunately they are not left to their own devices; instead Penn subjects them to a steady drumbeat of propaganda—the students describe it as political indoctrination—urging them to be "sensitive and accepting of difference," the consequence of which, as the students themselves admit, is a campus "obsessed, mesmerized, driven by an unceasing battle between the various racial, ethnic, and sexual groups."

This indoctrination begins with freshman orientation, when in separate programs black students are told, to put it simply, that the University of Pennsylvania is a racist institution, with a racist curriculum, a racist faculty and student body, and the whites in turn are harangued about their alleged racism.[5] Thus, as soon as they set foot on campus, students are informed, in effect warned, that depending on their race, they will be treated differently and unequally, and so they are, and so are professors.

The white student who shouts, "Shut up, you water buffalo," is charged with racial harassment, but the black students who steal and then destroy an entire press run of the student newspaper are not even reprimanded; the white Jewish professor who refers to himself and black students as "former slaves" is suspended for a semester without pay and is required to attend "sensitivity and racial awareness sessions," but the black professor who in public calls him an "asshole" is made head of the Center for the Study of Black Literature and Culture and is named to the search committee charged with finding a new president to replace the man who had presided over these events, Sheldon Hackney, who in turn is named chairman of the National Endowment for the Humanities by President Clinton.*

The situation at Penn is similar to that at Cornell in 1969 and, although not everywhere to the same extent, similar to that on most campuses today. Political correctness follows on affirmative action, and it is not at all clear that even its intended beneficiaries, to say nothing of the benefiting institutions, are the better off because of it. Many more black students are enrolled, but despite grade inflation, their dropout rate greatly exceeds that of white students. What effect this has on their pride, or, as we say today, their "self-esteem," is difficult to calculate but not to imagine. The university encourages them to attribute their difficulties to white racism, but the honest among them know this not to be the case. Even those who would have been admitted without it are forced to bear the stigma attached to affirmative action; they can never be sure they are not perceived by their white fellow students as the beneficiaries of racial preference. No one, especially no one otherwise qualified, likes it to be thought he is being admitted *because* he is black (or is being hired or promoted to tenure rank *because* she is a woman), but where affirmative action is the rule it is not easy to overcome the suspicion that this may indeed be the case. The highly qualified Susan Estrich, the first woman in ninety years to serve as president of the *Harvard Law Review,* said she did not know "a successful woman or minority who hasn't somewhere along the way, faced the assumption that they *[sic]* didn't quite deserve what they *[sic]* earned." As she put it, "We who are supposed to be its beneficiaries also pay the price of affirmative action."[6]

To say the least, these programs are of little use to the

---

*Informed of the newspaper theft, Hackney said that "two important values, diversity and open expression, appear to be in conflict." That "conflict" was resolved as Perkins would have resolved it. Instead of punishing the students who stole the newspapers, the university punished the campus police who apprehended them. According to the official report of the university's Judicial Inquiry Office, the police should have known that they were dealing with "a form of student protest [and not] criminal behavior."

blacks, they breed cynicism among the whites, and they have a corrupting effect on the institutions, but even if (as now seems likely) they are no longer to be required by the federal government, we are not likely to see the end of them in the private colleges and universities. They were initiated at Cornell and elsewhere because they were thought to be a way of alleviating a social problem, but they are retained probably because they make their champions feel good. They allow them to exhibit their compassion, and compassion, when detached from its religious foundations, is one way of expiating guilt. (Hence the limousine liberal.) Compassion is also accompanied—not always but frequently—by a sense of superiority; the healthy or wealthy one feels superior to the other who is sick or poor, because it is the other who is suffering and the one who can provide relief. Sympathy therefore, especially when one acts on it, is satisfying; it makes one feel good. As Clifford Orwin writes, "this is what lends credence to the Hobbesian view that sympathy is merely self-concern on vacation."[7]

Affirmative action for blacks was intended ultimately to bridge the economic and social gap between the races, but nothing similar to this can be said about women's studies courses, which, by somebody's count, now number in the tens of thousands. The more radical among them—Christina Sommers calls them "gender feminist courses"—can have no other purpose but to teach women to hate or despise men, and in the process they threaten to transform the university into a sort of boot camp for culture warriors.[8]

Unaware that it takes two to tango, even the moderate programs proceed on the assumption that women can be studied apart from men and have as their purpose to divide the sexes, not to bring them together. Yet there are few, if any, university presidents (still largely men) who object to the establishment of these programs. Like James Perkins before them, they apparently see no reason, or are too weak, to object, or perhaps they pretend ignorance of what is being taught in them.[9] Whatever the explanation, the situation brings to mind Tocqueville's prediction of what we can expect at the end of the women's project—namely, "weak men and disorderly women."[10]

Although a legacy of the sixties, affirmative action—for women or even for blacks—was not the principal cause for which the students took to the barricades in those turbulent times. True, they accused the universities of racism (as well as complicity in the draft and Vietnam War), but like their counterparts in France and Germany—remember Rudi Dutschke?—they fancied themselves part of a mass movement against the "repressive system" or the "technological culture" being imposed on them by the universities. According to the chroniclers of the Berkeley "rebellion," the students of the sixties were searching for "authentic values" and could not find them in the courses available to them.[11] The same complaints were heard at Cornell (as well as at Columbia, Harvard, Yale, and the rest), where students paraded as New Left "revolutionists," all the while expressing their contempt for "bourgeois society."*

The antibourgeois sloganizing, so popular, so easy at the time, was mostly cant, as Richard Nixon demonstrated when he put an end to the draft and, with it, the so-called student movement. The radical students of the sixties may have hated bourgeois society (and despised its representatives), but having no clear idea of what to put in its place, they abandoned politics for the drugs and sex of Woodstock. They should find the university much more to their liking today.

For the others, the sort of student who took no part in the sixties' rebellions, the universities continue their bourgeois ways. According to a recent report, more than 50 percent of the baccalaureate degrees now being awarded in our colleges and universities are in those most bourgeois of subjects: engi-

---

*The students took as their models Mao Zedong, Castro, and Che Guevara, but they might just as well have taken someone from Nazi Germany or Fascist Italy. I proved this when, to an American government class at the height of the Cornell crisis, I read some speeches analyzing the situation and calling for what ought to be done. The radicals in the class were enthusiastic until I revealed that the speeches were by Mussolini.

neering, business, and other professional programs (excluding education).

There is of course nothing despicable about learning how to make a living; on the contrary, providing for oneself (and for one's family) is, as Tocqueville points out, one of the things that distinguishes a free man from a slave.[12] But the radical students were justified in thinking that vocational training is not the proper business of the university. Americans have never had to be encouraged to look after the practical side of things; they do that for themselves. As Tocqueville said, "people living in a democratic age are quite certain to bring the industrial side of science to perfection anyhow," which is to say, without being encouraged to do so. This explains why the taxpayers and alumni who pay the piper are disposed to call an industrial or vocational tune. Yet, perhaps uncharacteristically, they continue to support the universities even though so much of vocational training—basic economics, business, accounting, computer science, and the like—could be provided at less than half the cost by the community colleges. (Less than 18 percent of Maryland's higher education budget is allocated to community colleges, even though they enroll 57 percent of the state's undergraduates.) They probably support the universities because they think it important that students— even prospective engineers, bankers, lawyers, doctors, accountants, and the like—should have some acquaintance with the humanities, or, as they might say (but with only the vaguest idea of what they mean by it), with "culture." Before contributing to the annual fund drives, however, they would do well to learn how these "culture" courses are being taught these days.

Although not the first to define the term as it is used in this context, Thomas Carlyle (in the 1860s) spoke of culture as the body of arts and learning separate from the "work" or "business" of society. This definition has the merit of reflecting (and that very clearly) the problem that gave rise to the culture movement in the nineteenth century. Carlyle was preceded by Coleridge, Keats, and Wordsworth (who, in his role as poet, saw himself as an "upholder of culture" in a world that had come to disdain it); by Shelley (who said that society could do without John Locke "but not without Dante, Petrarch, Chaucer, Shakespeare"); and by John Stuart Mill, for whom culture meant the qualities and faculties that characterize our humanity or those aspects of humanity that he, like Tocqueville, foresaw might be absent in a utilitarian or commercial society. Carlyle was followed by Matthew Arnold, for whom culture meant not only literary pursuits but—in a sentence that became familiar, if not famous—the pursuit of "the best which has been thought and said in the world."[13]

These critics and poets had a concern for the sublime (or the aesthetic) and a complaint against the modern commercial and bourgeois society in which the sublime, they feared, would have no firm place. The philosophical founders of this new society—particularly John Locke and Adam Smith—promised to provide for the needs of the body (and in this they surely succeeded); culture was intended to provide for the needs of the soul. Coleridge made this the business of his "clerisy," an official body—originally (as in the case of the Church of England) but not necessarily a religious corporation—set apart and publicly endowed for the cultivation and diffusion of knowledge. America assigned this task to the universities.

Of course no American university, or at least no public university, can ignore the task Jefferson assigned to the University of Virginia, that of paying "especial attention to the principles of government which shall be inculcated therein." He believed that students have to be prepared to live in a free society, to know what is required of citizens in that society. But one of the things required of them is to criticize it, for example, to call it to account for its racism or, as Coleridge and Company were doing in the nineteenth century, for its failure to inculcate respect for "the best which has been thought and said in the world." Unable, for constitutional reasons, to establish a clerisy, we assigned this task to the universities and, more precisely, to their humanities faculties. Unfortunately, as Allan Bloom wrote, "the humanities are now failing, not for want of support but for want of anything to say."[14] Or, as he might have said, what the humanities are now saying is a sophisticated version of what the radical students used to say.

Shortly after Bloom published *The Closing of the American Mind,* a trenchant account of the state of the humanities in this country, and especially in the universities, the American Council of Learned Societies assembled a group of distinguished humanities professors and charged them with writing a response to it. Their report acknowledges the book's "disturbingly popular" success but insists that the attacks on the humanities (by Lynne Cheney and William Bennett, as well as by Bloom) "would be comic in their incongruity if they were not taken so seriously by so many people, with such potentially dangerous consequences." It goes on to say that "such attacks mislead the public [and] give students quite the wrong impression about what the humanities are doing." Contrary to what the critics are alleged to be saying, students are reading the great books (or, as the report puts it by way of casting doubt on their greatness, the "great books"), but they have "to learn to think about them in ways that do not suppress the challenges of contemporary modes of analysis."[15] But in making that statement about the humanities having nothing to say, Bloom was referring to deconstructionism, the most prominent of those "contemporary modes of analysis," the mode of analysis then favored by—to quote the ACLS report—"the best scholars in the humanities today."

Deconstructionism was brought to America by the Belgian-born Paul de Man (among others). When de Man died in 1983, Yale (where he had been teaching after leaving Cornell) is said to have gone into mourning, and President A. Bartlett Giamatti declared that "a tremendous light for humane life and learning is gone and nothing for us will ever be the same." Giamatti himself was soon to resign and become, first, president of the National Baseball League and then baseball commissioner (neither one the most humane of vocations), but there is little doubt that in his eulogy of de Man he was speaking for the Yale literary faculties and, indeed, for the Modern Language Association, the governing body of contemporary humanities. When, in 1986, J. Hillis Miller became president of the MLA, he said, "the future of literary studies depends on maintaining and developing that rhetorical reading which is today called 'deconstruction.' " What, then, is deconstructionism?

An answer to this question is not easy to come by. As one might expect, there is a vast secondary literature on the subject, but when one leaves aside the polemical and therefore unreliable attacks written by its enemies, most of it is either unintelligible or (at least for someone not schooled in contemporary literary theory) incomprehensible. Consider the following passage from the pen of a Cornell professor of history:

> De Man's very understanding of language in his later works made dispossession, trauma, and mourning constitutive features of the linguistic process itself, and his continual critique of an "aesthetic ideology" of totalization, organicism, full rootedness, and the elimination of difference—in brief, the illusory realization of the imaginary—may in certain limited and problematic ways be read as applicable to the assumptions of the Nazi movement. I would also note that the undoing of the binary oppositions, while perhaps more marked in Derrida than in de Man, has been a crucial aspect of deconstruction in general and is very important for the critique of a scapegoat mechanism that resists internal alterity, is intolerant of mixed or hybridized forms, and requires a fixed, pure, and decisive divide between the integral self and the other.[16]

Any translation of this passage, indeed, any attempt to explicate its obscurity, would violate one of the principles of deconstructionism; obscurity is supposed to be a sign of profundity and, as such, is preferred over clarity.[17] Thus to attempt to give a coherent account of deconstructionism requires one, like it or not, to enter a bizarre world where meaning is meaningless, where "all interpretation is misinterpretation," where words have no referents, where (to bring this to an end) a dog is not a kind of barking animal but a "concept."

As explained by de Man himself, deconstructionism is a way of reading that claims to be superior to other modes of literary criticism because it is more cognizant of the problem of language and, therefore, of reading. "De Man," according to Geoffrey Hartman, one of his most devoted partisans, "always asks us to look beyond natural experience or its mimesis [its imitation or representation in a work of art or literature] to a specifically linguistic dilemma," and that dilemma derives from our inability to control "the relation between meaning and language." The fact that it does not, and cannot, convey meaning in any objective sense is, de Man says, "the distinctive curse of all language." A "text" does not convey its author's meaning; it has its own "textuality," independent of the author. A work of literature cannot be "reduced to a finite meaning, or set of meanings," which means that the critic's task is not to elucidate but to interpret; in a way, the critic's interpretative skills are more important than the work (or "text") being read. "And since interpretation is nothing but the possibility of error, by claiming that a certain degree of blindness is part of the specificity of literature we also reaffirm the absolute dependence of the interpretation on the text and of the text on the interpretation."[18] In effect there is no meaning, there is only interpretation—or as Gertrude Stein said of Oakland, "there's no there there"—and the more idiosyncratic, the better. Like some other modern critics, deconstructionists treat a work of literature the way a figure skater treats ice: as a surface from which to launch their linguistic versions of camels, toe loops, and double axels. Put otherwise, criticism is exalted over literature, or readers over authors, and according to one deconstructionist, whereas the history of criticism used

to be part of the history of literature, "now the history of literature is part of the history of criticism."[19]

As explained by Hartman (quoting de Man), "The fields of
critical philosophy, literary theory, and history have an inter-
linguistic, not an extralinguistic, correlative; they are secondary in relation to the original, which is itself a previous text.
They reveal an essential failure of disarticulation, which was
already there in the original. They kill the original, by dis-
covering that the original was already dead. They read the
original from the perspective of pure language *[reine Sprache]*,
a language that would be entirely free of the illusion of meaning."[20] Translated, this means that what is written by the critic
is related ("interlinguistically") to the work being criticized,
but neither the work nor the criticism is related to anything in
the world outside language. Language is not about anything
except other language. This is true of a Shakespeare play, a
Wordsworth poem, the Declaration of Independence, the Constitution of the United States, or a popular potboiler. As one
deconstructionist admitted, even newspapers and almanacs
can be deconstructed.

To say that nothing written has an "extralinguistic correlative" means that nothing written refers to, or is related to, anything existing outside the "text". It means that love,
friendship, and fidelity; envy and jealousy; justice, injustice,
slavery, tyranny, and tolerance; natural rights and constitutional wrongs, all the things written about by poets, playwrights, philosophers, historians, statesmen, and founders are
merely words, words without correlatives other than other
words. It means—here I quote Roger Kimball—that "the
atrocities we read about are merely literary phenomena, referring not to the sufferings of real people, real 'originals,' but
only to a 'previous text'!"[21] It means that neither Matthew
Arnold nor anyone else can speak of "the best which has been
thought or said in the world" because there is no basis for such
judgments, no basis for criticism. There is nothing outside the
text, and above all, as Allan Bloom put it, there is nothing
higher. "This," he said, "is the final step in making modern

man satisfied with himself."[22] The only thing the humanities can say to him is what the students were saying in the sixties: "Do your own thing."

Deconstructionism had its critics in the academy, but it ceased to be the reining mode of critical analysis for another reason. It was discredited largely because de Man was discredited. In 1987 it was revealed (first in the pages of the *New York Times*) that he had been a Nazi collaborationist during the German occupation of Belgium, having written 170 articles for the French-language *Le Soir* and ten others in *Het Vlaamsche Land,* a Flemish-language daily.[23] What is of interest here, because it speaks volumes about the condition of the contemporary university, is how the academy responded to these revelations.

De Man had made no mention of his Nazi connections when he came to the United States in May 1948, and it is easy to understand why. His benefactor, novelist and critic Mary McCarthy, and his academic colleagues, first at Bard College, then at Harvard, Columbia, Johns Hopkins, Cornell, and Yale, could not have been expected to welcome him had they known of his Nazi connections. Communism is one thing, but being pro-Nazi, then and now, puts one beyond the pale. And although many of the leading figures in the fields of comparative literature and literary theory were to deny it, some of them to excuse it as a product of youthful innocence, de Man had been pro-Nazi and, so long as the Germans were winning the war, had made no effort to conceal it. On the contrary, he had openly expressed his admiration of Hitler, had supported his war and his program; like Hitler, he had looked forward to a Europe without Jews.

He addressed the Jewish question in a *Le Soir* article of March 4, 1941, entitled "Les Juifs dans la littérature actuelle" (the Jews in contemporary literature), at the end of which he proposed his own version of Hitler's "Final Solution." Modern literature, he wrote, has not been "polluted" by Jewish influence because Jewish writers, especially in France, have always been second-rate, but the Jews were at least partly responsible for the decadence of European political life. Thus, by their being banished to a "Jewish colony, isolated from Europe," the political problem could be solved without any "deplorable consequences for Western literary life." Banishing writers of only "medicore value" would have the additional benefit of allowing Western literature to continue to develop or evolve "according to its own laws."[24]

In the October 28, 1941, edition of *Le Soir* he, like the notorious Martin Heidegger, rejected any attempt to distinguish between Germany and Hitlerism. Their similarity, or "closeness," he wrote, was evident from the beginning, and the war would only make it clearer that Hitler spoke for Germany; the war would unite "the Hitlerian soul and the German soul, making them into a single and unique power." He said this "is an important phenomenon because it means that one cannot judge the fact of Hitler without at the same time judging the fact of Germany, and that the future of Europe can be foreseen only within the framework of the possibilities and needs of the German spirit. It is not a question of a series of reforms, but, rather, of the definitive or final emancipation of a people who, in turn, are called upon to exercise a hegemony in Europe."[25] Question: From whom or what were the German people (and after them the people of Europe) to be emancipated?

In his essay "On the Jewish Question," Karl Marx had argued that the "emancipation of mankind from *Judaism*" depended on the "emancipation of the Jews" from Judaism, or as he put it in the last line of the essay, "the social emancipation of the Jew is the *emancipation* of society from *Judaism*." It might be said that Marx was one of the first to think actively about a solution to the "Jewish question" or, as it came to be called, the "Jewish problem," but as he was later to say, mankind poses for itself only such tasks as it can solve, and because he thought that at the time mankind had no solution in hand, he was content to wait until the Jews ceased to be Jews. Not being content to wait for that to happen, Hitler devised a solution, and in his own way so did Paul de Man.

As might have been expected, these revelations of his Nazi sympathies created a public scandal, but not among his academic admirers. The charges against him were said to be "groundless" (Rodolphe Gasché); the fact that his "writings during the occupation contain certain disturbing statements and positions with no parallel in his other writings before or after the occupation makes it difficult to read his newspaper articles as straightforward expressions of deeply held beliefs" (Ian Balfour); it is impossible to "understand what this allusion to 'a Jewish colony isolated from Europe' meant at that moment" (Jacques Derrida); "although [de Man] grants the maximum attention to the role that Germany or 'German genius' has played or ought to play in the destiny of Europe, although he recalls constantly the necessity of understanding thoroughly the history of the German nation in order to understand Hitlerism, although he is vigilantly opposed to the commonplace and the 'lazy and widespread solution' that comes down to 'supposing an integral dualism between Germany, on the one hand, and Hitlerism on the other [and] although his analysis leads him to judge German 'hegemony' in Europe to be ineluctable, this diagnosis seems rather cold and far removed from exhortation" (Jacques Derrida); "De Man's 'dirty secret' was the dirty secret of a good part of civilized Europe. In the light of what we now know, however, his [later] work appears more and more as a deepening reflection on the rhetoric of totalitarianism" (Geoffrey Hartman); "we are not now, and, in all likelihood, shall never be . . . in the position of being able to pass judgment on Paul de Man" (Leon Roudiez); de Man's so-called "collaborationist" journalism was "simply a job" (Fredric Jameson).[26]

Not content simply to defend de Man, his friends and intellectual neighbors proceeded to subject his academic critics (and there were many) to a torrent of abuse. To cite only the most extreme example, the Northwestern University professor Andrzej Warminski accused them of not being able to read, of deliberate misrepresentation, of "stupidity," of being sick, of being philistines, of being primarily committed to "the institution and institutional values and criteria," which, they thought, were being threatened by de Man and "anyone with intellectual values (which, by the mere fact of *being* intellectual values always represent a potential threat to the institution and its creatures)." But, he went on, even this was not enough to explain the "hysteria" provoked by the revelations. "What could make so many of these creatures crawl out from under the rocks of their pathologies?" To this he attached the following footnote: "Anyone who thinks that the reptilian figure here is exaggerated should read some of the slime that has passed for [academic] 'journalism' these last months."[27] One might well ask what it was that caused him to crawl out from under the rocks of *his* pathologies.

But there is a nonpathological explanation for Warminski's anger, if not for the way he expressed it. He and his friends saw the revelations and the ensuing attacks as an attempt by the bourgeois "establishment" to discredit not only Paul de Man but also his way, which was their way, of doing literary criticism. By responding as they did, however, they disclosed the intellectual and moral bankruptcy of deconstructionism, with the result that few literary theorists today are willing to be associated with it.

The assault on the universities, begun by the radical students of the sixties, was continued in a more subtle fashion by the deconstructionists in the eighties. Unlike the students, they did not strike, riot, occupy buildings, or take up arms, nor, as one of the Berrigan brothers was accused of doing— even as he was nominated for a Nobel Peace Prize—did they engage in a plot to kidnap Henry Kissenger and blow up the heating system of federal buildings in Washington. (The case ended in a mistrial.) All they did is teach (and teach the next generation of teachers), but what they taught is that the universities have nothing of importance to teach. Matthew Arnold would have had the universities teach the books containing the best that has been thought and said in the world, and Thomas

Jefferson wanted them to teach the Declaration of Independence and *The Federalist,* the "best guides [to the] distinctive principles of the government of the United States." But, according to Paul de Man, there is no best thought and no best guide because there is no text; there is only interpretation. As he said, "the distinctive curse of all language" is that it cannot convey meaning in any objective sense. Thus, about those things that mattered most to Arnold and Jefferson—all the things written about by poets, playwrights, philosophers, historians, statesmen, and founders—the humanities, indeed the universities, would have nothing to say.

In a way this is what the students were complaining about in the sixties: the irrelevance of the curriculum. For some of them the solution was to remake the university into a kind of countercultural welfare agency, and the extent of their success is evident in the prevalence of black studies, women's studies, and multicultural programs. For the others—the ones searching for "authentic values," in which phrase there is, perhaps, a hint of a longing for an education of the sort proposed by Coleridge and Company—what does the university offer? In the humanities it offers a politicized curriculum, the core of which is antirationalist, antihumanist, and antiliberal.

It used to be thought (and in some quarters is still thought) that Shakespeare is the greatest of our poets, the playwright who shows us, for example, the meaning of love and friendship, envy and jealousy, the character of good rulers and the fate of tyrants. In a word, he shows us human beings just as they are, a mixture of the high and the low, or as someone said, "his poetry gives us the eyes to see what is there." The political plays especially meant something for Abraham Lincoln. "Some of Shakespeare's plays I have never read," he said, "while others I have gone over perhaps as frequently as any unprofessional reader. Among the latter are Lear, Richard Third, Henry Eighth, Hamlet, and especially Macbeth. It is wonderful."[28] But for the New Historicism, currently the dominant movement in the field of Shakespeare studies, his plays simply reflect the prejudices of his day. They are said to be worthy of study only because in them can be found the seeds of racism, sexism, capitalism, classism, all the evils that are said to characterize bourgeois society. Reading Shakespeare in this way has the effect of reducing his stature in the eyes of the students. "Safely entrenched in their politically correct attitude," writes Paul Cantor, a critic of the New Historicism, "students are made to feel superior to Shakespeare, to look down patronizingly at his supposedly limited and biased view of the world."[29]

For the students looking for something "wonderful," for something not available to them in the bourgeois world from which they come and to which they must, willy-nilly, return, these antihumanists have nothing to say.

NOTES

1. The scientists' turn came in 1971, when students blew up the Mathematics Research Center at the University of Wisconsin, killing a postdoctoral fellow and destroying the lifework of five physics professors. Since then science as such has come under attack from feminists, Afrocentrists, and a variety of "postmodernist" professors. For a detailed account of this antiscience campaign, see Paul Gross and Norman Levitt, *Higher Superstition: The Academic Left and Its Quarrels with Science* (1994).
2. Berrigan was a campus hero, famous for leading the band of grim ecclesiastics who wrested card files from the hands of the clerk of the Catonsville, Maryland, draft board office and burned them in the parking lot with homemade napalm. When, in a public debate, I asked him whether they had given some thought to the possibility that some harm might come to the defenseless and probably terrified clerk, he replied, "Yes, we gave that *prayerful* consideration, but we decided the protest was so important that we had to run that risk. . . . Besides," he added after a short pause, perhaps recalling that they had not bothered to solicit the clerk's opinion on whether *she* was willing to run that risk, "anyone who works for the draft board deserves no more consideration than the guards at Belsen and Dachau."
3. Bayard Rustin, "The Failure of Black Separatism," *Harper's* (January 1970), p. 30.
4. Richard Bernstein, *Dictatorship of Virtue: Multiculturalism and the Battle for America's Future* (1994), p. 71.

5. Ibid., pp. 64–65, for a detailed account of this haranguing.
6. Susan Estrich, "Affirmative Action: Politics of Race," *USA Today*, February 23, 1995, p. 11A.
7. Clifford Orwin, "Compassion," *American Scholar* (Summer 1980), p. 323.
8. Christina Hoff Sommers, *Who Stole Feminism?: How Women Have Betrayed Women*" (Simon & Schuster, 1994), p. 28.
9. Students in a women's studies course at Georgetown University are required to read the "SCUM Manifesto," the flavor of which is contained in the following statement: "SCUM [Society for the Cutting Up of Men] is too impatient to hope and wait for the brainwashing of millions of [male] assholes. . . . SCUM will not picket, demonstrate, march or strike to attempt to achieve its ends. Such tactics are for nice, genteel ladies who scrupulously take only such action as is guaranteed to be ineffective. . . . SCUM will kill all men who are not in the Men's Auxiliary of SCUM."
10. *"On peut aisément concevoir qu'en s'efforcant d'égaler ainsi un sexe à l'autre, on les dégrade tous les deux; et que de ce mélange grossier des oeuvres de la nature il ne saurait jamais sortir que des hommes faibles et des femmes déshonnêtes."* Alexis de Tocqueville, *Democracy in America*, vol. 2, book 3, ch. XII, "How the Americans Understand the Equality of the Sexes."
11. Sheldon S. Wolin and John H. Schaar, *The Berkeley Rebellion and Beyond: Essays on Politics and Society in the Technological Society* (1970), p. 40.
12. Tocqueville, *Democracy in America*, vol. 2, part IV, ch. 6, "What Sort of Despotism Democratic Nations Have to Fear."
13. See Carlyle, *Signs of the Times;* Coleridge, *On the Constitution of Culture and Society;* Shelley, *Defence of Poetry;* John Stuart Mill, "Coleridge," and, for a general account, Raymond Williams, *Culture and Society* (1958).
14. Allan Bloom, *Giants and Dwarfs* (1990), p. 293.
15. George Levine et al., "Speaking for the Humanities," *ACLS Occasional Paper*, 7 (1989), pp. 2–3, 14.
16. Dominick LaCapra, *Representing the Holocaust* (1994), p. 114.
17. John M. Ellis, *Against Deconstruction* (Princeton University Press, 1989), pp. 146–47.
18. Paul de Man, *Blindness & Insight: Essays in the Rhetoric of Contemporary Criticism* (1971), pp. ix, 11, 141.
19. Jonathan Culler, *Framing the Sign: Criticism and Its Institutions* (1988), p. 40. See David Lehman, *Signs of the Times: Deconstruction and the Fall of Paul de Man* (1991), pp. 262–63.
20. Geoffrey Hartman, "Blindness and Insight," *New Republic* (March 7, 1988), p. 30.
21. Roger Kimball, "Professor Hartman Reconstructs Paul de Man," *New Criterion* (May 1988), pp. 42–43.
22. Bloom, p. 293.
23. *Le Soir* was Belgium's most widely read paper, with a daily circulation of 255,000. After its Belgian owners had fled to France, its name and facilities were taken over by the German authorities. All its articles were censored by the Militärverwaltung's Propaganda Abteilung (the Propaganda Divi-

sion of the Military Administration). The Flemish-language daily, *Het Vlaamsche Land*, was sponsored by the Germans and began publication in January 1941; its circulation was 21,000.

24. *"En plus, on voit donc qu'une solution du problème juif qui viserait à la création d'une colonie juive isolée de l'Europe, n'entrainerait pas, pour la vie littéraire de l'Occident, de conséquences deplorables. Celle-ci perdrait, en tout et pour tout, quelques personnalités de mediocre valeur et continuerait, comme par le passé, à se développer selon ses grandes lois évolutives."* Le Soir, March 4, 1941.

25. *"La guerre n'aura fait qu'unir plus étroitement ces deux choses si voisines qu'étaient dès l'origine l'âme hitlerienne et l'âme allemande, jusqu'à en faire une seule et unique puissance. C'est un phénomène important, car il signifie qu'on ne peut juger le fait hitlérien sans juger en même temps le fait allemand et que l'avenir de l'Europe ne peut être prévu que dans le cadre des possibilités et des besoins du génie allemand. Il ne s'agit pas seulement d'une série de réformes, mais de l'émancipation définitive d'un peuple qui se trouve, à son tour, appelé à exercer une hégémonie en Europe."* Le Soir, October 28, 1941.

26. Werner Hamacher, Neil Hertz, and Thomas Keenan, eds., *Responses on Paul de Man's Wartime Journalism* (1989) pp. 209, 7, 147, 139; Geoffrey Hartman, "Blindness and Insight," *New Republic* (March 7, 1988), pp. 30–31; Leon Roudiez, "Searching for Achilles' Heel: Paul de Man's Disturbing Youth," *World Literature Today* (Summer 1989), p. 438; Jameson, *Postmodernism, or, The Cultural Logic of Late Capitalism* (1991), p. 257. In 1991 Jameson's book won the Modern Language Association's James Russell Lowell Prize "for an outstanding literary or linguistic study."

27. Hamacher, Hertz, and Keenan, eds., *Responses on Paul de Man's Wartime Journalism,* pp. 389, 395.

28. Lincoln to James H. Hackett, August 17, 1863, in *Lincoln: Speeches and Writings* (1989), vol. 2, p. 493.

29. Paul A. Cantor, "Shakespeare—'For All Time'?" *Public Interest* 110 (Winter 1993), p. 44.

Two Cheers
for Professionalism:
The 1960s, the University,
and Me

ALAN WOLFE

I

Although partisan in tone and heavily ideological in approach,
critics such as Roger Kimball and Dinesh D'Sousza are fundamentally correct when they suggest a connection between academic working conditions and radical politics. Explanations of
this relationship vary from the high-minded (only when the life
of the mind is at stake can dissent be honorable) to the cynical
(tenure rewards intellectual irresponsibility). But there is little
doubt that the radical spirit of the 1960s remains more alive in
the conservative 1990s in university circles than anywhere else
in American life.

No matter how obvious this affinity may appear, one
should never lose sight of how unexpected it was. The protest
that erupted in Berkeley in 1964 was directed against the academy—indeed, against some of the practices, such as the organization of the university by departments, which now protect
the academic left. No wonder that it spawned few successful
academics. David Lance Goines has tried to identify everyone
arrested at Sproul Hall on December 3, 1964. His list includes
some who made careers as politicos, such as Los Angeles City
Council member Jackie Goldberg, and others, like Goines him-

self or Barbara Garson, who achieved fame in nonacademic pursuits. Yet I could find no more than 10 out of the 825 who have achieved even a modicum of academic renown.[1] Myra Jehlin, then an activist graduate student, was not arrested; the list of those who were includes Stephen Gillers, now an NYU law professor; Stephanie Coontz, a feminist historian; and Randall Collins, a distinguished sociologist.

There surely are reasons why young political activists at that time would find the academy an unattractive career option. A maddening calm, one that simply could not be ruffled by considerations of social justice, demands for relevance, or a preference for substance over process, dominated university culture. Between those whose lives were shaped by depression and war and those growing up in the affluent society lay a chasm. The former—cautious in all things, pleased with the security (although not the low pay) of academic employment, and suspicious of causes and extremism—could only look with dismay, if not fury, at the high expectations and impatience for results that characterized the latter.

In retrospect, what made academic professionalism so maddening was that it was so . . . unprofessional. Rather than careers open to talents, networks and connections rewarded some and punished others. Neutrality and objectivity *did* mask an unargued-for preference for the status quo. Self-governance was often a device to prevent any government at all; academics generally went unregulated, especially by themselves. One had to write and teach, but there was, in the gentlemanly atmosphere of the 1950s, a widespread conviction that one should not be too active, lest one be equated with Sammy Glick, Budd Schulberg's fictional antihero who would stop at nothing to succeed.

Faced with inbred academics who claimed professional status but acted otherwise, the radicals of the early 1960s rejected the whole business as inherently corrupt; they were more likely to become hip entrepreneurs than they were to get tenure. In this they were quite different from those born five to ten years later, for whom Vietnam and Watergate, not demands for student power, were the defining events. (Andrew Ross was eight years old when Berkeley erupted.) The "second generation" of 1960s radicals would expose the hypocrisy of academic professionalism not by turning their backs on careerism and rewards but by showing what true professionals were like. Radical politics did flourish in the American academy, as critics charge, but if the academy was changed as a result, it became even more like the university that inspired the first wave of protests against it.

II

Thus 1960s student radicalism has become 1990s faculty professionalism. A professional can be understood as a person who is committed to specialization in a particular discipline, engaged in producing work to be read primarily by other professionals, committed to a career in which the rewards are long-term, devoted to self-governance and critical of any outside interference, preoccupied with questions of method, and convinced that amateurs are unable to do what professionals do best precisely because they lack the commitments just described. Each of these elements is more triumphant in the academy now than they were a generation ago.

When the tale of the left's triumph in the academy is told and retold, the two most prominently mentioned institutions are the Modern Language Association and the Duke University English Department. Both of course are tied to an academic discipline. Nor are they tied to just *any* discipline. English literature represents not only the language itself but the entire culture fashioned by that language. We know, thanks to Gerald Graff's history, that the hows and whys of English departments have always been contested, but the debates of the past were narrow in scope.[2] Everyone accepted, until relatively recently, that whatever they might not be, English departments were one thing: elitist. Those who taught English were by definition holdouts from mass society, guarding the language and its literature against the corruptions of the quotidian.

In an age of deconstruction that quaint image of the English department is long dead. But it is still worth remarking how everything was deconstructed but the department. Although a substantial part of the early New Left critique of the university focused on specialization as a particular evil, academic leftists, once out of graduate school, outspecialized their mentors. Gone was the early New Left's demand for interdisciplinary approaches to knowledge; as Stanley Fish was to put it, "Being interdisciplinary is so very hard to do."[3] Even those whose careers flourished in brand-new academic disciplines, such as black studies or women's studies, mocked the organizational characteristics, if not always the academic standards, of the traditional disciplines.

Professional associations flourished along with departments. Much has been made of the politicization of the Modern Language Association, but before it could become a prize worthy of capture, it first had to expand in size and scope. Academic professional associations were transformed from *Gemeinschaft* to *Gesellschaft* as radicals came to power in the academy; indeed, the American Sociological Association, reflecting its professional understandings of these matters, changed its name from the American Sociological Society and moved to Washington in the early 1960s. Not only did these organizations develop professional staffs, financed by ever-increasing membership dues, but they also broke up into specialized units, each reflecting a particular tendency within the field. When disciplines were dominated by a few departments, academic professional associations were relatively unimportant. But as departments proliferated, trips to the annual meetings became, for the aspiring professional, a necessity. It was all part of the long march through institutions.

Professionals write for other professionals. Whatever the value of this activity, it is far different from the notions that originally inspired the early-1960s generation. Andrew Jamison and Ron Eyerman trace the "seeds of the 1960s" back to fifteen writers of the previous decade, from C. Wright Mills and Erich Fromm to Lewis Mumford and James Baldwin.[4] All were either nonacademics entirely or academics living on the margins of their disciplines.[5] And virtually none of them has been reproduced among those inspired by their ideas. There are, within today's crop of academic writers, a number who are read outside their professional discipline. Richard Rorty, Henry Louis Gates, Edward Said, Stephen Jay Gould, Michael Walzer, Cornel West, and Martha Nussbaum are examples. All of them, unlike the earlier generation, obtained tenure at elite universities. Only Camille Paglia comes to (my) mind as an example of an intellectual working in a marginal institution who reaches an audience the size of that reached by a Herbert Marcuse or a Margaret Mead.

The frank careerism of contemporary academic leftists also seems peculiar in the light of their origins. The general idea seems to be that one is absolved of unseemly behavior not only by confessing to it but by relishing in it. This "dirty little secret" rhetorical style particularly fits Stanley Fish, academia's bad boy, who believes that he has struck a fatal blow at bourgeois society by acting bourgeois.[6] Yet Fish speaks for a generation; when leftists maintain that the personal is political, they mean not only that decisions made in private have public consequences but that public positions have private motivations. Having ridden the postwar wave of economic growth into comfortable positions with enviable job security, radicals come to terms with earlier vows of purity or poverty by acknowledging the reality of their success. They will not, like an earlier generation of academics, pursue a career while denying ambition. They will instead make their career the touchstone of their ambition.

Self-governance is at the heart of professional self-definition; physicians think of themselves as physicians to the degree that they, and not oversight agencies, make the key decisions involving care. Peer review is the particular form that academic professionalism takes. Only colleagues in a similar field should judge the competence of a candidate for tenure.

Departments, not obtrusive administrators, make the decisions about hiring. The best work is that which passes tests of blind submission and blind review. In short, faculty, like professionals everywhere, pride themselves on their autonomy.

There was once a time when faculty autonomy was no doubt a positive thing. When administrators were powerful, they imposed their will on academic departments, and as they did so, they tended to drive out nonconformity and unorthodoxy. Nicholas Murray Butler pioneered that model of university governance at Columbia, and it lasted as long as McGeorge Bundy's deanship at Harvard. But these days the situation is quite otherwise; administrators tend not to participate in the intellectual life of the university, while faculty, in the name of autonomy, reproduce replicas of themselves. Professional autonomy in practice tends to become monopolistic control over otherwise more open markets. One need not accept the claims of the critics of political correctness to recognize that departments controlled by radicals tend not to hire conservatives—or even liberals.

If faculty autonomy has become a cornerstone of contemporary professionalism, university autonomy has not. The Berkeley radicals demanded that government keep out of academic affairs; to them, the university was a sanctuary, roughly like a church, and state legislators had no business telling professors and students what to do. By contrast, the state of New Jersey has, until very recently, funded an office charged with ensuring that issues of race, class, and gender are introduced into the curriculum of the state's institutions of higher education. Similarly, Leonard Jeffries of City College had little trouble appealing to outside agencies, including the courts, when his university stripped him of his department chairmanship. Very little of the agenda of the academic left—from affirmative action to sensitivity training—can be accomplished without the regulation of universities by political agencies. Faculties are increasingly autonomous within institutions that are not.

Academic professionals are especially preoccupied with

questions of method, sometimes to the point where substance drops out of their work altogether. In my own fields of interest, sociology and political science, the survival of quantitative methods is quite unexpected. There was, in the minds of the New Left radicals, an association between reliance on quantitative methods and the war in Vietnam; both were unseemly products of a technocratic mentality bent on using human subjects to further the designs of autocratic elites. Luddism characterized the 1960s' zeitgeist; the revolt against academic complacency and irrelevance took the special form of a revolt against positivistic methods.

A glance at any of the leading social science journals indicates that quantitative methods since that time have become even more ubiquitous than they were then. What was unexpected was how many former leftists would contribute to their hegemony. Some Marxists criticized every aspect of bourgeois society except counting; they would use the tools of the social science to demonstrate the persistence of class inequalities. Radical economists turned not to the early Marx but to neo-Ricardians who believed that one could actually measure the falling rate of profit or the rate of surplus value. Those whose work was not primarily quantitative nonetheless developed a methodological self-consciousness; they would prove that historical or qualitative methods were methods nonetheless. Just as leftist English professors developed a more arcane and theoretically driven style than the New Critics and philologists who preceded them, radical social scientists could crunch numbers as well as anyone else. The clash between the attack on method and entrenched ways of conducting academic life was no contest; the latter won, hands down.

The concluding impact of all these trends was to reinforce the professional's historic disdain for the amateur and, at the same time, to increase the distance between the university and the world around it.[7] Whatever else the university became as the academic left reached its prominence, it would not be a place that welcomed generalists. History departments had no room for narrative storytellers with large audiences, just as

English departments would be unwelcome to John Gross's "man of letters."[8] Sociologists known to the reading public found themselves uncomfortable among the junior faculty in their departments, not because the younger scholars were more leftists, although they were, but because their work seemed so narrow. A literary humanist named John Kenneth Galbraith, who also happened to be an economist, could never have gotten tenure at Harvard if he had been born fifty years after he was. Russell Jacoby's argument that universities killed the New York intellectual is not the issue; the important question is whether what he describes is a good thing or a bad one.[9]

III

Because I was a 1960s radical who is now teaching in a 1990s university, there are two reasons why I ought to find myself in agreement with Jacoby's preference for the world of the intellectual over the world of the professional academic. One is that I am, for better or worse, a New York intellectual. The other is that I came to academic life convinced that I would reject academic professionalism rather than advance it to new heights. Yet I am very uneasy concluding that the professionalization of the university is a bad thing; after all, I no longer believe all the things I believed in the 1960s, and surely that must include some of the intemperate things I once said about the academy. But this borders on saying something about myself, so perhaps the best course would be to do so more explicitly.

Although I was not at Berkeley in 1964, my own career follows chronologically the story I have summarized. Each important date in the history of the New Left was also a date in my education. Thus 1964, the year of the Berkeley revolt, as well as the first civil rights law, concluded my first year in graduate school; 1968, when Columbia broke out, began my first as an assistant professor. (One finished graduate school quickly in those days; I was a newly minted Ph.D. before my twenty-sixth birthday, like Newt Gingrich just in time to exempt myself from the draft.) To this day I cannot separate such personally traumatic graduate school experiences as oral exams and my thesis defense from such politically traumatic experiences as Vietnam and the Watts riots.

The first in my generation to go to college—my father, a high school dropout, was a carpenter who later, with his father and brothers, ran a construction business that went bankrupt—I took the subway each day from our home in Northwest Philadelphia to Temple University. My undergraduate major was accounting. Students in the College of Business Administration had yellow registration cards, and I can still remember, after I began to do well, how mine would stand out in the English professor's pile, the only one of its hue among the pink cards of the College of Liberal Arts. Although I realized by my third year in college that I was unlikely to be an accountant, I nonetheless was graduated with a degree in business, surely one explanation for my current passion with the liberal arts.

Determined to get away from home, but with neither money nor a prestigious degree, I was unable to win acceptance to a number of leading graduate schools. But Vanderbilt University gave me a generous fellowship to study political science, and I moved to Nashville in the fall of 1963, two months before Kennedy was assassinated. It did not take much to turn a completely apolitical Philadelphia Jew into a radical at that time and in that town. Within a month of arriving, I was arrested for blocking the entrance to a restaurant and passed my first experience with jail in the company of organizers from the Student Nonviolent Coordinating Committee. When news of my arrest reached the papers back home, my mother flew down to see what had overcome her son; as a result, she met people like the Reverend C. T. Vivian and got to hear Martin Luther King, Jr., speak in a black church in the South.

Halfway through my one year in Nashville I had already given up on most of my courses; the political life was simply too compelling. When a death in the family called me back to Philadelphia, I came home, uncertain what to do, only to receive a call from a professor at the University of Pennsylvania. One of the teaching assistants had dropped out of school, leaving an introductory course open. Would I teach it and enroll in graduate school there? Desperate for something to do, I grabbed the chance. Within three years I had my degree and was on the market. More exactly, the market was on me. I did not have to look for a job. There was an opening at Douglass College, the women's college of Rutgers, and I happened to be living in New Brunswick at the time. Before I knew it, I was an academic.

Douglass, a conservative place, was nonetheless touched by the 1960s. Siding with the students in their demands for less intrusion in their lives, urging them to protest after King was shot, I was clearly persona non grata in my department, and that suited me just fine. For the *New York Times* had run a story about a new experimental college that was going to open on Long Island. Harris Wofford, a former Peace Corps official and the man who had urged John F. Kennedy to write to Coretta Scott King while her husband was in jail, was Old Westbury's founding president, and he was speaking a language I could understand. I was simply determined to get the college to hire me. As it turns out, it did, and I joined a small faculty of nine, one of whom, Michael Novak, later achieved fame as a conservative and Catholic thinker. (I saw him again, a quarter of a century later, at a seminar on *The Bell Curve* at the American Enterprise Institute.) My two years at Old Westbury were the two angriest years of the New Left's existence, 1968 to 1970. Students at Old Westbury were no less angry than anywhere else, and in my role as their mentor I helped ferment their rage. Within just a few years Wofford's idealistic rhetoric began to sound suspiciously patronizing and elitist. For my students, as for me, coming to terms with the 1960s meant rebelling against the Kennedy administration—at Old Westbury, personified in one of Kennedy's key aides. A liberal idealist when I came to Old Westbury in 1968, I had turned against both liberalism and idealism by the time it refused to renew my contract in 1970.[10]

Jobs, however, were still plentiful, and I took one at a branch of the City University of New York on Staten Island. My attention shifted to my discipline. I had helped form the Caucus for a New Political Science in 1967; although it received support from such nonradicals as Daniel Patrick Moynihan and Morris Janowitz of the University of Chicago, the caucus quickly became a forum within the discipline for leftists of all stripes. Then, as now, I was preoccupied with the question of what it meant to be a professional. It was already obvious in the late 1960s that one strategy for radicals was to be *better* professionals than those they opposed. But I argued then against such a position, at least for leftist political scientists. "The demand for professional conduct," I wrote, "is a demand for conservative politics."[11] The field was, unlike sociology, too hopelessly reactionary for genuine reform.

The profession took care of me before I could do much about it. Jobs in political science were unobtainable for one of my inclinations, but jobs in sociology came calling. I switched fields, never imagining that I would come to be as unhappy with the unthinking leftism of sociology as I once was with the complacent conservativism of political science. Teaching sociology at the City University of New York gave one a couple of excuses for ignoring a professional career: Sociology itself was far less coherent than other social science disciplines, and CUNY was a world unto itself. So long as one loved living in Manhattan, the whole idea of striving for success in one's profession in order to move to a better academic position was unthinkable. Having Zabar's within walking distance was much more important than publishing in the *American Sociological Review*.

And so without ever planning the matter, I evolved into a New York intellectual. The outlet for my ideas became the *Nation*, upon whose editorial board I quickly sat, and I spent a considerable amount of time explaining to the readers of that magazine exactly what was wrong with American society. None of this "popular" writing interfered with my academic career. At CUNY raises each year were automatic; under the leadership of a faculty union the whole notion of merit had disappeared from the university's vocabulary. Tenure came simply by sitting in place and keeping busy, although I am not sure that the latter was necessary.

By the age of thirty-five I found myself with a relatively well-paying full-time job, guaranteed for life, and the opportunity to write whatever I wanted in whatever way I wanted to. The question of professionalization had resolved itself easily for me; unlike the academic careerists of a later generation, who would publish their highly specialized research in unread journals and advance to ever more prestigious universities, I would, true to the spirit of the early 1960s that inspired me, remain a critic of all that—an amateur and a generalist living at the margins of a vocation dominated by rigorous professionals. The odd thing is that it did not happen, or at least it did not happen that way. Success as a New York intellectual not only taught me the limits of that often envied way of writing and thinking but also renewed appreciation for the academic professionalism I thought I had disdained.

Rejecting tenure, at least the first time I was awarded it, I moved to, of all places, Berkeley; I had decided to experience my midlife crisis early. Living on the margins of the academy was no different, I discovered, from living in its center, except that the pay was less. I came back to CUNY, this time to Queens College, joining an institution composed of a remarkable number of people of my general age and political instincts. It was a great place to find colleagues but, alas, an increasingly awful place to teach. Although Queens was the "jewel" in CUNY's crown, the students were, with all too few exceptions, uninterested and uninteresting. It may have been the sociology majors—primarily female children of Catholic families whose parents had decided against investing St. John's tuition on them. Each year, despite simplifying my reading list and making my subjects as contemporary as possible, I found myself unable to bring their lives and my life into any common experience. If Queens was the best, I could scarcely imagine the worst; from my experience there, I am convinced that James Traub does not exaggerate when he concludes that the admission of too many unprepared students "presses City to kneel down rather than to lift up."[12]

It was also at Queens that I discovered, after having written a few books, that I finally had something to say; John Gross's point that "it might not be a bad idea if no one under thirty was allowed to undertake original research without special permission" certainly applied to me, although forty might be a more appropriate cutoff date.[13] Moreover, I wanted to say what I had to say in a more academic style than I had ever tried. The result: a reversal of the usual career pattern. Many academics publish their earlier books with university presses hoping eventually to write for a more general audience. I established my credentials as an intellectual first, only to find myself unhappy with the amateurism I encountered in that company. I submitted an article to the *American Journal of Sociology* that was accepted, not without difficulty, in the same week that I wrote my first article for the *New Republic*. And I followed that by writing two academic books developing a sociological approach to moral obligation, both published by the University of California Press.

This shift toward greater academic seriousness was not confined to my writing. I was named dean of the Graduate Faculty of Political and Social Science at the New School for Social Research in 1990. Founded originally as the University in Exile in 1933, the Graduate Faculty had moved far from the kultur of its culturally conservative, antitotalitarian, but politically liberal founders. Its Economics Department was explicitly Marxist, so much so that its members routinely denied this self-evident fact whenever challenged. Other departments were less sectarian, but despite an often brilliant faculty and some wonderful students, the place did suffer from the stultifying arrogance of people who not only believe that they understand the world but are equally convinced that the great majority of others do not. My increasingly centrist, but still leftist, politics clashed with the culture, as did my sense that "positivist" social science was not necessarily a bad thing.

Only at the New School could someone like me, whose academic career had been so marginal compared with the quantitative hotshots and cutting-edge theorists of my discipline, stand for more rigorous methodological training and an effort to meet the professional culture of American academia at least halfway. The New School's picture of itself made little sense to me. I did not believe that the American academic world had become so riven with trivial method and narrow-gauged research that only those inspired by the brilliance of European social theory were saving the culture from barbarism. I actually believed the opposite. European theory seemed intellectually lazy to me, relying on verbal firepower or endless explications of text to mask a lack of connection to the real world. The standards of American scholarship, in my opinion, were far superior. Our books were actually edited, whereas any well-known European thinker could publish random and repetitive thoughts without ever being challenged. I even came to respect American academic journals, not, certainly, for the brilliance of the writing found therein but for the admirable effort to see whether evidence actually supported a conventional understanding of how the world works.

I left the New School three years after my arrival, having made very little long-term impact on its way of doing business. Now I work at Boston University, a place usually regarded (incorrectly) as a bastion of the right. Lured to BU with the promise of some resources to help build the Sociology Department, I have tried to bring to the department serious scholars of both the quantitative and the qualitative persuasion. This effort has strongly reinforced what I had already begun to notice: Academic professionalism is better than any of its alternatives. At the very moment when all too many of my very successful academic friends look longingly at the opinion magazines and wish above all else to be asked to write for them, I look at quarterly journals and university press books and am impressed with the depth and seriousness they convey.

IV

As someone who appreciates both the critical urge associated with the 1960s and the professional discipline of the 1990s I find repeated efforts to set one of these values off against the other unhelpful. Academics once debated the relative weight that should be given to teaching versus research for decades before it became obvious to almost everyone that the two are not in conflict; those who fail to renew themselves through some kind of research cannot possibly be good teachers. A similarly false debate is taking place between those who say that the university has no place for general intellectuals and those who attack academic publication as trivial and overly specialized.

It is not the existence of professionalism within the academic left that is disturbing but the kind of professionalism one finds there. Russell Jacoby explores this ground well in *Dogmatic Wisdom;* academic leftists pride themselves on their ability to write in ways that few can understand, all the while denouncing their critics as, in Joan Scott's words, "marginal intellectuals."[14] Judith Frank, according to Jacoby, denounces one critic for expecting "the humanities to be utterly transparent to the general population, when the truth is that for those who us who have gone through graduate training, the humanities are a profession. . . ."[15] It is as if these kinds of academic leftists have decided to take all the negative aspects of professionalism—hermetic isolation from criticism, self-conscious mandarinism, a propensity to distinguish between the in-group and the out-group—and make those into their manifesto, all the while ignoring the side of professionalism that emphasizes pride in a job well done and a sense of obligation to share the work with others.

There is, in short, something unprofessional about the academic left's determination to trumpet its belief in professionalism; physicians, after all, strengthen their claims to professional status through clinical practice and research, not by writing essays about the meaning of professionalism. To the degree that English professors write about being English professors, they are not doing what professionals do, no matter how often, in those writings, they try to justify professional status.[16] The academic culture that produced Lionel Trilling was anything but professional in today's terms, yet Trilling's work is more "professional" in its seriousness of purpose and depth of learning than anything produced at Duke or Penn. For all its haughty disdain for mere amateurs, the academic left's commitment to professionalism is not very deep; that may explain why so many English department activists in the culture wars are now talking about themselves, thinking of working in restaurants, or bemoaning the fact that they have failed to write persuasively for the general public.

One shudders at the thought of what some of them may produce for a general audience. For just as there are serious professionals and insecure ones, so there are also good intellectuals and bad ones. Because I write for general magazines, I find myself in the odd position of being taken aside by a large number of scholars whose work I deeply admire—only to be told by them, in hushed whispers, that what they would *really* like to do is to review books for the *New Republic*. Would I mind looking over something they have written? They then thrust into my hand an essay about a grand theme, often badly written, poorly argued, and filled with generalizations they would never make in their scholarly writings. I want to tell them to stick to what they do best, but I sense this may crush them. Having reached the pinnacle of academic success—their books and articles establish them, in my view, as professionals in the true sense of the word—they wish now to say good-bye to all that, as if their secret ambition in life all along had been a front-page review in the *New York Times Book Review*.

What I do tell them is how much work goes into my essays

for the *New Republic*. The amount of time I spend ensuring
that my argument is as tight as it can be is far greater in the
popular things that I write than in the books I write and the
manuscripts I review for university presses; the standards of
the latter are shockingly low compared with the former. But I
know that this can fall on deaf ears, for as hard as it may be to
write like a good New York intellectual, it is easy to write like
a bad one. There are just as many intellectuals who write
poorly and reason sloppily as there are academics. The truth
is that an awful lot of the stuff that gets published by academic
generalists is bad stuff. Everyone in the academic world can
tell the story of the untenured assistant professor who chose
to write a popular book, even one that received widespread
attention, only to be turned down later for tenure. Often those
stories betray the tunnel vision of the academy. Yet just as
often they touch on an important truth, for such books can be
shoddy in their use of evidence, thin in documentation, and
determined to make some larger point at the expense of a far
more complicated reality.

This is not to praise all academic writing. There are far too
many things being published in the academic world, and a substantial proportion of them is awful. Any book-length manu-
script can find some publisher; any article, rejected by the top
journals, can find a place in another journal. Yet there is also no
doubt in my mind that overall, the standards one has to reach to
have a successful academic career have increased over the past
thirty years. The opening up of the academic world to greater
competition has produced something much closer to a meritoc-
racy now than at any previous time in the history of the American university. As simple a matter as the advertising of jobs—
unheard of when I entered academic life—has had a profound
effect in encouraging a greater reliance on merit. The disserta-
tion I wrote in the 1960s could not, and should not, pass muster
today; I routinely insist that my own graduate students outper-
form anything I did as a graduate student. An assistant professor job search over which I presided when at the New School
produced three strong finalists. As we were considering their

merits, the graduate students complained about their poor quality until one of my colleagues, a distinguished senior scholar, pointed out to them that all three were better scholars at that stage of their career than he, or I, had been at that stage of ours. The standards expected for tenure in the 1990s are much higher than they were in the 1970s, creating considerable intergenerational inequity—tenured incompetents routinely find fault with far more qualified untenured colleagues—but nonetheless improving the quality of academic life.

This general point is even true of my own field; sociology, is fragmented, politicized, and unable to define what it is, to the point where the entire field, according to Irving Louis Horowitz, has disintegrated.[17] I disagree, at least with half the indictment. Yes, the field is in awful shape organizationally, but it has also, I believe, produced work that would meet any standard established during its "golden age" in the 1950s and 1960s.[18] Both the quantitative and the qualitative work has had to rise to a higher standard to be considered serious social science. I am not sure how much "golden age" sociology could make it under these more stringent standards: Robert Merton's work certainly (there are few Robert Mertons), but to take just one field of inquiry, the writings of William Julius Wilson on race are better argued and documented than the exhaustive, but not very convincing, research that went into *An American Dilemma*.

One reason why academic standards have improved is the entry of women and minorities into university life. In order to make it in a closed world, they had to perform better than those whose networks and buddy-buddy chauvinism had excluded them, and even that did not guarantee success. For one brief shining moment the academic world became a place in which individual merit would be rewarded, driven by furious competition to produce better work. It did not last long. Misinterpreting these individual successes as products of group membership, an affirmative action mentality gripped the university, threatening to replace one buddy-buddy system with another.

The conclusion of this particular version of the-personal-is-the-political is a plea for universities to reward neither academic professionalism nor general intellectuals but the best of both. I remain, by age and temperament, an academic generalist; there are too many topics about which I want to write, and life is too short, to specialize in only one thing. Believing in what I do, I naturally think there ought to be a place for people like me in the university, even, if not especially, at research universities. Not every member of a department has to publish only in scholarly journals. There are, after all, students to teach, not just future professors to train. I long for the day when I no longer have to exclude from my vita some of the writing of which I am most proud.

Yet I would be appalled if everyone in the university were like me. I learn an enormous amount from those whose style of work is completely different from mine, both from the number cruncher who wants to find out if the data support someone else's received wisdom, as well as from those who labor laboriously over details in ways impossible for one of my temperament. The American university does itself a disservice when it expresses its choice as one between intellectual work and academic work. If it strove to recognize both, the result was be a modified kind of professionalism—professionalism, so to speak, without its most conspicuous deformities. Although intellectuals are generalists, they can also be professional in their attitude, their discipline, and the use of the scholarship that forms their opinions. Although scholars view themselves as professionals, the best of them have something to say for a larger audience, and a few are capable of saying it quite well.

The early student radicals of the 1960s who rejected the academy had at least one thing right: Grand ideas are worth fighting for. The later student radicals who transformed the New Left critique of the university into an avenue of professional careers also had one thing right: Universities matter. The academic world performs at its best when both ideas work together and performs at its worst when neither idea is taken seriously.

NOTES

1. David Lance Goines, *The Free Speech Movement: Coming of Age in the 1960s* (1993), pp. 526–62.
2. Gerald Graff, *Professing Literature: An Institutional History* (1987).
3. Stanley Fish, "Being Interdisciplinary Is So Very Hard to Do," *Profession 89* (1989), pp. 15–22.
4. Andrew Jamison and Ron Eyerman, *Seeds of the Sixties* (1994).
5. Of the entire group, only Mills and Marcuse could be said to have followed traditional academic careers.
6. See especially the essays collected in Stanley Fish, *Doing What Comes Naturally: Change, Rhetoric, and the Practice of Theory in Literary and Legal Studies* (1989).
7. These themes are explored in ways similar to those developed here in David Bromwich, *Politics by Other Means: Higher Education and Group Thinking* (1992).
8. John Gross, *The Rise and Fall of the Man of Letters: Aspects of English Literary Life since 1800* (1992).
9. Russell Jacoby, *The Last Intellectuals: American Culture in the Age of Academe* (1987).
10. My first publication dealt with my Old Westbury years. See Alan Wolfe, "Conditions of Community: The Case of Old Westbury," in *Power and Community: Dissenting Essays in Political Science,* ed. Philip Green and Sanford Levinson (1968).
11. Alan Wolfe, "The Professional Mystique," in *An End to Political Science: The Caucus Papers,* ed. Marvin Surkin and Alan Wolfe (1970), 296.
12. James Traub, *City on a Hill: Testing the American Dream at City College* (1994), 191.
13. Gross, p. 312.
14. Russell Jacoby, *Dogmatic Wisdom: How the Culture Wars Divert Education and Distract America* (1994), 165.
15. Ibid., p. 167.
16. For a lively example, see Bruce Robbins, *Secular Vocations: Intellectuals, Professionalism, Culture* (1993).
17. Irving Louis Horowitz, *The Decomposition of Sociology* (1993).
18. I argue this point at greater length, and with many examples, in "Weak Sociology. Strong Sociologists: Consequences and Contradictions of a Field in Turmoil," *Social Research* 59 (Winter 1992), pp. 759–79.

PART THREE

———

RACE

The Half-Life of Integration

ANITA LAFRANCE ALLEN

The 1960s began as a decade of intense debate in the United States about the felt requirements of racial justice.[1] One of these was "integration," especially the integration of pervasively segregated southern states. Integration was to the 1960s what emancipation had been to the 1860s: a moral lodestar, a mother lode, pregnant with abstract moral meanings, overdue for delivery as concrete political, legal, and social reforms.

By 1970 hopes of meaningful integration had begun to fade. Hostile white citizens resisted integration, much as they had resisted emancipation. Emancipation devolved into Jim Crow. Integration devolved into white flight and other acts of avoidance. Moreover, after the assassination of Martin Luther King, Jr., in 1968, frustrated African Americans increasingly ascribed "integration" the negative connotation it bears today: a hegemonic policy to assimilate decultured blacks into a culturally white society. Throughout the 1970s, 1980s, and 1990s intellectuals eschewed "integration" in favor of "black power," "nationalism," "Afrocentricity," and "multiculturalism." These alternatives rightly affirmed the legitimacy of distinct African American cultural forms and claims for autonomous coexistence with other population groups.

Integration is scarcely anyone's stated ambition today. Yet viewed as principled opposition to separatism, integration was a good idea in the 1960s and is still a good idea. Public laws and private hearts ought to unite against our nation's persistent culture of segregation, whereby racial turf artificially constrains decisions about how, where, and with whom we live.

MEANING IN THE MIST

For a short time in the 1960s integration was a widely supported public goal, propounded by individuals and organizations of all races. Although many African Americans and whites subscribed to the goal of integration, not all subscribers viewed it in just the same way. Not even the most compelling supporters of integration forged a specific, universally shared vision of an integrated America and how to achieve it. Liberals never reached consensus about what "integration" required, beyond the bare act of outlawing most forms of public-sector race discrimination. Integration was a functional norm, but like most norms, it subsisted in a conceptual mist of disparate and ambiguous meanings.

Our household nourished broad and idealistic understandings of integration. We were an African American military family. My parents had six children. For us, integration signified a state of affairs in which people of all races could do three things. They could, first, enjoy opportunity and access to material rewards in desegregated communities; second, expect civility and courtesy of others; and, third, be intimate with people of any racial description.

For my parents, the word "integration" chiefly meant the definitive end of legal segregation, combined with the beginning of real employment, education, and housing opportunities for blacks. They expected that after integration, they and other hardworking blacks would enjoy the material blessings most whites enjoyed.

For me, "integration" carried the second signification as well. Racism was incivility. Integration signified a triumph over racism. I thought of racism in personal rather than institutional terms. In an integrated world, prejudiced, menacing people would not snicker when I passed them in the street. They would not call me "nigger." They would not close doors in my face. They would not draw "queer" circles around me in the schoolyard.

Particularly when I was a teenager, "integration" held the third meaning. It signified a form of social life in which blacks and whites could enjoy authentic, intimate relationships marked by friendship and love. The relationships I imagined in the newly integrated society would bear no resemblance to the pathologic paradigm of animal curiosity and betrayal depicted years later in filmmaker Spike Lee's *Jungle Fever*. I was too young to understand that my utopian vision of integration, as relaxing private social barriers, was precisely the nightmare of racists (and many liberals) that long delayed and almost thwarted both school desegregation and the passage of the 1964 Civil Rights Act.

The process of integration seemed to be under way in the South in the mid-1960s once local authorities and private businesses responded to Congress and the courts by desegregating schools and places of public accommodation. Yet early integration efforts were so quickly followed by white resistance and black revolt that the more idealistic and utopian visions harbored by families like mine never got off the ground. Traces of our visions survived in the federal civil rights laws and in controversial practices that have included "busing," "affirmative action" in employment and education, minority business "set-asides," and racially mixed "planned communities."

Too many affluent whites immediately bought their way out of the formal integration demanded by law. They retreated to exclusive residential, social, and commercial enclaves. They sent their children to exclusive private schools. The low-income and middle-class whites who were left behind among the blacks surely got the message from the flight of elite role models that avoidance was the optimal response to integration measures.

Forced by law to open doors on a nondiscriminatory

basis, resentful whites were openly hostile to blacks or simply not welcoming. Disappointed blacks often participated in integration efforts with a certain ambivalence and attitude. It was scarcely a substantive change for the better to occupy social spaces with whites under subordinating conditions of prejudice and resentment. I am among the African Americans who benefited most from the civil rights reforms of the 1960s and the affirmative action policies of the 1960s, 1970s, and 1980s, but all of us who participated in integration to our benefit have also borne serious costs.

Integration in the 1960s was a frustrating truncation of the deep racial rapprochement for which many had struggled. Why did serious integration fail? Why are we still a racially divided nation? Why do we still seem to prefer segregated neighborhoods, college dormitories, high school cafeterias, and personal ties? The mutual acknowledgment of deep-running cultural dissimilarities may help explain the failure of the most utopian conceptions of integration: We are not all alike, and our unique differences inevitably separate us.

But my experience with integration efforts in the South in the sixties suggests that moral limitations blocked meaningful integration as well. Resistance, avoidance, selfishness, the absence of a commitment to live and teach the moral truth behind civil rights legislation, these also help explain the short life of integrationist idealism in the United States. The "real tragedy of contemporary race relations . . . is not that integration failed, but that it was barely tried."[2]

No Deliberate Speed

I was born in 1953, just in time for *Brown v. Board of Education*.[3] I ought never have experienced enforced public school segregation, but I did. The Supreme Court's 1954 decision in *Brown* held that racial segregation in public primary and secondary schools violates the Constitution. The Court considered expert testimony arguing that separate schools were inherently unequal. The experts said compelling black children to attend legally segregated schools made them feel that they were social inferiors. School segregation lowered African American children's self-esteem. This self-esteem claim remains controversial, but there could be something to it. After a couple of years in black primary schools, my older sister explained segregation on the ground that blacks, but not whites, have the shameful biological need to defecate and urinate.

Showing no urgent concern for the self-esteem or basic education of African American children, most southern towns responded slowly to *Brown*. Foot-dragging on public school integration was common in the South. The seemingly far-reaching *Brown* decision had not demanded that the states dismantle their segregated school systems immediately. *Brown* had instead required desegregation "with all deliberate speed."[4] The monumental Civil Rights Act of 1964 legislated integration of public accommodations and outlawed discrimination in housing, voting, and education. Yet foot-dragging on public school segregation continued in many places, prompting the Supreme Court to rule in 1965 that "delays in desegregating school systems are no longer tolerable."[5]

For me and other African American children, post-*Brown* foot-dragging had practical consequences. Foot-dragging by Anniston, Alabama, meant that in 1958, at the age of five, I took a solo bus and car journey each day miles from my home at Fort McClellan, Alabama, to reach a Negro kindergarten somewhere in Anniston. Foot-dragging by Atlanta, Georgia, meant that in 1959, at the age of six, I attended first grade at a Negro elementary school.

As it happens, I received a good education in these two segregated schools. When I left kindergarten, I could already read and write like a second grader. Luckily I was not the least bit aware of racial differences at the time. I suffered no conscious blows to my self-esteem and harbored no sense of racial injustice. Those things came later, when I attended a racially integrated public high school.

NEWT AND ME

The now-defunct Baker High School in Columbus, Georgia, counted Newton ("Newt") Gingrich as among its most illustrious graduates. Mr. Gingrich graduated in 1960. I also attended Baker High, graduating ten years later than the United States congressman who, in 1995, became the first Republican Speaker of the House of Representatives in decades. Even before he officially assumed the Speaker's office, Gingrich had declared war on what he termed the "Great Society, counterculture, McGovernik" legacy of the 1960s.[6]

The second half of the 1960s brought us comprehensive national civil rights laws banning discrimination on the basis of sex and race, along with antipoverty legislation and constitutional privacy rights. I have been personally acquainted with so many hardworking, poor, underemployed, and child-burdened black people that I view these legal reforms as nothing less than basic moral justice. Yet in the mind of Mr. Gingrich the 1960s killed morality in America. According to Gingrich, after 1965 there was no more "commitment to creating . . . character," no more "work ethic," no "honesty, right and wrong," no "vigilant . . . defense of liberty."[7] The glib representations of a powerful politician rewrite history only for the people who did not live it.

Speaker Gingrich and I went to Baker for the same reason. We were both "army brats," the children of military men at one time stationed at Fort Benning, Georgia.[8] Although Fort Benning operated its own elementary and middle schools reserved solely for military children, it did not operate a high school. Typical secondary school-age children who lived at Fort Benning traveled in a convoy of olive green buses to nearby Baker or one of Muscogee County's other public high schools.

In many respects Baker High was the same school in 1960, when Gingrich graduated, as it was in 1970, when I graduated. It was a plain complex of two-story red-brick buildings on a scruffy baked lawn. It overlooked "Victory Drive," a soldier's playground of cheap motels, hamburger stands, porn shops, girlie shows, and car dealerships. It had a decent academic curriculum and a decent football team.

But in one key respect Gingrich's Baker High School and mine were very different. When Gingrich graduated, the Columbus schools were segregated. In fact, barely any public facilities or private businesses open to the Columbus public were available to blacks and whites on equal and nondiscriminatory bases. Gingrich's Baker High was what southerners used to call a white school. A "white" public school rarely knowingly enrolled "colored" (or, as we were also called, "Negro") children.

Like Newt Gingrich, my older sister attended a segregated high school. Years of post-*Brown* foot-dragging in Columbus meant that when she was ready for secondary school in 1963, Fort Benning military authorities had no choice but to transport her to a black school twice as far from home as Baker High would have been. A fourteen-year-old accustomed to racial diversity in military neighborhoods, churches, and schools, my sister was forced to separate herself from her peer group and go to a "colored" school. If experts cited in *Brown* were correct that legally compelled segregation harms the self-esteem of African American children, consider the effects of legally compelled *re*segregation of a military dependent accustomed to racial diversity.

Both my parents came from very poor Atlanta families. My father joined the military in the early 1950s to escape denigrating economic prospects. My parents had attended "colored" high schools in Atlanta, where they studied from outdated used textbooks cast off from white schools. They believed with warrant that the "colored" high schools in Columbus would have fewer and poorer resources than the white schools. As a consequence, they could not explain why my sister had to go to a Negro school in ways that did not make all three of their school-age children feel sad and inferior.

Under a so-called stair step plan adopted in 1964, Columbus school authorities had planned to desegregate the student bodies (but not teachers or staffs) of its public schools one grade at a time over a twelve-year period, beginning with the twelfth grade. A federal lawsuit brought by African Americans forced school authorities to abandon their dilatory twelve-year plan.[9] Under the watchful eye of the federal courts, Muscogee County administrators moved more quickly to desegregate. By 1967 Columbus had enrolled a significant number of blacks in its previously white schools. Gingrich's Baker became an "integrated" school.

SECOND-WAVE INTEGRATOR

The first wave of youthful African American school integrators went to white schools throughout the South in the early 1960s surrounded by police, politicians, and protesters. The photographic images of their brave moments are unforgettable. I was a second-wave black integrator. I attended a white school in the months and years after the white community had ceased to fight school desegregation with shrill protests and brute force. Resistance had gone underground. We second-wave integrators at Baker High required no federal marshals to escort us safely to our classes. But we might have used a good psychologist.

I am reluctant to tell anyone who did not live through the sixties that I attended an "integrated" high school. An "integrated" school in this period was usually a formerly white school that had begun to enroll a quota of blacks to comply with—or to avoid—court-ordered desegregation. To say that I attended an integrated school might falsely suggest that I went to a racially diverse high school in which black and white students coexisted on equal footing. The truth of the matter is that I attended a school whose administrators seemed to view integration solely as a matter of permitting blacks to enroll in a white school and take their chances.

During the years that I attended Baker, the faculty and staff remained virtually all white. Despite the presence of African American, Hispanic, Asian American, and Jewish teenagers, many from military families, a white southern Protestant Christian ethos permeated the place. (Many students and teachers used the word "Christian" as a synonym for "good.") Nearly all the school's academic and social honors went to white students.

Needless to say, there were no 1970s-style black studies programs, nothing of what in the 1980s came to be known as multicultural education. In my classes we did not read a single book, essay, or poem written by a person who was not a white American or European. Even more surprising, we were not instructed about our immediate situation, about the fact that we were part of a historic effort to end a regime of racial separatism.

A great deal of credit must be given to the resilient African American teenagers at newly integrated schools who tried to have normal high school experiences. At Baker blacks threw themselves into sports, drama, and ROTC. Many excelled. Many did well academically too. Early in our freshmen year another black student and I were skipped to the tenth grade. Like Newt Gingrich, I received a National Merit Award and scholarships to college.

Despite successes, we African Americans were keenly aware of our minority status at Baker and of the low regard in which blacks were held generally in our school and town. We could not put so looming a reality out of our minds. We were full of bravado, but insecure, always trying to prove ourselves worthy of the white world into which we had been partly admitted. I worried to the point of numb fingers and headaches that I would not receive appropriate recognition. And sometimes I did not. One year my English teacher passed over me and took a white student with a lower grade point average to the Honor Banquet to which each teacher was supposed to invite her best student. Newt Gingrich secretly dated one of his Baker High teachers; I found it hard even to speak to mine.[10]

Minority exclusion from the elite social realm of the school was particularly dispiriting. No black woman could hope to be elected cheerleader, prom queen, or homecoming queen. No black could expect to be voted "Most Beautiful" or "Most Handsome." The absence of black cheerleaders (of all things) came to symbolize racial exclusion. During the 1970–71 school year turmoil erupted over the cheerleading issue, and someone burned down the gymnasium.

A number of black students found Baker's peculiar brand of integration intolerable and transferred to one of the black public high schools across town. Black students from military families were accustomed to living and going to school among whites. But even we openly fantasized about attending one of the black schools to escape the pressures of integration.

For those of us who stayed behind, our peculiar integration had its lighter moments. Black students sometimes took advantage of teachers' xenophobic distrust. Once a black student ostentatiously rolled something white between his fingers and, in his best imitation of a thug, asked our English teacher if she knew what he had in his hand. Determined to take charge of a presumably dangerous situation, the teacher demanded that he turn over his "marijuana cigarette." The class erupted into hysterical laughter and the teacher turned crimson when the suspected big bad possessor of illegal drugs revealed that his "joint" was nothing more than a bit of twisted notebook paper.

And then there was the "Afro pick" ban. Afro picks were the combs of choice for black students wearing the "natural," "Afro," or "bush" hairdos that school officials discouraged as expressions of radical rebellion.[11] One day the school principal announced that Afro picks were no longer permitted on campus. Why? We were told that the sharp-toothed picks, some of which resembled angel food cake cutters, might be used as weapons. To cope with the ban, some students took to grooming their Afros with table forks.

A DIVIDED CAFETERIA

The presence of blacks on a white campus does not alone achieve meaningful racial integration. Within my integrated high school, segregation was the social rule. The demise of my close relationship with a white friend is illustrative.

As middle schoolers at Fort Benning, Pam Wilson and I had been neighbors and inseparable pals. We dressed alike, in twin miniskirts, poor-boy tops, and white go-go boots. Together we danced the pony and the jerk to hits by Diana Ross and the Supremes. Together we got into trouble with our parents for playing spin the bottle, the notorious heterosexual kissing game.

Shortly after beginning the eighth grade, I moved a hundred miles away to the Atlanta Army Depot. Pam and I maintained our friendship through letters. She seemed happy to learn, eighteen months after our separation, that my father had been reassigned to Fort Benning and that I would attend her high school, Baker High School. Soon after my arrival at Baker, Pam and I ran into each other in the cafeteria. But after making eye contact and waving from across the room, we felt restrained by the unwritten rule against racial intermingling. She sat at a table with white friends. The trapped look in her eyes pushed me to a table of blacks. Unable to resume the old relationship, we had none at all.

VIETNAMISH WARS

The racially segregated character of my life in the era of putative integration moved beyond Baker's walls in 1969, when my father was sent to Vietnam. We had to leave Fort Benning once again. This time we moved just a few miles, to Columbus, to await his safe return. Columbus neighborhoods were still de facto segregated. We moved to Dawson Estates, then a shiny new middle-class black neighborhood. For some time thereafter the close human contacts that constituted my social world—the neighbors, friends, dates, parties, and telephone calls—were overwhelmingly with other African Americans.

This life of rigid black-white segregation was typical of the lives lived by residents of Columbus. But it sent me to war against myself. My multicultural preferences could not be reconciled with my segregated behavior. I had no problem with having African American friends and neighbors; my problem was with being forced to exclude and deny feelings for people who were not African Americans.

The U.S. military is often thought of as a conservative force in American society. My college classmates viewed it that way in the early 1970s, when "military-industrial complex" was a ritual sneer. In key respects the military is a conservative institution. But the comparative social equality of the races among military families in the 1960s cultivated liberal expectations in me.[12] Integrated housing, schools, churches, swimming pools, health care, friendships—they got under my skin. They became norms against which I continue to judge social arrangements.

For southern black families like mine, taking up military life in the 1950s and 1960s meant an opportunity to taste what America could be like if everyday life were not ordered around principles of discriminatory race segregation. I had had plenty of white, Hispanic, and Asian friends in the past, and now I was cut off from all such people. I was not comfortable with segregation in the way that civilians seemed to be. Segregation felt unnatural. Because I subjectively experienced my social choices as constrained by segregation, my relationships with most people seemed dictated. I felt more caged than free.

In the last semester of my senior year the war within was complemented by a war without. A friendly whisper escalated into a major battle with Baker High. While in study hall, an hourlong period of monitored individual schoolwork, I whispered a few words about a Latin homework assignment to a classmate. Talking was against the rules, and I was ordered to write the sentence "I will not talk in study hall" one hundred times. When I refused the silly punishment for what I thought was a technical and justifiable breach, the study hall teacher sent me to see our principal, Oscar P. Boyles. I expected Mr. Boyles to side with me. Instead he ruled as insolence my articulated disdain for repetitive sentence writing. He then meted out the most severe punishment within his powers, a weeklong suspension from school.

I had not imagined anyone could be kicked out of school for so minor an infraction. It was 1969! Young people were burning down buildings, abusing drugs, carrying weapons. At Baker suspension was a devastating sanction usually reserved for recidivist bullies and thieves. Because suspension was normally handed out to serious offenders, many campus organizations shared a rule that suspension meant an automatic ban from further participation. Moreover, teachers were not required to permit suspended students to make up missed examinations. I faced all these harsh consequences.

I believed I was suspended because of my race. I was smart and cooperative. I had done too well at Baker. I had to be brought down a notch or two. "Anita," Mr. Boyles explained, "I've got to make an example out of you for the sake of the other nigra [sic] children." When Mr. Boyles announced my suspension, I flew into an emotional rage. I initially refused to leave his office. I left only after my mother arrived, promising that she would immediately appeal to the local board of education. But she did not know how to go head to head with white officials. She broke her promise to me and tried to shield me from shame by attributing my intransigence to stress over my father's absence in Vietnam.

The suspension transformed me. Thereafter I had nothing but contempt for Baker High administrators. I began to associate closely with the school's few self-described rebels, existentialists, and atheists, most of whom were white. Once or twice I invited my white friends into my black neighborhood. My poetry turned political, my clothing outrageous, my Afro large. I knew almost nothing about the civil rights movement, the women's movement, the black power movement, the antiwar movement, and radical youth culture but began to look as if I belonged to all of them.

I graduated from Baker in June 1970 at commencement exercises held at the Columbus Municipal Auditorium. I was still feeling wronged. It was all I could do to balance the mortarboard atop my Afro for the duration of the ceremony. Three months later I headed to college. My mother hoped I would accept a scholarship from Emory University, an established white school in Atlanta. Instead I chose New College, an experimental college in Sarasota, Florida, with a radical philosophy of personal freedom.

HAPPY RETURNS

Despite the "good-bye and good riddance" sentiment with which I had left Baker High, something drew me to my twentieth class reunion in 1990. Maybe I was curious. Maybe I felt especially good about myself and wanted to show off. Baker had not ruined my life! I was prepared to forgive and forget. I was happily married. I had a Ph.D. from the University of Michigan, a law degree from Harvard, a tenured position on the faculty of Georgetown University Law Center, and a long résumé.

The officers' club at Fort Benning was the reunion site. One other black alumna, a Hollywood actress named Peggy Blow, showed up for the event. My integrated high school's twentieth reunion, like my integrated high school itself, was a white affair. Undaunted, I moved about the ballroom, starting conversations with people who looked trapped. I left early, wondering how these graduates of Baker felt about the fact that their white school, in the years after integration, had become run-down and mostly black.

In 1993 I went back to Columbus yet again, this time to give an invited speech at the public library during Black History Month. I was stunned by the celebrity treatment I received in the hands of the African American community.

The day before my talk a chauffeur-driven stretch limousine transported me to a reception at Columbus College. Prominent local black lawyers, judges, and politicians came to shake my hand. Some of my black classmates from Baker came by as well.

Among the sprinkling of whites at the reception was Oscar P. Boyles, now retired, the unprincipled principal of days past. I was stunned to see him. Boyles made a point of saying that he had been planning to do some house painting that day but had postponed the task just so that he could come to congratulate me. I could not resist asking the old man for his views on school integration in Columbus. Without waiting for his answers, I gave him mine. After listening to me for a while, he smiled wryly and said, "Y'all taught me a lot; yes, y'all did."

The next evening I spoke to a full auditorium at the main branch of the public library. After my talk the black mayor pro tem of Columbus presented me with a rolled parchment signed by the white mayor, citing my high moral character and declaring the last week in February as "Anita Allen Week." Little girls shyly asked for my autograph. A local television station covered the event, which was the number two story on the evening news. My photograph ran on the front page of the local black newspaper.

This exalted VIP treatment was all due to black citizens' extraordinary pride in the modest successes of an African American graduate of the local school system. They thought it remarkable that a black graduate of Baker High School was a published scholar and had appeared on national television. Although Columbus has produced numerous black professionals, black residents of the city are demoralized by the frequently low achievement of young blacks. When a black librarian learned about my accomplishments from a chance encounter with my father, she spearheaded the effort to bring me to Columbus as a guest of the city and a role model for young people. I was genuinely touched and appreciative.

Columbus does not seem so bad anymore, although it remains a profoundly segregated city. Many neighborhoods, schools, churches, and businesses serve only one race. But there has been a major change for the better since the 1960s: African Americans have a little political power. They share power with whites and other groups, enjoying black political representation in local, state, and national government. It is not clear how much power and influence blacks in Columbus have acquired with respect to the things that trouble them most. But by 1993 they had achieved just enough political clout to persuade the Muscogee County School District to celebrate Black History Month, to finance my visit, and to extract a flattering declaration from the mayor's office. The power to involve the public in events that build racial self-esteem surely contributes to making community life more tolerable for African American citizens.

TURF PEACE

Journalists use words like "Balkanization" and "tribalization" to decry the situation in which American population groups battle over turf. As disturbing as the imagery and reality of "turf wars" may be, I am disturbed as well by aspects of our national "turf peace"—by the phenomenon of power-sharing racial groups politely living lives divided by physical and perspectival boundaries. Power sharing among minority and majority groups is a good and just development for a constitutional democracy. But power sharing is only part of the integration dream for melded lives that some of us began to nurture in the 1960s.

Historian John Hope Franklin has remarked that we cannot "have a . . . multiracial society when people are parceled or separated out, ghettoized, Balkanized or however you want to say it."[13] Some parceling is inevitable since most ethnic and other cultural group differences are as real and worthy of preservation as individual ones. But the extensive segregation currently found in the United States is an imposed evil, linked to illusions of white supremacy.

Today the physical and perspectival division between African Americans and whites is particularly sharp. Throughout the country blacks and whites live by choice or fate in single-race neighborhoods, attend single-race schools, work in single-race settings, and have single-race social lives. As opinion polls often conclude, blacks and whites hold starkly divergent, even antagonistic perspectives on political and legal topics. Black workers tend to view affirmative action remedies as just, while white workers tend to view them as unjust reverse discrimination. Many whites thought the degree of force used by Bernhard Goetz and by the Los Angeles police officers videotaped beating Rodney King was justified, although many blacks condemned such violence as white prejudice run amok. Black intellectuals discerned critical scholarly insight in Lani Guinier's voting rights proposals, while think thank whites ridiculed the same proposals as the undemocratic radicalism of a "quota queen." O. J. Simpson may have seemed like an innocent hero framed by a white racist cop to many blacks, but to many whites the black hero was a tragically guilty fallen star.[14]

Beyond Partisan Politics

In the 1980s and 1990s a number of conservative Republican politicians campaigned against "affirmative action," the generic name for a cluster of education, labor, and voting reforms defended in the 1960s as practical means for achieving integration. President Ronald Reagan aggressively attacked affirmative action by appealing to the moral justice of the "free market," "personal responsibility," and a "color-blind society."

During the civil rights movement, Martin Luther King, Jr., himself pressed for a color-blind society. Conservative politicians' more recent calls for a color-blind society have seemed to some liberals like coded demands—made on behalf of putative white male victims of affirmative action—for the abandonment of a public commitment to justice for racial minorities.

Republican political reforms proposed for the end of the twentieth century include the eradication of affirmative action programs, along with reductions in welfare benefits to the poor, tax cuts for middle- and upper-income groups, and additional restrictions on reproductive choice. Newt Gingrich has characterized these reforms as repairing damage to the nation done by the 1960s. Repairs may be in order; it would be foolish to insist that policies legislated a quarter century ago are beyond review and revision. Legislative reforms are doubtless needed in some areas. Yet to demonize the 1960s is to denigrate a vibrant decade of overdue moral emphasis on fairer, freer, and more collaborative lives.

When it comes to domestic policy reforms, no decade in American history can claim a greater righteousness than the 1960s. Domestic policy acquired its long-awaited conscience in the sixties. The nation's federal courts and Congress finally took definitive steps to acknowledge fully the humanity of its nonwhite and female citizens. The moral ideals of the 1960s included a radical new commitment to equality that cut across racial, economic, and gender lines. Poverty programs implemented in the 1960s were designed to sustain the poorest families with dependent children, many of whom were black.

At first the predominant conception of equality informing public policy in the sixties was a color-blind equality of opportunity rather than a color-conscious equality of results. But both Democratic and Republican policy makers were at a loss as to how they could demonstrate that equal opportunity had become the law of the land, unless racial minorities were in fact getting the jobs, promotions, school admissions, business contracts, and public offices from which whites had previously excluded them. In 1965 President Lyndon B. Johnson turned "affirmative action" into the centerpiece of federal labor policy because he believed it would open up meaningful opportunities for minorities. White House support for affirmative action continued into the administration of President Richard M. Nixon.

Policy makers' desire to make progress toward equal opportunity for minorities and white women objectively discernible drove the eventual expansion of affirmative action to include numerical goals, quotas, timetables, and set-asides. After the 1960s these affirmative action devices were increasingly controversial. But liberals widely defended quantitative measures as necessary for achieving not only meaningful equal opportunity but also culturally "diverse" schools and racially "balanced" workplaces.

In reality the 1960s and its leaders were neither morally pure or morally bankrupt. The discovery of imperfections in race and poverty programs begun in the 1960s says nothing adverse about integrationism itself. The integration ideal, along with the policies and people inspired by it, deserve to be credited. The project of integration demands bipartisan respect as the just sequel to the emancipation of African American slaves. A nation of people once divided by law into superior and inferior races should labor to eliminate those cruel divisions.

In recognition of our common humanity, we should yield to our capacities to live together as friends and equals. And we do have such capacities, or so I was first persuaded through exposures to integration in the military. It is unclear for how long politicians seeking political advantages will continue to caricature the sixties as an immoral decade. Their caricatures may be effective as a short-term strategy, but strategy should not be confused with history.

COHABITATION

Relative to what I believe to be its potential, the ideal of integration has lived too briefly and incompletely in the United States. Its life has been a half-life. Yet despite overall patterns of separation and disagreement, many African Americans and whites live in the same neighborhoods, learn in the same schools, and work for the same employers. Among the affluent classes in particular, many share cultural affects, personal aspirations, religions, politics, moral values, friendships, and love. A union of the races is coming about with sexual intercourse and intermarriage among blacks and whites. Vocal offspring of these interracial couplings are rejecting traditional racial categories of self-definition. At the same time, biologists, social scientists, and philosophers are questioning whether the concept of "race" makes much sense at all.

This picture of the United States suggests racial unification. But racial division seems to be the truer national portrait at the moment. Hopes formed in the 1960s—that judicially mandated school desegregation in combination with federal civil rights and poverty programs would lead to deep racial unity—barely survived the 1960s. Power sharing and turf peace are the images of race relations proffered the richly multicultural but still-segregated Generation X.

The 1960s are memorable for the optimistic ideals of racial rapprochement that spirited civil rights advances. The revival of a similar optimism would be useful today to compensate for the atomistic, turf-protective tendencies of multicultural politics. "Integration" is probably too freighted, too outmoded a term to resurrect. We have yet to name the postmulticultural ideal of diverse population groups truly cohabiting the nation.

NOTES

1. In December 1963 the National Opinion Research Center polled a sample of adult Americans to find out what they considered "some of the most important problems facing the United States today." Integration and related race issues were the most frequently cited cluster of "problems." Of those polled, 46 percent named "civil rights, segregation, integration, race relations, [and the] negro problem" as among the most important problems. Only 24 percent, the next highest percentage, named "unemployment, automation, loss of jobs, depression, economic growth, high prices, cost of living, low wages"; only 20 percent named the "Cold War, International Communism, Russia . . ."; only 13 percent named "govern-

ment spending, budget, taxes and public debt"; only 16 percent named "threat of war, maintaining peace, . . . nuclear war"; only 5 percent named "loss or lack of religion . . ."; and only 2 percent named "public health, Medicare for the aged, medical costs. . . ."

2. Peter Applebome, "Keeping Tabs on Jim Crow: John Hope Franklin," *New York Times Magazine* (April 23, 1995), p. 34.

3. 347 U.S. 483 (1954).

4. 349 U.S. 294, 301 (1955).

5. Bradley v. School Bd. of Richmond, 382 U.S. 103, 105 (1965).

6. Maureen Dowd, "G.O.P.'s Rising Star Pledges to Right Wrongs of the Left," *New York Times,* November 10, 1994, pp. A1 and B3.

7. Ibid.

8. Jim Auchmutey, "Mr. Speaker: The Family Man Gingrich's Life No '50's Sitcom," *Atlanta Constitution,* January 14, 1995, p. A8.

9. Lockett v. Bd. of Education of Muscogee Cty. Sch. Dist., 342 F.2d 225, 226 (1965).

10. Auchmutey, op. cit. In 1962 Gingrich married his former Baker High math teacher, Jacqueline Battley. She was seven years his senior. They were later divorced.

11. Chemically or heat-straightened hair was once the rule for well-groomed African Americans whose hair was naturally kinky. See David Llorens, "Natural Hair—New Symbol of Race Pride," *Ebony* (December 1967), pp. 139–44.

12. Ranked by some as among his greatest accomplishments, President Harry S. Truman signed an executive order on July 26, 1948, "calling for equal treatment and opportunity in the armed forces." See Brady Prauser, "Support of Civil Rights Seen as His Greatest Feat," *Kansas City Star,* April 30, 1995, p. H2. The complete integration of military personnel and their families has been hampered by the fact that blacks and other "minorities have tended to be concentrated in support jobs and other positions less opportune for rapid advancement than such specialties as aviation and combat arms." See Bradley Graham, "Military Short of Victory in War on Bias; Numbers Suggest Leadership Posts Elude Minority Servicemembers," *Washington Post,* April 29, 1995, p. A01.

13. Applebome, p. 34.

14. In a Harris poll published at the beginning of Simpson's trial, 61 percent of white respondents said Simpson was guilty, while only 8 percent of blacks said he was guilty. Of black respondents, 68 percent said Simpson was innocent; the rest were undecided. Arthur Brice, "The Simpson Report News and Notebook Items," *Atlanta Constitution,* February 11, 1995, p. A7.

Reflections on
Black Power

RANDALL KENNEDY

The "Black Power" slogan became prominent nationally in June 1966, when Stokely Carmichael declared in Greenwood, Mississippi, that the "only way we gonna stop them white men from whuppin' us is to take over. We been saying freedom now for six years and we ain't got nothin'. What we gonna start saying now is Black Power!" He stated this at a rally soon after being freed from jail for defying an order to refrain from raising tents on the grounds of a black public school to house civil rights demonstrators, his twenty-seventh jailing in connection with civil rights activism. Carmichael was in Mississippi to continue James Meredith's March against Fear. Meredith had planned to walk from Memphis, Tennessee, to Jackson, Mississippi, to dramatize the determination of African Americans to exercise long-denied freedoms. Only one day after beginning his trek, Meredith was ambushed and wounded by gunshot. Leading activists from across the ideological spectrum of the civil rights movement rushed to the scene to resuscitate the march. The best-known of these, Martin Luther King, Jr., continued to articulate the theme of interracial fraternity and sorority that he had sounded so memorably at the March on Washington in August 1963. His slogan remained "Freedom Now!" and he eschewed the new chant "Black Power!" "I'm not interested in power for power's sake," he declared. "I'm interested in power that is moral, that is right and that is good."

He also maintained that since blacks are only 10 percent of the population of the nation as a whole, it would be misguided to believe that they could prevail by themselves. "There's going to have to be a coalition of conscience," he insisted. By contrast, Carmichael and other of King's competitors within the movement for racial justice had reached the point where they were no longer willing to accept what they viewed as excessive compromises by blacks for the sake of coalitions with white liberals. They were also angered by abundant evidence that even after a decade of highly publicized marches, boycotts, sit-ins, and petitions, the consciences of many Americans were still lamentably dull when it came to the problem of racial inequality. Angry too were many in the audience in Greenwood who had seen first hand over lifetimes the ugliest consequences of blacks' weakness relative to whites. Challenged to tell the world what they wanted, many in the restless crowd echoed Carmichael: "Black power! Black power! Black power!"[1]

These reflections proceed in three stages. The first describes the purposes, tactics, and idiom of proponents of black power. The second focuses upon the influence of the black power initiative, showing how it has permeated institutions and conditioned habits of thought. The third evaluates the black power tendency, concluding that on balance, it has had a detrimental effect on the arduous task of extracting racial justice from a poisoned social landscape.

I

"Black Power" is a slogan that has been invested with many meanings.[2] Four predominate. One is separation from whites as fully as practicable. An example of this tendency is the demand of Robert S. Browne that the United States be partitioned along racial lines so that blacks can govern their own sovereign nation. A second conception of black power lays primary emphasis on cultural regeneration through the cultivation and celebration of distinctive practices and a unique aesthetic. The best example of this tendency are the teachings of Maulana Ron Karenga, who champions adopting African names, learning Swahili, wearing (what was thought to be) African garb, and creating new, distinctively African American cultural forms, such as the celebration of Kwanza, an alternative to the traditional, "white" approach to the Christmas celebration. A third conception of black power defines it as the American variant of a global ideology aimed at subverting capitalist imperialism in favor of a socialism largely inspired by Third World revolutionaries. Exemplifying this strand of black power is the Black Panther party under the leadership of Huey Newton and Eldridge Cleaver.

A fourth conception of black power aims to enable blacks to participate fully and equitably in all phases of American life and maintains that the best way to accomplish this end is for blacks to make demands on the American polity as a unified, independent, self-reliant, and militant group that is willing to pursue its agenda by any means necessary. Its proponents borrow rhetoric and ideas from the other varieties of black power. Proponents of this fourth strand, for instance, often suggest that black Americans must celebrate their African roots, engage in strategic separations from whites, and see themselves as part of a worldwide revolt of colonized colored peoples. But at its heart this fourth variant of black power is an African American variant of black power is an African American variant of interest group pluralism that has long been a feature of American political culture. This is the conception of black power that has been most influential and that shall therefore be the focus of my remarks.

Soon after the furor over "Black Power" arose in 1966, the *New York Review of Books* published an essay by Stokely Carmichael entitled "What We Want." Unfortunately he did not explain in a direct, comprehensive, detailed way what he and his allies sought. Nor did he do so later, when he coauthored, along with Charles V. Hamilton, *Black Power: The Politics of Liberation.*They recognized this. "We do not offer a blueprint," they acknowledged.[3] "[O]ur aim," they said, "is to offer a framework" suggesting certain "guidelines."[4] At the center of that framework were notions of self-determination and effective influence regarding all matters of governance. In the words of Carmichael and Hamilton, "The goal of black self-determination and black self-identity—Black Power—is full participation in the decisionmaking processes affecting the lives of black people."[5] Among the most central of the guidelines constituting this framework was the precept that black people must "consolidate behind their own, so that they can bargain from a position of strength" for an "effective share in the total power of the society."[6] Adding a bit more specificity, Carmichael and Hamilton asserted:

> Black Power means, for example, that . . . where black people have a majority, they will attempt to use power to exercise control. This is what they seek: control. When black people lack a majority, Black Power means proper representation and sharing of control. It means the creation of power bases, of strength, from which black people can press to change local or nation-wide patterns of oppression— instead of from weakness."[7]

"[I]t was by building Irish Power, Italian Power, Polish Power," Carmichael and Hamilton argued, "that these groups got themselves together and operated from positions of strength."[8] To do so, according to Carmichael and Hamilton, proponents of black power would have to nurture "a sense of peoplehood: pride rather than shame in blackness, and an attitude of brotherly, communal responsibility among all black people for one another."[9] They would also have to insist that the struggle for the advancement of black people be designed by blacks and for blacks. "Black organizations," Carmichael and Hamilton maintained, "should be black led and essentially black staffed, with policy being made by black people."[10]

Much of the content of black power derives from critiques

of two forces that occupied prominent positions in the imagination of its proponents: the leaders of the civil rights establishment and white liberals. The civil rights establishment refers to the persons and organizations that the federal government, the largest foundations, and the most influential press outlets perceived as the leaders of the movement to advance the status of African Americans. In 1966 the black civil rights establishment consisted of, among others, the NAACP, headed by Roy Wilkins; the SCLC headed, by Martin Luther King, Jr.; and the Urban League, headed by Whitney Young.

Proponents of black power derided the civil rights establishment, rejecting its "old slogans and meaningless rhetoric."[11] "One of the tragedies of the struggle against racism," Carmichael and Hamilton remarked, is that "there has been no national organization which could speak to the growing militancy of young black people in the urban ghettos and the black-belt South."[12] Questioning the authenticity of the civil rights establishment, Carmichael and Hamilton claimed that its voice had become adapted to a white middle-class audience, serving as a buffer between that audience and angry young blacks. "It claimed to speak for the needs of a [black] community," they lamented, "but it did not speak in the tone of that community. None of its so-called leaders could go into a rioting community and be listened to."[13]

The black powerites argued that the civil rights establishment had failed to obtain meaningful, positive changes for the masses of black folk. They acknowledged that the black civil rights establishment and its allies had succeeded in obtaining the enactment of the Civil Rights Act of 1957, the Civil Rights Act of 1964, and the Voting Rights Act of 1965. They acknowledged too that this establishment had succeeded in altering social arrangements in such a way as to open up new possibilities for some of the most well-educated, best-positioned African Americans—people like Robert Weaver, who became in 1965 the first African American member of the cabinet as secretary of the Department of Housing and Urban Development; Thurgood Marshall, who became in 1965 the first black solicitor general and in 1967 the first black Supreme Court justice; Andrew Brimmer, who became in 1966 the first black member of the Federal Reserve Board.

The black powerites maintained, though, that these developments were principally cosmetic, that they would aid only the most well-off Negroes and be of little relevance to the day-to-day lives of most blacks, particularly the black poor, that such changes covered up the deeply rooted dynamics of racial subordination that would perpetuate pigmentocracy even without the continued assistance of whites who actively and self-consciously sought to hold blacks down, and indeed, that cosmetic "advances" were actually counterproductive insofar as they misled Americans of all hues into believing that the country's race problem was finally being appropriately addressed.

According to the black powerites, the failure of the black civil rights establishment was primarily attributable to three errors. The first was the belief that racial justice could be accomplished by integrating Negroes into all of the institutions of American life from which they had formally been racially excluded. Carmichael and Hamilton charged:

> The goals of integrationists are middle-class goals, articulated primarily by a small group of Negroes with middle-class aspirations or status. Their kind of integration has meant that a few blacks "make it," leaving the black community, sapping it of leadership potential and know-how. . . . [T]hose token Negroes—absorbed into a white mass—are of no value to the remaining black masses. They become meaningless show-pieces for a conscience-soothed white society.[14]

Pressing their attack, Carmichael and Hamilton went on to assert:

> "Integration" as a goal today speaks to the problem of blackness not only in an unrealistic way but also in

a despicable way. It is based on complete acceptance
of the fact that in order to have a decent house or
education, black people must move into a white
neighborhood or send their children to a white
school. This reinforces . . . the idea that "white" is
automatically superior and "black" is by definition
inferior. For this reason, "integration" is a subterfuge
for the maintenance of white supremacy.[15]

The second error of the civil rights establishment,
according to black powerites, was its insistence upon engaging
in coalition politics. "All too frequently," Carmichael and
Hamilton complained, "coalitions involving black people have
been . . . dictated by terms set by others and for objectives not
calculated to bring major improvement in the lives of the black
masses."[16] They charged that the civil rights establishment had
naively relied upon allies—the labor movement, the liberal
wing of the Democratic party, the liberal church groups—that
"neither look[ed] upon the blacks as co-equal partners nor
[perceived] the goals [of the coalition] as any but the adoption
of certain Western norms and values."[17] What the civil rights
leadership had failed to recognize, Carmichael and Hamilton
alleged, was that "the political and social rights of black people
have been and always will be negotiable and expendable the
moment they conflict with the interests of their 'allies.' "[18]

The great object lesson deemed to illustrate this point perfectly was the fate of the Mississippi Freedom Democratic
party (MFDP) at the National Democratic Convention in
Atlantic City, New Jersey, in August 1964.[19] At the convention
the primary aim of the leader of the national Democratic
party—President Lyndon Baines Johnson—was to ensure a
trouble-free convention that would give him a big, enthusiastic
sendoff for his campaign against the Republican nominee, Senator Barry Goldwater. That aim was complicated by the simultaneous presence of two delegations from Mississippi, both of
which claimed to be the authentic representatives of Democrats in that state. One delegation was comprised of segregationists who represented the traditional state party and did all

that they could to exclude blacks from all forms of political participation. The other delegation, known as the Freedom Democrats, was comprised of representatives of the MDFP, a multiracial alternative to the lily-white regular party.

The nationally televised hearings before the Credentials Committee of the convention highlighted one of the most dramatic moments of the sixties. Its highpoint was the anguished, heart-stopping testimony of Fannie Lou Hamer, the youngest of twenty children raised in poverty by sharecropper parents. A cotton picker since the age of six, Mrs. Hamer related that it was not until she attended a meeting sponsored by the Student Nonviolent Coordinating Committee (SNCC) when she was forty-six that she learned that she even had the right to vote. She also detailed how she was unlawfully beaten in jail by Mississippi law enforcement officers to dissuade her from voting.

Initially leading white liberals and black civil rights leaders supported the demand of the Freedom Democrats that they be accredited by the convention. That support, however, quickly melted away under pressure brought to bear by Johnson and Senator Hubert H. Humphrey, who was soon to be selected by the president as his running mate. Secure in his grip on the white liberal and black vote, Johnson wanted to minimize defections by southern whites on account of his liberal civil rights record and deprive Goldwater of any opportunity to claim that he had backed down at the convention in the face of black militancy. In the end the convention was willing to offer the dissidents only a compromise: two seats for the Freedom Democrats; seating of the regular (i.e., white segregationist) delegates if they signed a loyalty oath agreeing to support the party's nominees in the November general election; a promise to bar all racially discriminatory delegations in the future. The Freedom Democrats refused to accept it. "We didn't come all this way," Mrs. Hamer objected, "for no two seats."[20] To the Freedom Democrats and their staunchest allies, the compromise represented nothing less than a victory for white supremacists, who were not planning to vote for Johnson anyway. They felt betrayed and embittered and brought to future dealings with white liberals and the black

civil rights establishment a deep sense of agrievement and suspicion that seeped into the black power tendency.

According to the black powerites, the third error of the
black civil rights establishment was its purportedly uncondi-
tional embrace of nonviolence. "From our viewpoint," Carmichael and Hamilton declared, "rampaging white mobs and
white night-riders must be made to understand that their days
of free head-whipping are over. Black people should and must
fight back"[21] because "a 'non-violent' approach to civil rights
is an approach black people cannot afford and a luxury white
people do not deserve." "[T]here can be no social order," they
threatened, "without social justice."[22]

The other main target of black powerites' scathing criticism was white liberals. They were condemned for being
unreliable, for harboring a sense of racial superiority notwithstanding their verbal allegiance to racial egalitarianism, for
exploiting the civil rights movement for voyeuristic "kicks,"
and for ignorantly failing to recognize the detrimental effect
their participation would have on blacks' efforts to organize
themselves. Carmichael and Hamilton's handbook is peppered
with attacks on white liberals, such as the one that follows:

> All too frequently . . . many young, middle-class,
> white Americans, like some sort of Pepsi generation,
> have wanted to "come alive" through the black com-
> munity and black groups. They have wanted to be
> where the action is—and the action has been in those
> places. They have sought refuge among blacks from
> sterile, meaningless, irrelevant life in middle-class
> America. They have been unable to deal with the sti-
> fling, racist, parochial, split-level mentality of their
> parents, teachers, preachers, and friends. Many have
> come seeing "no difference in color," they have come
> "color blind." But at this time and in this land, color
> *is* a factor and we should not overlook or deny this.
> The black organizations do not need this kind of ide-
> alism, which borders on paternalism.[23]

Blacks powerites acted on this dissatisfaction. In SNCC, for example, they suggested informally that it was improper for whites to occupy position of leadership in an organization dedicated to the advancement of black people. Then they discouraged white members from organizing in black communities, arguing that the proper place of white activists was in white communities. Finally, hard-line black powerites succeeded in expelling all whites from SNCC on the ground that black people needed all-black organizations to develop the racial confidence and militancy needed for black liberation.

II

Black power has exerted tremendous influence since the midsixties. It has served as a role model for sectors of the women's liberation movement, the gay liberation movement, and the white ethnic revival. It has also affected deeply the political culture of African Americans. It is this feature of the legacy of black power that I shall be most concerned to chart.

The fate of black power was not at all clear when it first emerged as a slogan. Certain prominent white liberals and black civil rights leaders attacked it in harsh terms. In an editorial entitled "The Politics of Frustration," the *New York Times* declared:

> Regardless of other interpretations that could reasonably be offered of the term "black power," Mr. Carmichael and his SNCC associates clearly intended to mean Negro nationalism and separatism along racial lines—a hopeless, futile, destructive course expressively merely of a sense of black impotence. . . . Effective politics for Negroes, as for any other group, means bringing pressure to bear at the right times and places and taking part in shifting alliances with other groups. But most of the militants . . . have no taste or talent for the arduous practice of sophisticated pol-

itics. They are taking refuge from the hard fact of the
dwindling effectiveness of direct action by escaping
into black nationalism.[24]

Referring to black power in an address to the annual convention of the NAACP, Vice President Humphrey asserted:
"[R]acism is racism—and there is no room in America for racism, of any color. We must reject calls for racism, whether
they come from a throat that is white or one that is black."[25]
The executive director of the NAACP, Roy Wilkins, was even
more condemnatory: "No matter how endlessly they try to
explain it, the term 'Black Power' means anti-white power.

"Ideologically, it dictates 'up with black and down with
white' in precisely the same fashion that South Africa reverses
that slogan.

"It is a reverse Mississippi, a reverse Hitler, a reverse Ku
Klux Klan."[26]

Similarly dismissive was A. Philip Randolph, the grand
old man of the black civil rights establishment. "Black Power,"
Randolph wrote, "is a menace to racial peace and prosperity.
No Negro who is fighting for civil rights can support Black
Power which is opposed to civil rights and integration."[27]

Not only did Wilkins, Randolph, and some of their close
allies upbraid the black powerites verbally, but they also
moved against them in action, attempting to isolate the black
power initiative. Even before the banner of black power was
unfurled at the continuation of the Meredith march, the
NAACP and Urban League withdrew from the march, aware
that Carmichael and others were intent upon turning the struggle for African American advancement in a direction to which
they were deeply opposed.

The opponents of black power failed, however, in their
attempts to isolate it. For one thing, many progressives who
disagreed with black power were unwilling to distance themselves aggressively and openly from it. Martin Luther King,
Jr., for instance, did not withdraw from the Meredith march as
did Wilkins and Young. He jousted with Carmichael for the

hearts and minds of audiences. But he continued to march with Carmichael and the other black powerites. Similarly hesitant were many white liberals. When black powerites in SNCC, acting on a racial basis, ousted all whites from the organization, those who had been racially excommunicated disagreed but generally refused to air their opposition publicly. There were many reasons for this reaction. One was a recognition that black powerites in the Deep South in the mid-sixties had bravely faced white supremacist violence in order to challenge Jim Crow pigmentocracy. They had paid dues that, in the minds of many, entitled them to respect and deference no matter what one thought of their new tendency.

Another reason why black power escaped isolation is that its most vociferous white liberal and black establishment critics were themselves bereft of what was needed to address unemployment, poverty, social disorganization, and the other massive problems that lay at the root of the dissatisfactions that Black Power both reflected and fed. These problems appeared to loom larger in 1967 than 1957, in part, because of the very success of the civil rights movement in removing from the nation's landscape the most blatant symbol of black subordination—de jure segregation. Having accomplished that large task, some leaders in the civil rights establishment (i.e., Roy Wilkins) had no new ideas to propose. Others (i.e., Bayard Rustin) had new ideas to propose but no effective political machinery with which to effectuate them.

Some blacks experienced this vacuum as a bitter disappointment, if not betrayal. This leads to yet another reason why the attempt to isolate black power failed. Its proponents spoke to the frustrations of blacks who perceived that their day-to-day lives had not been much affected by the civil rights movement. The black powerites in other words had a constituency—the angry, restless, undisciplined, volatile elements of black communities across the nation, the element that had surfaced periodically in miniriots during the high tide of the civil rights movement in 1960–64 and that surfaced more dramatically in the dozens of major riots that erupted during "the long hot summers" of 1965–67, when the influence of the civil rights movement ebbed markedly. Black powerites delivered to this constituency recognition of its frustrations and acknowledgment that these frustrations were grounded in realities and justified. Black powerites also gave this constituency something else: psychological thrills—the thrill of observing black figures bathed in publicity who appeared to care more about speaking to blacks than to whites and the thrill of listening to blacks who defiantly trampled racial taboos by making defiant, militant statements that theretofore would surely have consigned them to obscurity, insane asylums, jail, or death.

Black power also escaped isolation because it offered other sectors of American society valuable goods. It offered the ambitious spokesmen of black power a way of outflanking their elders and seizing the spotlight. It offered journalists— the directors of the spotlight—dramatic, controversial news. And it offered to white countercultural leftists a more exotic, flamboyant, and fascinating array of partners in disruption than the earnest, proper, unapologetically religious and patriotic figures of the early sixties who had pioneered the sit-ins, mounted the Freedom Rides, and braved the Klan in the depths of the Deep South.

Black power did more than escape isolation. It established the premises, tone, rhetoric, and style that many of the most prominent black activists of the past thirty years have embraced and adopted. Nothing better illustrates the transformative power of the black power tendency than its evolution within the nation's most venerable civil rights organization, the NAACP. Roy Wilkins was one of black power's most vociferous critics. But by the nineties the NAACP was willing to select as its executive director Ben Chavis, a figure thoroughly imbued with the black power ethos. In the sixties the NAACP under Wilkins objected to the creation of black dormitories on predominantly white college campuses or the establishment of black studies departments formed on the basis of academic criteria other than those that governed other departments. For the NAACP to object now would create an uproar, for the practices that Wilkins criticized have become so widely accepted.

As a result of the black power tendency, black caucuses have sprung up within practically every institution, association, or profession imaginable: the Congressional Black Caucus, the National Association of Black Journalists, the Black Law Students Association, the Black Silent Majority Committee, the National Association of Black Social Workers, the national Black McDonald's Operators Association, et cetera. There was a time when race-oriented black groups were formed of necessity when whites prevented blacks from participating with them in various endeavors. Such was the basis for the National Medical Association, the National Bar Association, and the American Tennis Association. (Note that these groups, formed largely, if not wholly, by blacks, avoided defining themselves racially in their titles.) In the aftermath of black power, by contrast, it became a virtual imperative for blacks to organize a racially defined pressure group whatever the nature of their relationship to white colleagues.

In the mid-sixties, among those seeking to advance the fortunes of black folk, black powerites led the way in deriding "color blindness" and caused quite a stir by doing so. Nowadays criticism of color blindness is old hat; many progressives extol race consciousness. Carmichael and Hamilton asserted in 1966 that black power would mean that "where black people have a majority, they will attempt to use power to exercise control." A quarter century later this aspiration had become a matter of federal governmental policy—majority-minority electoral districting—pursuant to the Voting Rights Act. In the sixties some child welfare agencies began to shed what had been a rigid, uniform policy of placing a child of a given race only in the foster care or adoptive home of adults deemed to be of the same race as the child. Animated by the black power ethos, the National Association of Black Social Workers demanded that racial matching be rigidly reinstituted, at least with respect to black children, a demand that has often been heeded (to disastrous effect). The *New York Times* merely reflects conventional wisdom when it editorializes blithely, with no felt need to offer justification, that "of course" racial matching is preferable for children to a process that affirmatively disregards racial distinctions in making custody decisions. Black powerites in academia, churches, and the arts called for the recognition of a distinctively "black" sociology, political science, philosophy, theology, and aesthetic. A generation later the concept of a "black" voice and a black mode of thinking is widely accepted. In these and scores of other ways, large and small, black power has deeply tinctured American politics, culture, and society. It has played a major role in bringing to the fore what Iris Marion Young approvingly terms *Justice and the Politics of Difference* (1990).

III

One's stance toward black power will depend in large measure on how one thinks the United States can and should be organized. I reject the premises and aspiration of black power because I believe that the United States can and should be organized in a way that minimizes the significance of racial difference, particularly in the public sphere. I reject racial pluralism as the underlying paradigm by which to judge and design social policy. I reject the aim of creating cabinets, juries, schools, legislatures that racially look like America because I want an America that looks beyond looks. It is from this starting point that I criticize black power and the tradition in American culture that is has strengthened, the tradition of racialism.

Let me be clear. I am *not* saying that black power is necessarily racist; below I shall turn to the relationship of black power and racism. What I mean to say now is simply that black power is self-evidently racialist. In terms of both aspiration and tactics, the proponents of black power want to accentuate the racial consciousness of Black Americans. They want black Americans' affections and loyalties to be triggered by race or, more precisely, by blackness. They want black people to have racial pride or, more precisely, a pride in being black. "We," from the point of view of black powerites, means a racial "we," as in we black folks. Black powerites, at least the ones with whom I am principally concerned, are not racist in the sense that they believe nonblacks to be inferior and that their inferiority justifies their subordination. But black powerites do believe that nonblacks are different—and should be kept different—and that blacks can justifiably exclude nonblacks from "their" activities and associations. Black powerites are racialists in that they accept the notion of resources being defined racially and then apportioned pursuant to some appropriate racial formula so that blacks get their proper cut.

I reject these aims and tactics as the building blocks for the society I want to live in and bequeath to my children. I do not want the American pie defined racially and therefore oppose the notion of a white cut, a red cut, a brown cut, a black cut, et cetera. I do not want Americans of any stripe to have racial pride. One of the cultural landmarks of the sixties was James Brown's "Say It Loud—I'm Black and I'm Proud." Taken literally, that statement is unobjectionable. But what it came to mean (and perhaps what Brown intended it to mean) was this: "Say it loud, I'm proud to be black." This notion of having pride in one's race is widespread and deep-seated. "Every true man," Justice John Marshall Harlan declared in his dissent in *Plessy v Ferguson*[28], "has pride of race." But I do not think that a person should have "pride of race." A person should not be ashamed of whatever group he or she is affiliated with by dint of birth. No one chooses or creates his or her parents. By the same token, no one should take pride in an affiliation to which he or she was born. An ascribed status is not something one achieves but merely something one inherits, like arms, or money, or one's hometown.

I am ultimately critical of black power, then, because it situated itself within a tradition of racial group pluralism. It militantly rejected the notion that whites should wholly dominate the society on the basis of a racial privilege. That was good, and the risks that some black powerites took to press this message in the face of violent white supremacists was positively heroic. Black power, however, accepted the idea of racial shares in the society, simply demanding that blacks, as a group, be accorded a bigger share than they had been granted in the past. That was mistaken. They should have aspired for more.

This criticism obviously takes on something larger than black power. It takes on the broad range of racist and racialist conceptions of the good society that have governed the United States throughout its history. Very few have envisioned and attempted to bring into existence a society in which affection and loyalty are not organized racially, in which the signals given by skin color are of no moral or political significance, in which individuals are free of the prison of racial ascription, in which there is such a withering away of racial division that perceived racial difference no longer stands as an impediment to a white American's genuinely feeling love for a black American and a black American's genuinely feeling love for a white American. Attempts to make this possible have emerged at various times. During the First Reconstruction some reformers attempted to inscribe upon the federal Constitution the idea that public authorities should be totally and absolutely prohibited from distinguishing between citizens on the basis of race. Wendell Phillips, an avowed racial amalgamationist, proposed that the Fourteenth Amendment to the federal Constitution prohibit states from making "any distinction in civil rights and privileges . . . on account of race, color, or descent."[29] But his proposal was rejected in favor of a Fourteenth Amendment whose language would permit the states and the federal government to make racial distinctions, as they routinely do today.

During the Second Reconstruction some reformers again attempted to eradicate all racial divisions. That aim was what participants in a civil rights march in Boston in the early sixties sought to dramatize when white women marchers handed over their children to black women marchers and black women marchers reciprocated. That aim was what at least some activists meant to advance when they linked arms and hands with other activists of different hues and sang "Black and white together/We shall overcome someday." That is the aim to which an activist dedicated herself when describing to police a man who had mugged her, she purposefully (though unwisely) declined to mention the fact that he was black not because she wanted him to escape apprehension but because she wanted the police to have to apprehend him without using a racial identification to do so. That is what reformist attorneys had in mind when they challenged the racial classification system of the United States census and the practice in some locales of indicating the race of candidates on ballots.

The congressional and executive branches of the federal government made steps in this direction by prohibiting racial discrimination in many types of facilities (such as restaurants and hotels), in many types of employment, and in certain sorts of housing transactions. The Supreme Court did so as well, finally invalidating de jure segregation and antimiscegenation statutes. No agency of government, however, pressed home the proposition that public authorities should *never* allocate burdens or benefits on the basis of racial group identity. Nowadays some conservatives claim that they support this idea. But they typically champion it opportunistically in the context of attacking racialistic affirmative action programs designed to elevate the fortunes of racial minorities. The color blindness orientation of conservatives does not typically entail aggressively rooting out old-fashioned antiblack racial discrimination. Nor does it often entail challenging other sorts of state-sponsored racial distinctions, such as police officers' routine practice of using racial identity as a basis for assigning a higher degree of suspicion to blacks than to others. At present the Supreme Court permits government officials to distinguish between persons on a racial basis in a wide variety of areas. And as a matter of day-to-day social practice, people of many hues and ideological dispositions assert racial distinctions with a vengeance.

The pervasiveness of racial distinctions cannot be laid at the foot of black power, of course. There were other, far more powerful social forces at work than the black power initiative—i.e., antiblack racism, the white ethnic revival, and other expressions of assertive racial groupism—that prevented the polity from diverting from the avenue it had long been traveling, the avenue of racial pluralism. But black power was a contributor to the failure to pursue a different road, the one that some of the earliest pioneers in SNCC and CORE and other civil rights organizations attempted to chart and pave in the early sixties, the road that Martin Luther King, Jr., had in mind when he spoke of transforming Alabama into a place where little black boys and black girls would be able to join hands with little white boys and white girls and walk together as sisters and brothers.

I am critical of black power on a second level that is largely, if not wholly, separable from the first. My second-order criticisms of black power can be embraced and have been made by people who largely accept the aspirations of the pluralist black powerites.

The first of these criticisms is that black power lowered the moral stature of the struggle for racial justice. Two deficiencies in particular warrant comment. The first has to do with a lack of both generosity and gratitude. My point of departure regarding this point is the statement, quoted above, by Carmichael and Hamilton, complaining that:

> All too frequently . . . many young, middle-class, white Americans, like some sort of Pepsi generation, have wanted to "come alive" through the black community and black groups. They have wanted to be where the action is—and the action has been in those places. They have sought refuge among blacks from sterile, meaningless, irrelevant life in middle-class America. . . . Many have come seeing "no difference in color," they have come "color blind." But at this time and in this land, color *is* a factor and we should

not overlook or deny this. The black organizations
do not need this kind of idealism, which borders on
paternalism.[30]

In this statement Carmichael and Hamilton acknowledged
something that is sometimes denied: that although in political
and economic terms blacks are often weaker than whites, even
the poorest and most vulnerable blacks are by no means powerless. Even in the midst of Mississippi in the mid-sixties, facing the wrath of aroused white supremacists, blacks were not
powerless. They had certain assets. They had a morally
appealing cause that was attractive to some people, including
whites seeking refuge "from sterile, meaningless, irrelevant
life in middle-class America." Carmichael and Hamilton
begrudged giving this refuge to the few whites who sought it.
They hoarded "their" movement and displayed resentment
toward whites who had already joined it or wanted to participate. This was a distinctly ungenerous stance and one that was
impolitic, besides, given that the movement for racial equality
required generosity from people who, using the criterion of the
black powerites, could aptly have said that the blacks' struggle
for advancement was no concern of theirs.

Along with a lack of generosity, black powerites also
showed—and have continued to display—a striking lack of
gratitude. It is undoubtedly true, as many have charged, that
some of the white activists who participated in the antiracist
struggles of the sixties showed naiveté about the obstacles
blacks faced and annoying pretensions about their capacities
that were probably reflective to some degree of a sense of
racial superiority. At the same time, regardless of their shortcomings, *any* white person who went to the front lines in the
struggle against Jim Crow segregation is entitled to respect and
gratitude for what he or she did. After all, such people risked
ostracism, jail, beatings, or even death. Some escaped the
threatened risks. But some did not. James Goodman, Michael
Schwerner, James Reeb, Jonathan Daniels, and Viola Liuzzo
are white Americans who were killed because they were what

segregationists referred to as "nigger lovers": whites willing to fight for justice alongside blacks. For blacks or any other Americans to resist feeling and expressing gratitude toward such people is deplorable. But such resistance has been offered, and its baleful ramifications continue to ripple. The commitment of some whites to the struggle for racial justice has remained at a high level despite the off-putting responses of black powerites. These responses, however, have regrettably (though understandably) dampened the commitment of others. It is simply bad politics for any group carelessly to alienate potential allies.

There are other criticisms. Thus far we have discussed the most restrained, responsible side of black power. We have been considering black powerites on good behavior. Although Carmichael and Hamilton criticized the black civil rights establishment for tailoring its voice to middle-class whites and serving as "a sort of buffer zone between that audience and angry young blacks," this is precisely the strategy of presentation behind *Black Power: The Politics of Liberation.* In it one finds neither explicit appeals to antiwhite prejudice nor reckless calls for retaliatory violence. One does find, however, a studied ambiguity with respect to both these issues.

Carmichael and Hamilton went to some lengths to refute the claim that their call for black power was tantamount to racism in reverse. It was a good thing that they did so, an indication that in fact, they did care about the sensibilities of those in their audience whose support might be affected one way or another by their response. On the other hand, in a nod to another sector of their audience—the sector indifferent to those attentive to the matter of antiwhite prejudice—Carmichael and Hamilton wrote that white society is not "entitled" to reassurances that Black Power in power will not resort to antiwhite measures.

Similar equivocation seeps into their discussion of violence. On the one hand, they avoided making any call for retaliatory violence. On the other hand, they said nothing expressly championing anything other than lawful, self-defensive violence. They also wrote that "a 'non-violent' approach to civil rights is an approach black people cannot afford and a luxury white people do not deserve. . . . White people must be made to understand that they must stop messing with black people, or the blacks will fight back."[31]

This coy ambiguity is important. For one thing, it signaled tolerance for antiwhite prejudice and violent rhetoric and action, a tolerance seized upon by other, less careful black powerites, who gave observers good reason to associate their beliefs and aims with angry bigotry and swaggering menace. A year after Carmichael launched the black power initiative in Mississippi, SNCC's Chicago office declared in a position paper that genuine seekers of black power "must fill [themselves] with hate for all white things," "must stop fighting a 'fair game,' " and instead "hate and disrupt and destroy and blackmail and lie and steal" and make Uncle Tom traitors "fear to stand up like puppets for . . . white men."[32] Carmichael himself became increasingly narrow, strident, extreme, and derogatory, deriding whites as "honkies," insisting that blacks follow "an African ideology which speaks to our blackness and nothing else," threatening that blacks are "going to build a concept of peoplehood in this country or there will be no country," and embracing every Third World dictator accessible, from Fidel Castro to Sékou Touré to Ho Chi Minh.[33] H. Rap Brown, Carmichael's successor as head of SNCC, only deepened the descent. Here is how he ended his memoir, *Die Nigger Die!:* "This country has delivered an ultimatum to Black people; america says to Blacks: you either fight to live or you will live to die. I say to America, Fuck It! Freedom or Death Power to the People."

This ugly, reckless, machismo-obsessed, overbearing, intolerant side of the black power initiative must be taken into account not only because of its effects on whites but, perhaps more important, its effect on blacks. Julius Lester, who was for a time an outspoken black powerite, wrote a book in 1967 entitled, revealingly, *Look Out, Whitey, Black Power's Gon' Get Your Mama!* The sad irony is that black power ended up "getting" many of its own black children. The urge for purging once loosed is hard to cabin. After the black powerites in

SNCC and CORE and other organizations got rid of whites for not being black enough, they turned on blacks who were too light-skinned, or too middle class, or otherwise insufficiently black to understand the "truly black" position on this and that. Sometimes this led to excesses that would be comic were they not so tragic. Because he eventually questioned certain (highly contestable) nostrums embraced by his black powerite colleagues, Lester was not only ostracized by his former "brothers and sisters" but seriously threatened with physical harm. The same fate befell Stokely Carmichael (who was purged from the Black Panther party) and other black powerites, such as James Forman. This problem with managing criticism within black communities remains alive today and continues to have as a salient feature that the more a person or organization emphasizes black unity, the more such a person or organization is likely to repress black dissidents. No one has been more insistent on the need for black pride and togetherness than Minister Louis Farrakhan of the Nation of Islam. And no one has been more ruthless in his policing of black "traitors," in a chilling line running from Malcolm X (who sparked the anger of Minister Farrakhan for daring to criticize the hypocrisy of Elijah Muhammad) to Milton Coleman (a newspaper reporter who sparked the minister's anger for daring to reveal that candidate Jesse Jackson regularly used in private an anti-Jewish expression).

Finally a word needs to be said about the way in which black powerites have portrayed their relationship to other activists and the consequences of that portrayal for current understandings of recent American history. Put simply, Black Powerites often suggest that with the exception of Malcolm X, prior to their entrance onto the scene, the struggle to advance the fortunes of black people lacked "manhood" and militancy, realism and resolve, that the movement lacked what it takes to create "real" change in America. The influence of this interpretation explains, to some degree, why it is that in the historical imagination of many, particularly young blacks, "the sixties" conjure up images of Malcolm X and Huey Newton, not Fannie Lou Hamer, Medgar Evers, Amzie Moore, Fred Shuttlesworth, Herbert Lee, Septima Clark, or the scores of others whose remarkable acts of heroic and effective sacrifice warrant much closer attention than they currently receive. The creeping triumph of the black powerite interpretation also explains, in part, why Martin Luther King, Jr.'s reputation has taken a dip among young black activists, who mistakenly see him as a wimp.

I do not doubt that black power has unleashed energies and aspirations that have contributed in salutary ways to the lives of many blacks and through them to the nation as a whole. If it has played a bad role in the racial politics of the country, it has played a good one as well, focusing attention on the continuing presence of social inequities and channeling dissatisfactions into organized pressure. But the most effective and exemplary campaigns for racial change in America were not organized in the sixties under the banner of black power. The black-led community uprisings against racial oppression in Montgomery and Selma, Holmes and Amite, did not deride white people, indulge in violent rhetoric, reject aid from sympathetic outsiders, or place a racial limitation on their aspirations. The support and maintenance of these communal declarations of independence required unity, assertiveness, and discipline, all of which were produced without appeals to antiwhite prejudice or resentment.

Perhaps the rise of black power was inevitable. We should beware, however, of the error of thinking that what happened had to happen. Perhaps racialism is an unavoidable part of our future. We should try to imagine, however, a different road with a better destination.

NOTES

1. Descriptions of the Meredith march on which I have relied are found in John Dittmer, *Local People: The Struggle for Civil Rights in Mississippi* (1994), pp. 389–407; Charles Payne, *I've Got the Light of Freedom: The Organizing Tradition and the Mississippi Freedom Struggles* (1995), pp.

376–77; David J. Garrow, *Bearing the Cross: Martin Luther King, Jr., and the Southern Christian Leadership Conference* (1986), pp. 475–89.

2. A particularly useful taxonomy of competing conceptions of black power is found in William L. Van Deburg, *New Day in Babylon: The Black Power Movement and American Culture, 1965–1975* (1992), pp. 112–191.

3. Stokely Carmichael (now known as Kwame Toure) and Charles V. Hamilton, *Black Power: The Politics of Liberation* (1992 edition, with new afterwords by the authors), p. xvi.

4. Ibid.

5. Ibid., p. 47.

6. Ibid.

7. Ibid., p. 46.

8. Ibid., p. 51.

9. Ibid., p. xvi.

10. Ibid., p. 83.

11. Ibid., p. 50.

12. Ibid.

13. Ibid.

14. Ibid., p. 53.

15. Ibid., p. 54.

16. Ibid., pp. 59–60.

17. Ibid., p. 62.

18. Ibid., p. 63.

19. For Carmichael and Hamilton's view of this controversy, see their chapter in *Black Power* revealingly titled "Mississippi Freedom Democrats: Bankruptcy of the Establishment," pp. 86–97. For a clear, detailed, scholarly account, see Dittmer, pp. at 272–302.

20. Quoted ibid., p. 302.

21. Carmichael and Hamilton, p. 52.

22. Ibid.

23. Ibid., p. 83.

24. Quoted in Charles E. Fager, *White Reflections on Black Power* (1967), p. 44.

25. Ibid., p. 53.

26. Ibid., p. 42.

27. Ibid., p. 55.

28. 163 U.S. 537, 554 (1896).

29. See Andrew Kull, *The Color Blind Constitution* (1992), p. 62.

30. Carmichael and Hamilton, p. 83.

31. Carmichael and Hamilton, p. 53.

32. See *Black Protest Thought in the Twentieth Century,* 2d ed., ed. August Meier, Elliott Rudwick and Francis L. Bruderick (1971), pp. 484–90.

33. See *Stokely Speaks: Black Power Back to Pan-Africanism* (1971).

What the Civil Rights Movement Was and Wasn't

(with Notes on Martin Luther King, Jr., and Malcolm X)

———

CASS R. SUNSTEIN*

———

The white man has reveled as the rope snapped black men's necks. It is only right for us to be joyous when our God inflicts pain on our enemy. . . . We all have a common enemy. Whether he's in Georgia or Michigan, California or New York. He's the same man—the same man. . . .   —Malcolm X

We're all black to the white man, but we're a thousand and one different colors. Turn around, look at each other!   —Malcolm X

Less and less do we transform private troubles into public issues. There is no willingness to take risks, no setting of dangerous goals. The time has come for a reassertion of the personal.   —Tom Hayden, 1962

On a theoretical level you can say that we believed in wanting to achieve civil rights. But there was something else. The whole emotion of defining not only yourself, but also your life by risking your life, and testing whether you are willing to die for your beliefs, was *the* powerful motive, I believe.

—Tom Hayden, 1988

* Karl N. Llewellyn Professor of Jurisprudence, University of Chicago.

> I have a dream that one day, down in Alabama, with
> its vicious racists, with its governor having his lips
> dripping with the words of interposition and nullifica-
> tion, that one day, right there in Alabama, little black
> boys and little black girls will be able to join hands
> with little white boys and white girls as sisters and
> brothers.   —Martin Luther King

What claims were made by people involved in the civil rights movement of 1960s? What changes did they seek for society and for law? And what are the implications of the civil rights movement for the issues that face us today?

In this essay I venture some answers to these questions. As we will see, the civil rights movement was mostly conservative and backward-looking. It attempted to reform American practices by reference to long-standing American ideals. These ideals include *freedom from desperate conditions* and *opposition to caste,* in the form of second-class citizenship based on skin color. The reformers of 1960s were not at all enthusiastic about the judiciary; they sought to use *political rather than judicial* channels for producing change. But they were not committed to the principle of color blindness. Although color blindness is in many ways an attractive ideal as we enter the twenty-first century, the attack on affirmative action is a revisionist and even cynical rereading of what people in the 1960s actually said and did.

Those who are trying to reclaim the best aspects of the civil rights movement of the 1960s should stress, above all, the opposition to racial caste—a central theme in the work of both Martin Luther King, Jr., and Malcolm X. Along the basic dimensions of human well-being, African Americans remain way below white Americans, to the point where whites, standing along, would rank first among the nations of the world, whereas African Americans would rank thirty-first (right below Estonia). We should return to the anticaste principle as an animating goal for civil rights policy. What is important for my purposes here is an understanding of that principle, not any particular political initiative. Probably job programs are better than welfare programs; certainly efforts to spur the private economy are better than government employment initiatives. The key point is that any system with castelike characteristics is a system in need of reform; the question of strategy is important but secondary.

I offer a related suggestion. Whatever the participants in the 1960s civil rights movement may have thought, we now know that race-neutral remedies are generally better than racially based remedies. What is crucial in the legacy of the movement is the emphasis on the problem of second-class citizenship and the insistence on doing something about that problem. For the 1990s, and in the foreseeable future, much progress can be made in a race-neutral fashion, through initiatives that are designed to work against the problem of caste. Very much in keeping with the spirit of the 1960s, those initiatives call for political rather than judicial reforms.

There are of course great hazards in describing a large and diverse political movement, with so many different defining strands, in a short space. I will be shamelessly selective and impressionistic. As my principal texts, I use the writings of Martin Luther King; the writings of Malcolm X; and the founding document of the Students for a Democratic Society (SDS), the "Port Huron Statement." My goal is mostly descriptive, though not surprisingly, my own evaluations will appear from time to time.

SURPRISING CONSERVATISM: WHAT THE CIVIL RIGHTS MOVEMENT WAS *FOR*

Deviation between Practice and Ideal

The basic documents of the civil rights movement show that the movement was conservative and backward-looking. At least in its earliest stages, and to a significant extent thereafter, its defining aspirations came from America's own stated ideals. Participants in the movement tried to identify those stated ideals and to insist that the nation should live up to them. In this way many members of the movement sounded much more like Edmund Burke than like the French revolutionaries, looking to the past to help define the appropriate content of the future.

Participants in the movement did not try to find basic commitments in places outside the American culture. Certainly most of them did not challenge the American culture itself. On the contrary, they described racial inequality as an anomalous institution entirely inconsistent with the basic thrust of American ideals and practices. (This came to be one of the most visible divisions between Martin Luther King, Jr., and Malcolm X, with the latter repudiating American ideals as fundamentally infected with racism.) Thus the civil rights movement borrowed a conventional and often highly effective reformer's strategy: to invoke a widely shared and time-honored ideal and to show that the practice at issue violated that ideal.

For example, the "Port Huron Statement" insisted that "[t]he declaration 'all men are created equal . . .' rang follow before the facts of Negro life in the South and the big cities of the North."[1] The student authors emphasized "the hypocrisy of American ideals."[2] Martin Luther King challenged the same thing in the same words—"the hypocrisy of American ideals"[3]—and insisted, "All we say to America is—Be true to what you said on paper."[4]

King's speeches frequently looked backward for the nation's core commitments. It is hard to read the famous "I have a dream" speech as if it were fresh and new, but it is worthwhile to try to do this with King's claim that his "is a dream deeply rooted in the American dream that one day this nation will rise up and live out the true meaning of its creed— we hold these truths to be self-evident, that all men are created equal."[5] What is striking here is that effort to associate the movement for racial equality with "the American dream," with the nation's own "creed," and with words from the Declaration of Independence. Thus King suggested, "One day the South will know that when these disinherited children of God sat down at lunch counters, they were in reality standing up for what is best in the American dream."[6] Thus King self-consciously invoked "the American dream" and the Declaration of Independence on numerous occasions, emphasizing their "amazing universalism" and treating discriminatory practices as "strange paradoxes."[7]

I have given simply a few illustrations of a pervasive claim in the civil rights movement. The basic objection—that racial inequality was inconsistent with American ideals—was a defining feature of the movement. As the movement became more radical, some of its members urged that racial inequality was an ineradicable part of American practice, rather than an isolated anomaly. Black nationalism—urging racial separation and even separate nationhood as a response to racism—was a response to this claim.

FREEDOM FROM DESPERATE CONDITIONS

The civil rights movement stressed two major strands in American political thought. Both of these are time-honored ideals. The first involves *freedom from desperate conditions;* the second involves *opposition to caste.*

American political thought has never been egalitarian, and the civil rights movement was not in fact egalitarian. On the contrary, American political thought has consistently rejected equality of condition, or of income and wealth, as inconsistent with liberty, unnecessary, and even counterproductive. But the belief in *freedom from desperate conditions*—emphatically not an egalitarian ideal—has long roots in the American political tradition. This form of freedom was enthusiasticaly supported by both James Madison and Thomas Jefferson.[8] Thus Madison offered this list of means of combating the "evil of parties": "1. By establishing a political equality among all.

2. By withholding unnecessary opportunities from a few, to increase the inequality of property, by an immoderate, and especially an unmerited, accumulation of riches. 3. By the silent operation of laws, which, without violating the rights of property, reduce extreme wealth towards a state of mediocrity, and raise extreme indigence towards a state of comfort." Thus Jefferson wrote:

> I am conscious that an equal division of property is impracticable. But the consequences of this enormous inequality producing so much misery to the bulk of mankind, legislatures cannot invest too many devices for subdividing property, only taking care to let their subdivisions go hand in hand with the natural affections of the human mind. . . . Another means of silently lessening the inequality of property is to exempt all from taxation below a certain point, and to tax the higher portions of property in geometrical progression as they rise. Whenever there is in any country, uncultivated lands and unemployed poor, it is clear that the laws of property have been so far extended as to violate natural right. The earth is given as a common stock for man to labor and live on.

Freedom from desperate conditions received one of its most celebrated endorsements in the 1944 State of the Union address by President Franklin Roosevelt. Roosevelt urged a "second Bill of Rights," including "the right to earn enough to provide adequate food and clothing and recreation," "the right of every family to a decent home," "the right to adequate medical care and the opportunity to achieve and enjoy good health," and "the right to a good education."[9]

In this light we cannot say that the commitment to freedom from desperate conditions was some socialist innovation or even a creation of the civil rights movement or the 1960s. But ideas of this sort did reemerge in the period, and in dramatic fashion. Such ideas were spurred by Michael Harrington's extremely influential book *The Other America.*[10] Answering John Kenneth Galbraith's *The Affluent Society,*[11] Harrington contended that in fact many Americans lived in desperate conditions. Though this "other America" was often invisible, it included, according to Harrington, millions of poor people. The book of course helped contribute to the now-controversial War on Poverty inaugurated by President Johnson.

An emphasis on desperate conditions was a crucial part of the civil rights movement, and it helped define its basic goals. Thus the "Port Huron Statement" suggested, "A program against poverty must be just as sweeping as the nature of the problem itself. It must not be just palliative, but directed to the abolition of the structural circumstances of poverty. . . . [E]xisting institutions should be expanded so the welfare state cares for everyone's welfare according to need."[12] King wrote in the same vein that "[t]he time has come for us to civilize ourselves by the total, direct and immediate abolition of poverty."[13] A particular concern was joblessness; hence King stressed not welfare but jobs: "Let us do one simple, direct thing—let us end unemployment totally and immediately."[14]

More concretely, and echoing Roosevelt, King proposed a bill of rights for the disadvantaged, including equal opportunity and a right to training. His statement of overall objections included: "Economic security, decent sanitary housing, and quality education for every American."[15] King urged that "A Bill of Rights for the Disadvantaged could mark the rise of a new era, in which the full resources of the society would be used to attack the tenacious poverty which so paradoxically exists in the midst of plenty."[16]

Most dramatically King proposed toward the end of his life a "poor people's march," designed to dramatize the plight of the disadvantaged. He wrote:

> There are millions of poor people in this country who have very little, or even nothing, to lose. If they can be helped to take action together, they will do so with a freedom and a power that will be a new and unset-

tling force in our complacent national life. Beginning
in the new year, we will be recruiting three thousand
of the poorest citizens from ten different urban and
rural areas to initiate and lead a systained, massive,
direct-action movement in Washington. . . . [W]e
will move on to Washington, determined to stay there
until the legislative and executive branches of the
government take serious and adequate action on jobs
and incomes. . . . The many people who will come
and join this three thousand, from all groups in the
country's life, will play a supportive role, deciding to
be poor for a time along with the dispossessed who
are asking for their right to jobs or income—jobs,
income, the demolition of slums, and the rebuilding
by the people who live there of new communities in
their place; in fact, a new economic deal for the
poor.[17]

This endorsement of "a new economic deal" was the practical
effort that followed the commitment to freedom from desperate conditions.

On the eve of the twenty-first century America is quite
ambivalent about these aspects of the civil rights movement.
Perhaps programs intended to produce freedom from desperate conditions actually "trap" people in a position of dependency. To the extent that this is so, it shows what should not
be surprising: Government policies may fail. And as the law
professor Karl Llewellyn liked to say, "Technique without
morals is a menace; but morals without technique is a mess."
In some ways the programs that emerged from the civil rights
movement have produced "a mess," even if it would be much
too crude to say that the programs are a universal failure. This
practical point is independent from what I am emphasizing
here: The commitment to freedom from desperate conditions
is a long-standing American ideal, and it animated the civil
rights movement.

OPPOSITION TO CASTE

An important feature of the civil rights movement should be described as an *anticaste principle*. This principle finds its origins in the original constitutional rejection of the monarchical legacy and the explicit constitutional ban on titles of nobility. The principle was fueled by the Civil War amendments and the New Deal. The underlying objection entails an effort to eliminate, in places large and small, the caste system rooted in race.

There is something like a caste system whenever a highly visible but morally irrelevant characteristic is associated with second-class citizenship—in the form of systematic disparities in well-being along the most important dimensions of social welfare. Claims of second-class citizenship were quite central in the civil rights movement. Consider in this regard the "Port Huron Statement," which begins its discussion of discrimination with the claim "Our America is still white."[18] The authors supported this claim with reference to sharp disparities between blacks and whites with respect to literacy, salary, work, unemployment, housing, education, and voting.[19]

Second-class citizenship was a huge theme in the writings and speeches of Malcolm X. Indeed, Malcolm X stressed this very idea in urging not government assistance but self-help remedies, which he thought necessary to overcome dependent status: "The American black man should be focussing his every effort toward building his own businesses, and decent homes for himself. As other ethnic groups have done, let the black people, wherever possible, however possible, patronize their own kind, hire their own kind, and start in those ways to build up the black race's ability to do for itself. That's the only way the American black man is ever going to get respect. One thing the white man never can give the black man is self-respect!"[20]

In fact an important feature of any caste system involves

corrosive effects on the self-respect of its victims, and self-respect was a key issue in the civil rights movement of the 1960s. The interest in racial integration—central, of course, to King—had a great deal to do with such effects. For King, racial segregation was unacceptable because it was a daily reminder of a perceived inferiority. "Any law that degrades human personality is unjust. All segregation laws are unjust because segregation distorts the soul and damages the personality. It gives the segregator a false sense of superiority and the segregated a false sense of superiority."[21] Part of the problem with segregation was that it injured self-respect: "Segregation scars the soul of both the segregator and the segregated. The segregator looks upon the segregated as a thing to be used, not a person to be respected."[22]

Ironically, the interest in black nationalism stemmed from quite similar concerns. In a system of integration blacks would inevitably be dependent on whites; hence the problem of dependency loomed large. For black nationalists, it was clear that equal status could not be achieved in America. Malcolm X favored racial separation on these grounds: "[A]s long as our people here in America are dependent upon the white man, we will always be begging him for jobs, food, clothing, and housing. . . . The Negro in America has been treated like a child. A child stays with the mother until the time of birth!"[23] Much of Malcolm X's attack on the movement for integration consisted of a claim that blacks did not need to be with whites in order to succeed. He thus wrote: "[R]espect as human beings! That's what America's black masses want. That's the true problem. The black masses want not to be shrunk from as though they are plague-ridden. They want not to be walled up in slums, in the ghettoes, like animals. They want to live in an open, free society where they can walk with their heads up, like men, like women."[24]

On this count at least, King spoke similarly: "The negro must boldly throw off the manacles of self-abnegation and say to himself and the world: I am somebody. I am a person. I am a man with dignity and honor. I have a rich and noble history, however painful and exploited that history has been."[25] Thus both radicals and moderates on civil rights embraced some traditional American ideals. Malcolm X's comparative radicalism—his embrace of racial separatism—stemmed less from his rejection of those ideals than from his hopelessness that the white majority would ever live up to them.

PARTICIPATION, CITIZENSHIP, AND NONJUDICIAL MEANS FOR SEEKING CHANGE

The 1960s were a time of extraordinary judge-led developments, with the Warren Court at its ascendancy, using the Constitution to invalidate racial segregation and other practices of racial exclusion. But the civil rights movement was not at all focused on judges and courts. On the contrary, civil rights advocates thought that reform through courts was counterproductive because it would lead to a dangerous form of political passivity.

It should come as no news to say that the notion of participatory democracy enjoyed a large-scale revival in the 1960s. The revival has had continuing effects on American law and politics. The "Port Huron Statement" is characterized above all by this theme: "We seek the establishment of a democracy of individual participation, governed by two central aims: that the individual share in those social decisions determining the quality and direction of his life; that society be organized to provide the media for common participation." Thus the authors lamented that "almost no students value activity as citizens." They urged that "politics has the function of bringing people out of isolation and into community." They sought a political life based on the principles "that decision-making of basic social consequence by carried on by public groupings" and that "politics be seen positively, as the art of collectively creating an acceptable pattern of social relations."[26]

Ideas of this sort played a substantial role in the civil rights movement. In its early stages the movement had been highly court-centered, above all in Thurgood Marshall's attack on segregation under the name of the Constitution. But the "Port Huron Statement" urged a quite different direction, saying that "the historic Supreme Court decision of 1954, theoretically desegregating Southern schools, was more a proclamation than a harbinger of social change—and is reflected as such in the fraction of Southern school districts which have desegregated, with Federal officials doing little to spur the process."[27] Hence the student movement relied little on courts.

Rejecting the judge-focused approach, Martin Luther King sharply criticized reliance on courts alone. Indeed, he suggested that judicial forums bred passivity: "When legal contests were the sole form of activity, the ordinary Negro was involved as a passive spectator. His interest was stirred, but his energies were unemployed."[28] In a similar vein, King wrote on the inadequacy of legal decrees standing by themselves: "The law tends to declare rights—it does not deliver them. A catalyst is needed to breathe life experience into a judicial decision by the persistent exercise of the rights until they become usual and ordinary in human conduct."[29]

King also placed a premium on citizenship. To be sure, he was not a participatory democrat of the SDS variety; he saw participation mostly as instrumental to other social goals, not as an end in itself. But he nonetheless urged widespread involvement in politics: "I do have a graduation thought to pass along to you. Whatever career you may choose for yourself—doctor, lawyer, teacher—let me propose an avocation to be pursued along with it. Become a dedicated fighter for civil rights. Make it a central part of your life. . . . You will make a greater person of yourself, a greater nation of your country, and a finer world to live in."[30]

Hence King emphasized the political process above all: "The chief weapon in our fight for civil rights is the vote. I can foresee the Negro vote becoming the decisive vote in national elections."[31] One of King's most powerful early speeches is titled: "Give Us the Ballot—We Will Transform the South."[32]

The speech is focused on the need to supplement the judicial branch with democratic forums: "So far, only the judicial branch of the government has evinced this quality of leadership. If the executive and legislative branches of the government were as concerned about the protection of our citizenship rights as the federal courts have been, then the transition from a segregated to an integrated society would be infinitely smoother."[33]

On this count King and Malcolm X were closely allied. Malcolm X similarly expressed support for nonjudicial arenas: "The polls are one place where every black man could fight the black man's cause with dignity, and with the power and the tools that the white man understands and respects, and fears, and cooperates with. . . . The cornerstones of this country's operation are economic and political strength and power. The black man doesn't have the economic strength—and it will take time for him to build it. But right now the American black man has the political strength and power to change his destiny overnight."[34]

Similarly, Malcolm X said, "I might put out that I am 100% for any effort put forth by Black people to have access to the ballot." Perhaps ironically, his now-famous phrase "by any means necessary" found a principal place here, as he urged that people use "any means necessary to secure these rights"—the rights of access to the ballot.[35] Here too we find an important commonality between civil rights moderates and radicals: a commitment to democratic politics, rather than to judge-led social reform.

THE CYNICAL CALL FOR RACE NEUTRALITY

Do modern-day opponents of affirmative action carry the banner of the 1960s civil rights leaders? Was the civil rights movement opposed to all racial distinctions? The answer to both question is no. The attack on affirmative action may be right, but the effort to enlist Martin Luther King, Jr., in its favor is at best crude and probably worse than that.

Many people are familiar with a recent and especially prominent "reading" of the civil rights movement that characterizes the movement as opposed to all racial classifications. On this view, a prime target of the civil rights movement—if only its own principles are rightly characterized—is affirmative action. Martin Luther King is thus described as an opponent of any and all race-conscious approaches. But this is a misunderstanding, an appropriation of King's legacy for ends that King would not likely have accepted.

To be sure, King's "I have a dream" speech referred movingly to the possibility that "my four little children will one day live in a nation where they will not be judged by the color of their skin but by the content of their character." These words have appeared in prominent attacks on affirmative action policies. But participants in the civil rights movement were emphatically not committed to a norm of color blindness. Though King wrote in terms of race neutrality as an ultimate ideal, he was speaking not abstractly but in a particular context at a particular historical moment, and he meant to make a particular historical point, one very much connected to issues of lower caste status. He was certainly not speaking to the issue of affirmative action. In fact King was urging a form of social transformation of which affirmative action is, at least plausibly, a part. The norm that he urged was not incompatible with affirmative action schemes and indeed could well have been used to supported them.

In fact King spoke directly to the issue of affirmative action. He wrote: "It is impossible to create a formula for the future which does not take into account that our society has been doing something special against the Negro for hundreds of years. How then can he be absorbed into the mainstream of American life if we do not do something special for him now, in order to balance the equation and equip him to compete on an equal basis?"[36] Asked in 1965 whether it was "fair to request a multibillion-dollar program of preferential treatment for the Negro, or for any other minority group," King flatly replied: "I do indeed." In 1964 King criticized the idea that once blacks had been granted simple equality before the law, no further action should be taken. "On the surface," he wrote, "this appears reasonable, but it is not realistic. For it is obvious that if a man is entered at the starting line a race three hundred years after another man, the first would have to perform some impossible feat in order to catch up with his fellow runner."[37]

King was a proponent of affirmative action policies, and the 1960s civil rights movement is best conceived as favoring such policies. It is ahistorical or worse to suggest that King opposed such policies or that his statements suggest a principle of color blindness whatever its purposes and effects.

IMPLICATIONS FOR CURRENT PROBLEMS

Does the civil rights movement have implications for us? Does it bear on the 1990s or the twenty-first century? To say the least, the 1960s were a complex historical period, and maybe we should think through our problems without thinking hard about what civil rights advocates sought a long time ago. But the civil rights movement, and Martin Luther King, Jr., and Malcolm X in particular, have been prominently used in recent debates, and it is only human nature to make sense of our present by making sense of our past. It therefore seems reasonable to ask whether the movement has implications for the current period or whether it offers a legacy that we might actually use—if not today, then perhaps tomorrow.

I think that the civil rights movement suggests a distinctive and still-promising understanding of the issue of racial equality. That understanding grows directly out of the moral heart of the movement, the attack on racial caste. I offer a few words on that understanding here. My goal is to offer a brief generalization, or a reading, of what participants in the civil rights movement of the 1960s were attacking.

The motivating idea behind an anticaste principle is that

differences that are both highly visible and irrelevant from the moral point of view ought not, without very good reason, to be turned, by social and legal decisions, into systematic social disadvantages. A systematic disadvantage is one that operates along standard and predictable lines in multiple important spheres of life and that applies in realms that relate to basic participation as a citizen in a democracy. There is no simple algorithm by which to identify those realms. As a provisional working list, we might include education, freedom from private and public violence, income and wealth, employment, political representation, longevity, health, and political influence. (Recall the analogous list in the "Port Huron Statement.") Of course I do not suggest that in nature or extent the castelike features of modern American society are identical to those of traditional caste societies. I do suggest that to the extent there is a problem of racial inequality, the underlying difficulty has everything to do with castelike features in the nation in which we now live.

In the area of race discrimination a large part of the problem of inequality consists not only in identifiable acts of discrimination—though they are indeed objectionable—but also in this sort of systemic disadvantage. A social or biological difference has the effect of systematically subordinating members of the relevant group—not because of "nature" but because of social and legal practices. It does so in multiple spheres and along multiple indices of social welfare: poverty, education, political power, employment, susceptibility to violence and crime, and so forth. Consider in this regard—and also by way of comparison to the similar effort in the "Port Huron Statement"—the Human Development Index in the United Nations Development Program's 1993 *Human Development Report*. The index, based on longevity, educational attainment, and per capita income, is itself somewhat crude. But it is highly revealing that the United States as a whole ranks sixth, that white Americans by themselves would rank first, and that blacks by themselves would rank thirty-first (next to Estonia).

Now compare some data from the *Statistical Abstract of the United States*. The median income of white households is $31,435, compared with $19,758 for black households. Nearly one third of black Americans live below the poverty level, compared with about one tenth of white Americans. Of whites over sixty-five, 10 percent live below the poverty line, compared with about a third of blacks. Perhaps worst of all, 45 percent of African American children live below the poverty line, compared with 16 percent of white children. About a third of black households earn less than $10,000 per year, compared with less than 13 percent of white households.

Consider also the fact that nearly 80 percent of whites have completed high school, compared with about two thirds of African Americans. About 23 percent of whites have completed four years of college, compared with about 12 percent of African Americans. The life expectancy of a white American is six years more than the life expectancy of an African American. From about 1970 to the present, eight to eleven people per 100,000 were murdered. This figures includes between six and ten white men, but between forty-eight and seventy black men and between two and three white women, but between eleven and fifteen black women. In 1991, thirty-eight whites out of one thousand were subject to a crime against persons, down from forty-three in 1973; but sixty-one blacks were subject to such a crime, up from fifty-three in 1973. Now these disparities have many possible sources and many possible remedies. What I am suggesting here is that when skin color is associated with systemic disparities of this kind, there is a serious problem calling for social response.

As Martin Luther King and Malcolm X both emphasized, differences of this sort will produce frequent injuries to self-respect, the time-honored constitutional notion of "stigma." If you are African American, you will encounter one or another aspect of a caste system every week and probably more than that, during encounters with the police, or shopkeepers, or gas station attendants, or the people you meet on the street. To say the least, self-respect ought not to be distributed along the lines of race. When someone is a member of a group that is systematically below others, and when the group characteristic is highly visible, insults to self-respect are likely to occur all the time. An important aspect of a system with castelike features is that social practices produce a range of obstacles to the development of self-respect largely because of the presence of the highly visible but morally irrelevant characteristic that gives rise to castelike status.

Of course the law cannot provide self-respect, at least not in any simple or direct way. But group membership tends to fuel a cycle of discrimination, in which, for example, employers rely on statistical discrimination; group members adjust their aspirations to this reliance; statistical discrimination because it is all the more rational; and so on. That is an important aspect of the caste system to which a good legal system will attempt to respond.

In the area of race, denials of basic respect, usually based on prejudice of some sort, are a large part of what it means to have a caste system. With blacks, for example, dark skin color is associated with a range of stereotypes that can have harmful effects during encounters with an enormously wide range of people. These rank among the injuries that the civil rights movement of the 1960s was attempting to eliminate. I suggest that an anticaste principle is the best reading of its animating spirit.

It is important as well to note that any such principle should be used by legislative and executive bodies, not by courts, and that the focus of the civil rights movement was on nonjudicial bodies as well. Courts should play a secondary role. They lack the power of initiative, the fact-finding capacity, and the democratic legitimacy to bring about systematic social change on their own. On this count participants in the 1960s movement were very much on the right track. Their substantive goals were well connected with this institutional choice and with refusal to see the judiciary as the foundation for social reform.

FOR REMEDIES—BUT
AGAINST RACE CONSCIOUSNESS

There should be no *constitutional* objection to genuinely remedial race- and sex-conscious policies, at least as a general rule.
If a basic constitutional goal is opposition to caste, affirmative
action policies are ordinarily permissible. Partly this is a lesson
of the history of the Civil War amendments; if history is relevant, it is extremely hard to support the view that affirmative
action programs are invalid. There is no good evidence that
the drafters and ratifiers of relevant constitutional provisions
sought to eliminate affirmative action programs, and there is a
lot of evidence that they did not intend to do this.[38] A great
historical irony is the fact that in the 1980s and 1990s many
people who usually insist on judicial restraint and close attention to history have tried to persuade the Supreme Court to
invalidate affirmative action programs on constitutional
grounds.

To be sure, it may be possible for adventurous and creative people seeking to use the identity for their own purposes
to generalize from the Civil War amendments a form of broad
opposition to the use of skin color as a basis for the distribution
of social benefits and burdens. Perhaps we should say that
under the Fourteenth Amendment, government ought never or
rarely to consider skin color in its official decisions because
use of skin color has bad educational and expressive effects
and because it legitimates the view that people should see one
another, and themselves, in racial terms. As a matter of policy,
this view is sensible, but as a matter of constitutional law, it
seems unacceptable. It is historically adventurous, to say the
least, and it would also involve a exceptionally intrusive role
for the courts. Race-conscious programs occupy a wide range.
They can be found in education, employment, licensing, and
elsewhere. They have been accepted at local, state, and federal levels, by courts, administrators, presidents, and legisla-

tures; they have come from people who hold sharply divergent views, including conservatives and liberals alike; both Democrats and Republicans have supported them. In these circumstances judges should be extremely reluctant to say that there is anything like a flat ban on race-conscious programs.

It might be tempting to conclude, from what I have said thus far, that race- and sex-conscious remedial policies are not only unobjectionable but mandatory under an anticaste principle. Perhaps such policies are necessary in order to counteract second-class status; certainly many people think so. But it is now time to acknowledge that many such policies have been only a mixed success and, in some places and ways, a conspicuous failure. A few platitudes are worth repeating: In some places race-conscious judgments have stigmatized their purported beneficiaries, by making people think that African Americans are present only because of their skin color. In some places such judgments have fueled racial hostility and increased feelings of second-class citizenship. Some people who would do extremely well in some good institutions— schools or jobs—are placed, by affirmative action programs, in positions in which they perform far less well, with harmful consequences for their self-respect. Ironically, affirmative action programs can aggravate problems of caste, by increasing the social perception that African Americans are less competent than whites.

In part the failures of affirmative action programs have stemmed from white resistance to any remedies at all for the legacy of discrimination. We should not discount the extent to which opposition to affirmative action may really be opposition to any change in the status quo. But in part the failures have come from a general and in many ways honorable conviction: that skin color (and gender) should not matter to social outcomes. In view of both history and principle, that conviction should not be discounted or trivialized. It is notable in this regard that many defenses of affirmative action programs are hard to offer in public. Often the true nature of affirmative action programs is not discussed publicly because it would be humiliating to the supposed beneficiaries or intolerable to the public at large.

To say this is not to say that all or most affirmative action programs should be abolished. There is too much variety to allow for sensible across-the-board judgments. But we know enough to know that such programs have often failed and that it is often better to try race-neutral alternatives.

All this suggests that there should be a presumption in favor of race- and gender-neutral policies and also that there is a great need—for those interested in carrying forward the best elements of the 1960s' civil rights movements—to develop legal reforms that are not gender- or race-conscious. Race-neutral programs would not give rise to widespread fears that government is playing favorites or is subject to the lobbying pressure of well-organized private groups. And it would be possible to administer an anticaste principle in race-neutral terms—indeed, in terms that make it hard to identify the resulting initiatives with any particular political position.

We can think of many examples. These include broad-based anticrime and antidrug measures; literacy and educational programs; policies designed to protect children from poor health and from poverty, including neonatal care and childhood immunizations; and programs designed to discourage teen pregnancy and single-headed families. Policies of this kind could easily be designed in race-neutral terms, and such policies would be directed against many of the important problems faced by both African Americans (and women as well).

Since the 1960s the public is widely said to have become "antigovernment," and perhaps the "antigovernment" posture of the 1980s and 1990s should be taken to argue against anticaste initiatives of the sort I have outlined. But despite their rhetoric, recent critics of government are not truly "antigovernment." They are extremely enthusiastic about many forms of government intervention, including those that protect rights of property. They are most enthusiastic about the forms of government intervention that are embodied in the principles of the common law (establishing property rights and contract rights, both under law). They very much like those forms of government intervention reflected in use of the criminal law to protect private property and to prevent private violence.

In fact almost no one is really "antigovernment." The fruitful question is not whether we seek government intervention but whether particular forms of government intervention are likely to promote our goals. In the area of racial inequality, race-neutral programs—designed to reduce violence, to promote education, to give children decent life prospects, to make drug use less attractive, to counteract single motherhood, to increase employment prospects—are the best ways of reclaiming the aspirations of participants in the 1960s' civil rights movement.

These are brief and inadequate remarks. I set them out here only to suggest some of the directions in which equality law might move in the future. It is ironic but true that a new stage of civil rights policy, directed most self-consciously against racial caste, might also be self-consciously designed—for reasons of policy and principle—so as to avoid race and gender specificity.

DEHUMANIZATION

I now venture into more difficult and speculative territory. It has to do with issues of character, and with the way that we characterize and interact with people with whom we disagree or even people whom we consider fundamentally different or oppressors. The point has everything to do with modern-day politics, perhaps above all in the area of race relations.

Begin with the opening quotation from Tom Hayden, which reveals a part of the picture. Hayden writes that it is time to reassert the personal. Often it is said, and revealingly so, that "The Personal is the Political." This slogan, from 1970s feminism, means that personal injuries, especially in the area of sex equality, can be an outgrowth of political injustice. Individual insults and harms may result from the distribution of political power; individual insults and harm may be what they are, and do what they do, only because of the distribution of political power (consider the allocation of labor within the family or the issue of sexual harassment). But what I want to suggest here is that the converse is also and equally true: *The political may be the personal,* in the sense that one's claims about politics are often a product of one's personal issues as well.

We need not get very Freudian, or speculate about psychological forces, in order to recognize this point. The second quotation from Hayden, writing in 1988, makes things very clear. In Hayden's retrospective view, personal desires of a certain kind ("defining not only yourself, but also your life by risking your life") were dominant, and civil rights claims were in a sense secondary. To put things a bit crudely, an important aspect of the 1960s' movement, especially among student activists, consisted of the playing out of personal issues in political guise. (This does not of course disparage the political claims, which stand or fall independently of their origins.)

There is a deeper point. In many radical movements, left and right, those who seek social change portray themselves as more than human, while they portray their enemies as less than human or as fundamentally other than human. Or they *define* both themselves and their opponents just in terms of what separates them, so that there are no other common links. Often, of course, this is a strategy of those seeking to promote or maintain racial inequality; consider the rhetoric of the Nazi party or of the Ku Klux Klan. Hate speech typically has this form. Or consider modern-day rhetoric by people who complain about "the socialists" or "the radical right."

In talk radio this form of rhetoric is omnipresent; it is no accident that Rush Limbaugh refers to "the liberals" rather than just "liberals." But the same strategy is often used by people who are seeking to overcome discrimination and oppression. There was an unmistakable tendency by some participants in the 1960s' civil rights movement to caricature and even to dehumanize certain groups of people, to refuse, at least in their rhetoric, to see them as human beings or as individuals with narratives, sufferings, and life histories of their own.

We can see an example in Malcolm X's frequent description of his oppressors as the "white man"—as if there were only one. Recall the passage at the beginning of this essay: "The white man has reveled as the rope snapped black men's necks. It is only right for us to be joyous when our God inflicts pain on our enemy. . . . We all have a common enemy. Whether he's in Georgia or Michigan, California or New York. He's the same man—the same man. . . ." In fact Malcolm X frequently used singular and plural forms for rhetorical effect. Compare, along the dimension of distinguishing among people in apparently the same class, his statement, also quoted at the beginning of this essay, "We're all black to the white man, but we're a thousand and one different colors. Turn around, look at each other!" This "looking" at particularity works, ironically, to establish common ground.

We can see something similar in Malcolm X's famous reaction to the assassination of President Kennedy, to the effect that the "chickens have come home to roost."[39] The oddity of the reaction and the horror it caused come from the fact that Kennedy's personal history—his life, his family, his role in promoting or undermining racial equality—was treated as quite beside the point. A human being was murdered after all; Malcolm X's reaction seemed to obscure this point.

Of course there are strategic and other reasons for speaking in these ways. Acknowledgment that, for example, members of the Nazi party were also human beings may complicate and in that way undermine our effort to capture what the Holocaust was about. Acknowledgment that people who contributed to a system of racial caste were not all the same, or that they were as human and as capable of suffering as anyone else, may deflect attention from the project of calling attention to the caste system. Such an acknowledgment may lead to a kind of distorting evenhandedness and easy sentimentality that make social change and looking at reality hard to accomplish.

These strategic issues—and the associated moral issues—cannot be resolved in a few paragraphs. But it seems right to say that many participants in the 1960s' civil rights movement dehumanized their adversaries, depicting them as members of a monolithic force sharing little or nothing with those who fought to end injustice.

Martin Luther King insistently avoided this form of dehumanization. Instead he attempted at all times to combat it. In doing so, he raised two different points: the effects of this distinctive form of hatred on those who hate and the erasure of particularity and individuality that is brought about by group-based hatred.

Thus King wrote, "I have also decided to stick to love. . . . I'm not talking about emotional bosh when I talk about love, I'm talking about a strong, demanding love. And I have seen too much hate. I've seen too much hate on the faces of sheriffs in the South. I've seen hate on the faces of too many Klansmen and too many White Citizens councilors in the South to want to hate myself, because every time I see it, I know that it does something to their faces and their personalities and I say to myself that hate is too great a burden to bear. I have decided to love." Thus King wrote, "Hate is just as injurious to the person who hates. Like an unchecked cancer, hate corrodes the personality and eats away its vital unity."[40]

But most of King's response was connected with the need for particularity and with the need too for humility and for seeing each person as an individual. In his view, this understanding was interestingly connected with a commitment to human universality. Rejecting sharp polarities between good people and bad people, he said, "[T]here is some good in the worst of us and some evil in the best of us. When we discover this, we are less prone to hate our enemies." Thus he wrote, "The one thing about bitterness is its blindness. Bitterness has not the capacity to make the distinction between some and all."[41] And the "Port Huron Statement" reflected a similar view: "In social change or interchange, we find violence to be abhorrent because it requires generally the transformation of the target, be it a human being or a community of people, into a depersonalized object of hate."[42] The key term here is "depersonalized object," something that is also accomplished through the rhetorical ploy of using a singular to describe a group ("the white man," "the Jew," "the liberal," and so forth).

In his famous statement after his trip to Mecca, Malcolm X spoke in terms that assert both particularity and universality, in a way that connected with some of King's own writing. Thus Malcolm X said: "During the past 11 days here in the Muslim world, I have eaten from the same plate, drunk from the same places, and slept in the same bed with fellow Muslims, whose eyes were the bluest of blue, whose hair was the blondest of blond, and whose skin was the whitest of white. And I felt the same sincerity that I felt among the black African Muslims of Nigeria, Sudan, and Ghana. We were all truly the same."[43] The insistence on seeing people in their particularity—as individuals with life histories of their own—helped promote a vision of brotherhood.

On this score it will be useful to close with the final discussion in an influential and very popular book on the 1960s, *Destructive Generation.*[44] The authors are Peter Collier and David Horowitz, former editors of *Ramparts* magazine turned Reagan Republicans. Much of the book is focused on the supposed threat to America posed by its internal enemies, subversive left-leaning intellectuals—"the adversary culture"— without real loyalty to America. The book ends with an anecdote. The authors sought out Susan Sontag, who had recently delivered an influential speech whose theme is captured in its title, "Communism Is Fascism with a Human Face." Collier and Horowitz, now staunch anti-Communists, praised Sontag for that speech, but "[w]arming to the occasion," reprimanded her for having republished without critical comment a 1969 essay about Communist North Vietnam in which she appeared to glorify communism. Collier and Horowitz also asked why Sontag had not offered "further challenges to the adversary culture's conventional wisdom about America and democracy." (Note the terms "adversary culture" and "conventional wisdom.") Collier and Horowitz added that Europe had produced Hitler and that it was America that had rescued Europe "from the barbarisms of the East." (Note the terms "barbarisms" and "the East.")

Sontag responded, "I'm not really interested in having this discussion. You're just projecting your own Manichaean politics onto the world. I don't want to enter your world, where you push everything to extremes." The book ends with a suggestion that Sontag "was right—we did push things to extremes." But according to the authors, her "judgment on us was also a judgment on her and others who understood the political stakes but didn't push things far enough."

What may be especially interesting is that in their incarnation as 1980s Reagan Republicans Collier and Horowitz showed the same character and sensibility as they showed in their incarnation as 1960s student radicals. This is a character and a sensibility that are attracted not only to sharp and simple distinctions between good people and evil people, and not only to a unduly clear sense of precisely which people stand with us and which stand against us, but also and precisely for the same reason to a form of dehumanization. The seeds of violence can usually be found here. This is the world that Sontag, in my view rightly, did not "want to enter."

It is also the world of much of modern politics—a part of the culture of the sound bite—where people attack one another's motives, hopelessly caricature one another's positions, and fail to see commonalities across political divides. In the area of race relations this form of dehumanization is especially common; consider, as just one example, the disgraceful attack on Lani Guinier as a "quota queen." We should deplore this way of discussing race relations and insist that King was right to see, in an insistence on human individuality, the seeds of a commitment to human universality. And we should be able to see this without denying, as King did not, that in the area of race relations very large issues divide us.

Some people believe that America has had one or perhaps two constitutional "moments"; others think that the New Deal qualifies as a third such moment or even that America has had a large number of constitutional moments. I think that any such picture would be artificial and far too simple for reality. America's constitutional development has been jagged and somewhat unruly. It has many of the characteristics of a Burkean common law process of incremental development— but a common law process that is punctuated by periods of public upheaval, in which the common law process becomes less cautious and incremental than it usually is. The civil rights movement of the 1960s was one such period of public punctuation, and its principal actors were, in that modest and nontechnical sense, constitution makers.

What is remarkable is that in the 1990s—thirty years later—the meaning of the civil rights movement has yet to be settled. I have urged that the movement was surprisingly conservative and backward-looking, that it pointed to time-honored American ideals, that it was focused on democratic rather than judicial channels of reform, and that it saw freedom from desperate conditions and opposition to caste as its defining commitments. In a period in which Martin Luther King's legacy is often said to be found in a thin conception of "color blindness," celebrating current practice, it is worthwhile to explore what King and others actually said. For those of us in search of a usable past, the anticaste principle—probably the leading theme of the movement—very much speaks to us today. That principle does not lead to any particular set of reforms. But it enables us to understand what the problem of racial inequality is really about, and it encourages us to seek initiatives that work to eliminate it or at least to reduce its most damaging features.

NOTES

1. Jim Miller, "Democracy Is in the Streets," (1977), 330.
2. Ibid.

3. Ibid., p. 282.
4. Ibid., p. 282.
5. Martin Luther King, *A Testament of Hope: The Essential Writings of Martin Luther King*, ed. James Washington (1986), p. 219.
6. *The Wisdom of Martin Luther King, Jr.*, ed. A. Ayres (1993), pp. 11–12.
7. *A Testament of Hope*, p. 330.
8. James Madison, (1983), vol. 14, pp. 197–98. Thomas Jefferson, *The Papers of Thomas Jefferson* (1953), vol. 8, pp. 681–82.
9. Franklin Roosevelt, *Public Papers and Addresses of Franklin D. Roosevelt*, (1969), vol. 13, p. 41.
10. M. Harrington, *The Other America* (1964).
11. J. K. Galbraith, *The Affluent Society* (1961).
12. Miller, p. 364.
13. *The Wisdom of Martin Luther King, Jr.*, p. 181.
14. Ibid., p. 224.
15. Ibid., p. 180.
16. Ibid., p. 22.
17. *A Testament of Hope*, p. 651.
18. Miller, p. 352.
19. Ibid.
20. Malcolm X, *The Autobiography of Malcolm X* (1964), p. 275.
21. *The Wisdom of Martin Luther King, Jr.*, p. 198.
22. Ibid.
23. Malcolm X, p. 246.
24. Ibid., p. 272.
25. *The Wisdom of Martin Luther King, Jr.*, pp. 199–200.
26. Miller, pp. 333–34.
27. Miller, p. 353.
28. *A Testament of Hope*, p. 566.
29. Ibid., p. 165.
30. Ibid., p. 22.
31. *The Wisdom of Martin Luther King, Jr.*, p. 230.
32. *A Testament of Hope*, p. 197.
33. Ibid., p. 198.
34. Malcolm X, *The Autobiography of Malcolm X*, Harold Bloom, ed. (New York: Chelsea House Publishers, 1995), p. 313.
35. Malcolm X, *February 1965: the final speeches* (New York: Pathfinder, 1992), p. 24.
36. Ibid., p. 68.
37. Martin Luther King, Jr., *Why We Can't Wait* (New York: Harper & Row, 1964).
38. See Eric Schnapper, "Affirmative Action and the Legislative History of the Fourth Amendment," *Virginia Law Review* 71 (1985), p. 753.
39. See Malcolm X, p. 301.
40. *A Testament of Hope*, pp. 250, 102. To this Malcolm X responded: "I do not agree with MLK that one should love a racialist whether he is lynching you or whatever he is doing. I believe in fighting a racialist physically." *Final Speeches*, p. 67.

41. *The Wisdom of Martin Luther King, Jr.*, p. 26.
42. Ibid., p. 333.
43. Malcolm X, p. 340.
44. P. Collier and D. Horowitz, *Destructive Generation: Second Thoughts about the Sixties* (1989), pp. 337–38.

Afterword

TODD GITLIN

I

The nineties are haunted by the sixties, but not because the sixties are lurking about, plotting the proverbial exile's return. The politics that has seized the initiative in the United States of America is the politics of repeal—restoration of the status quo ante in the name of revolution. During the early days of the 104th Congress, House Majority Leader Dick Armey, Republican of Texas, forthrightly articulated the new conventional wisdom: "To me all the problems began in the Sixties."[1] In the words of his superior, Speaker and Ph.D. Newt Gingrich, American history breaks in half in the sixties. During the years 1607 through 1965, Gingrich said not long after assuming the leadership of the House, "There is a core pattern to American history. Here's how we did it until the Great Society messed everything up: don't work, don't eat; your salvation is spiritual; the government by definition can't save you; governments are into maintenance and all good reforms are into transformation." Then came the watershed, Gingrich continued. "From 1965 to 1994, we did strange and weird things as a country. Now we're done with that and we have to recover. The counterculture is a momentary aberration in American history that will be looked back upon as a quaint period of Bohemianism brought to the national elite"—the notorious "counterculture McGoverniks," an elite that "taught self-indulgent, aristocratic values without realizing that if an entire society engaged in the indulgences of an elite few, you could tear the society to shreds."[2]

Thirty years on, leading politicians and pundits are expected to take positions and answer true / false quizzes about a decade when few of them were old enough to be at work expressing the very work ethic they now enshrine. That myth-begotten era when all the authority idols were being smashed, was it a gift to civilization or a defeat? Did you inhale or didn't you? Exercises in contempt, bravado, contrition, and self-extenuation are ritual elements of political nominations and campaigns nowadays, as also of movies, comedy routines, best-selling books. How odd it is that the mythic sixties remain a subject for active love and loathing may be illustrated by contrast. In the sixties no one was pressed to take a position on the thirties.[3] Few ran for office either vindicating the thirties or proposing to repeal them. Unforgiving Roosevelt haters were quaint, not powerful. When, in 1964, Barry Goldwater so much as intimated that Social Security might be expendable, his campaign exploded. During that sinful decade not even Marilyn Quayle, who properly reminded the 1992 Republican Convention that "not everyone [in the sixties] demonstrated, dropped out, took drugs, joined in the sexual revolution or dodged the draft,"[4] was boogying to the music of the thirties, fashioning thirties costumes for thirties parties, or (excepting Pearl Harbor, just over the edge) commemorating the great or terrible moments of that faded sepia decade.

Yet in the not very gay nineties a president identified with those years, whether he likes it or not, has had to devote considerable energy to wriggle away from the reputation, while his nemeses vilify the sixties as the onset of the decline of civilization—"a comprehensive disaster" that did "measureless harm," as Harvey C. Mansfield writes concerning the latter part of that decade, in an essay more imposing for breathtaking extravagance than nuance. The only comparable period of obsessive contentiousness in American history is the 1860s, which for decades were said to have been the time of either the Civil War or the War between the States, depending on who asked the question and where. Everyone could agree that something enormous had happened, and so it is with the sixties.

During the sixties many of the terrible simplifiers were on the left or dwelt, like Charles Reich of the virtually forgotten *Greening of America,* in those countercultural zones where willfulness passed for insight. Today virtually all the terrible simplifiers are on the right. Only a few desperate, unreconciled souls today embrace what is called the sixties wholeheartedly, sharing with the party of repeal the belief that the ensemble of movements, tactics, images, tones, and styles were indissoluble and have to be (in a slogan of those days) loved or left. The hard core has softened. The absolutist passions of the late sixties inevitably relented in the press of practical exigency, in the flush of semisuccess or the afterglow of defeat. Despite the furies of extremity, few feminists or sexual liberationists today retain the confidence that they are making a new social order from scratch. The liberationist impulse that these movements expressed when they were fresh and extravagant is beleaguered: by the rise of the right; by AIDS; by the impoverishment of women; by internal conflicts and self-doubts.

If rock aficionados and drug freaks express untempered enthusiasm for their bygone achievements, they can do so with half-straight faces only because in the society of instant gratification there are many mansions, and the rebellion industry, thanks to free markets, occupies more than a few. The marketing of transgression is a tribute to a society devoted to sales and surfaces as much as it is to the particular forms of transgression popularized in the sixties. Soi-disant conservatives, denouncing semipornography and gangsta rap as if the corporations they love to deregulate had nothing to do with the images they loathe, are, like the rest of American culture and politics, beholden to the culture of celebrity, which is one of the most enduring and least fruitful residues of the sixties. In a nation obsessed with what's hot and what's not, Schwarzenegger, Oliver Stone, Pat Robertson, Louis Farrakhan, Madonna, and Johnnie Cochran are brothers and sisters under the skin, celebrating celebrity, surfing the crests and troughs of publicity, titillating their fans with whatever license and libertinism their handlers fancy.

In an era of whining, the restorationist critics, like the self-proclaimed victims they mock mercilessly, exaggerate the enemy's conquests. After more than a quarter century of Republican ascendancy and an unprecedented rollback in the authority of the federal government, they are indefatigable when it comes to claiming past defeats and blaming them on liberals and the liberal state. The libertine thrust of American culture frightens and ignites them. Multiculturalism taps time-honored insecurity about whether the national cement shall long endure. The government, school prayers or no, is largely helpless to roll back the cultural zeitgeist, but there is plenty of political capital in demonizing "the government,"[5] neglecting the fact that multinational corporations also spawn regulations galore and exercise power not because of the reforms of the sixties but despite them.

But even the restorationists, in their hearts of hearts, must know that it is easier to curse the sixties than to pretend them away. The truth is that everyone today, the right as much as the left, stands on the ground of the sixties. The mainstream as much as the countercurrents presupposes the cultural changes that have been lumped together as "the counterculture." Today ponytailed ranchers rail against government regulation; antiabortionists claim the mantle of Martin Luther King, Jr.; antifeminists leave their children at home to travel the country giving speeches or blocking abortion clinics. People pick and choose their particular sixties to savage or to defend, but whatever their particular choices, they are fatally marked by the sixties. The savagers are the sixties' shadow, the negative double of that decade, energized by its hideous memory, dependent upon it for self-definition. The sixties are the decade they love to hate.

For one thing, they share the unbridled individualism that

was one of that decade's principal styles—and indeed the one they boast of despising. Gingrich and his supporters are obsessed with "self-indulgent values" but feel entitled to take any money from anyone. What is that if not self-indulgent? Their love of entrepreneurship shares American roots with the counterculture's libertarian strain. So does restorationist indifference toward the need for social supports. Restorationist ideas of family obligation diverge, of course, from hippie ideas, but the two, unacknowledged, do share an extravagant idea of the power of human will to carve out a sphere of freedom from social restraints.

Second, Gingrich's legions share the sixties' sense of extremity. The restorationists presuppose the breakdown of value consensus. They relish polarization and wildness. Gingrich's go-for-broke thundering, his absolute self-righteousness, his bombast, his refusal to honor limits recall the double-or-nothing spirit of the wackiest part of the sixties, the part that brought us slogans like "The Sky's the Limit" and "By Any Means Necessary." Gingrich's generation of members of Congress, like Ronald Reagan's ideologues before them, toss the word "revolution" around rather lightly. The collapse of communism hardly left them complacent but rather pumped up their sense that America trembles on the edge of a chasm. Thus Irving Kristol in 1993: "There is no 'after the Cold War' for me. So far from having ended, my cold war has increased in intensity, as sector after sector has been ruthlessly corrupted by the liberal ethos. . . . Now that the other 'Cold War' is over, the real cold war has begun. We are far less prepared for this cold war, far more vulnerable to our enemy, than was the case with our victorious war against a global Communist threat."[6] Thus Gingrich's characterization of President Bill Clinton as "the enemy of normal Americans" during the run-up to the election of 1994. Why take prisoners in a war to the death?

Apocalyptic intemperateness, paranoia, a loathing of compromise, a demonization of the enemy: on the right today, as on the left a generation ago, these are more than articles of faith. The style of extremity, millennialism, intolerance of ambiguity is an operating principle, widespread and entrenched, agitating the larger number of pragmatists in the respectable political parties. Today's Christian Coalition deplores the decline of civilization as fervently as the most apocalyptic environmentalist or hippie antimaterialist of the late sixties. Right-wing activists despise Bill Clinton ("COW-ARD, LIAR, SOCIALIST," in the words of one bumper sticker) with a venom reminiscent of the left's fear and loathing of Lyndon Johnson and Richard Nixon—except that the damage imputed to Clinton is mainly moral and symbolic, not corporeal, except perhaps for a few murders imputed to him and his wife. Jesse Helms's comment that Clinton had "better have a bodyguard" if he visited North Carolina[7] brings to mind the late-sixties' button "Where is Lee Harvey Oswald now that we really need him?"—except that those who wore such buttons did not chair the Senate Foreign Relations Committee.

If anything, the countercultural spirit has spawned a reaction at least as intense and consequential as the original. Not even during George McGovern's doomed candidacy did the left have the influence on Democratic policy that the right has on Republican—except perhaps on (admittedly, important) procedural questions like primary rules and delegation makeup. No leftist with crackpot views comparable to Pat Robertson's on the international (wink, wink) banking conspiracy commanded a key bloc of Democrats during the campaigns of 1968 or 1972. The resurrection of the Dixiecrats, complete with a refurbished rhetoric of states' rights—now known as block grants—has been accomplished by Republicans running against the sixties. As in the late sixties and early seventies, the major party's custodians of the ideal of victory have to watch out lest their fervent far wing frighten the moderate center. They beef themselves up when they crusade against smut, immigrants, deficits, and (perhaps) affirmative action, not abortion choice or low Medicare premiums.

II

Today, on every political and cultural front, the question is not whether to question authority but which authority to question. In the pages above, for example, Harvey C. Mansfield, Jr., Jeremy Rabkin, and Walter Berns assume that the powers that be are the counterculture McGoverniks and that it is necessary to roll them back. In Professor Mansfield's reckoning, from the counterculture McGoverniks came nothing more or less than a brainless, reckless will to power. His essay represents the id of what Sheldon Wolin calls the Countermyth—the pure form of repudiation, the will to counterpower. The war is on, and no quarter shall be given. On the environment he follows the either / or logic of the Third Worldists of the late no-longer-so-New Left, who used to claim that any virtues of Cuba or Vietnam were the accomplishments of the Revolution while vices, if any, were forced upon the pure of heart by the Imperialists. Contortedly Professor Mansfield doubts that the cleaner air and water we have since the sixties stem from the movements he detests and presumably thinks that the costly improvements were undertaken thanks to the goodness of corporate souls. So too for Professor Berns, who does not say that he disapproves of the growth of the numbers of black students since the sixties but does not tell us how these students would have gotten there without the messy and frequently deplorable student movement he deplores. Surely the deconstructionists whose power—and political energy—he wildly overrates have been too preoccupied with their unstable texts to take power in admissions committees.

Likewise, Professor Jeremy Rabkin, after properly calling attention to the extravagance of much of the feminist rhetoric of the late sixties, would have us believe that feminist overkill is the principal cause of family instability. It is undeniable that the radical women's movement of the late sixties, fueled by the free-floating rage and utopianism of the time, was (to put it mildly) cavalier about the virtues of families. But a bit of comparison shows that the erosion of family life cuts far deeper than the absurdities of liberationist rhetoric. From the sixties onward, divorce and unmarried cohabitation soared and families crumbled in societies where the feminist movement was weak, France and Italy, for example, as well as those where feminism was strong, like the United States and Scandinavia.[8] Utopian fantasies about female autonomy can be only one root of the family breakup. Professor Rabkin is silent on economic pressures that have tempted men into desertion and pushed women into the labor force where they might not have otherwise made that choice. And since he cites me as an authority on the liberationist streak in the late-sixties' women's movement, let me exercise an author's prerogative and italicize a phrase he quotes but does not remark on: "In the mid-Sixties, the sexual revolution surged through the New Left *as everywhere else*." The whole society was in convulsion—if not transforming the way people have sex (who has conclusive data?), at least making it legitimate to talk about the way people have sex or wish they did. As for much-noted humorlessness, the self-righteousness of feminists is surely not greater than the self-righteousness of antifeminists, as that of the pro-choice movement does not dwarf that of pro-lifers. Absolutism in the defense of passions respects no political monopoly. The sixties that were seedbeds of fanaticism were the sixties of George Wallace as well as Jerry Rubin, police goons as well as the Black Panther party, napalm as well as flag burning.

The interesting, genuinely divisive question is which sixties to embrace and which to criticize, and here is where the contributors to this volume diverge, as is right and proper for them to do, since a set of movements so sweeping and unsettling as those of the sixties could not help inspiring opposition as various, sometimes shrill and unremitting as the movements frequently were themselves. Sweeping, unsettling—and mysterious, since they surged up with no advance warning, anticipated by virtually no one, disturbing to everyone's theories about the stability of the affluent society, and melted away almost as rapidly as they had come, leaving perplexity and acrimony galore and enough continuing controversy to fuel demagogic political campaigns and stereotypic documentary films into the next millennium.

The sixties continue to perplex partly because, whatever the sound biters may think, the currents and movements did not line up neatly with one another. Although partisans and antagonists alike saw a single "spirit of the sixties," there were (as Sheldon Wolin points out above) crosscurrents and zones of confluence, tensions and interference patterns. For the analytical purpose of clarifying the tendencies, permit me to overdraw one distinction. One strand was individualist and libertarian. The beat, the hippie, the libertine were antinomian. The means and end were the maximum of personal freedom. Expression and transgression were normalized. The emphasis was on private life, even if the project was to display private life in public. ("Why don't we do it in the road?") Those who placed the emphasis on the quest for personal freedom wished to gratify desire. They wanted sex, drugs, rock 'n' roll; pleasure, rhythm, emotion—and they wanted them, as the saying goes, now. The enemy was repression, control, whether internally by the superego or externally by the police. The self-sufficient individual was the beginning and the end, the law. This spirit survives today as entrepreneurship. The slogan of the *Whole Earth Catalog* was: "We *are* as gods and might as well get good at it." Today's god is equipped with PC, modem, and scanner and is good at surfing the Net. His drug of choice is electronic.

Freedom was far from the only objective that brought the sixties to a boil. The other was an amalgam of equality and fraternity—in particular, solidarity with the poor and the low-caste. The civil rights movement was the seedbed, the War on Poverty a continuation, and a host of other projects from the Peace Corps to the revolutionism of the Third World, whatever their obvious differences, rang variations on the same theme. Throughout the variations the hope was to regenerate a public sphere: to universalize political rights; to move the grass roots closer to power; to animate public-mindedness; to oppose illegitimate authority in the name of a public that was the proper source of sovereignty. Individualism was suspect, value placed on cooperativeness, collective projects, and at the maximum, "the beloved community." The heroes were variously Martin Luther King, Jr., Malcolm X, Che Guevara, or anonymous Vietcong cadres, but not Alan Watts or Timothy Leary. Self-realization was to come through sacrifice, not the gratification of desire.

Between the libertarian and the solidarity strains, there were plenty of collisions and "contradictions," though also room for overlap. "NOT WITH MY LIFE YOU DON'T," an SDS antidraft slogan of 1967, could be applied with equal force to the Pentagon, a strip-mining company, or a battering husband. Many a sixties radical gambled that the two strands could be woven together. Frequently, at least for a while, they did make a home in the same breast. Anarchism nestled into the civil rights movement. Civil rights workers sang "Do What the Spirit Say Do" along with "We Shall Not Be Moved." The faith was that love would be the solvent of contradiction. "Make Love, Not War" was an attempt to finesse the differences. But they could never be erased. "We Shall Overcome" was not "I Shall Be Released." One pole usually overwhelmed the other, and individuals like Abbie Hoffman migrated from solidarity to libertarianism. The celebrity culture encouraged that sort of giddy migration. A rich society rewarded it.

Complexities multiplied. Even among the forces of solidarity, there were tensions over the question, Solidarity with whom? The crucial distinction was between universalist and particularist strands. Within the student movement there was tension from the beginning between the spirit of politics for others (civil rights, for example) and the spirit of politics for selves (student power, for example). Berkeley's Free Speech Movement attempted to extrapolate from one to the other. Anger at white supremacists spilled over into anger at the authoritarian paternalism of University of California administrators, so that an activist could believe that self-liberation was tantamount to, or inexorably coupled with, solidarity with oppressed blacks. (As Sheldon Wolin rightly notes, the goals and tactics of the Free Speech Movement were so modest, so frankly American one is amazed, thirty years on, at how hysterical the officials were.) This sort of hybrid politics kept cropping up, breaking down, and cropping up again. Activists kept on seeking an ideological Holy Grail in which they could dissolve all their dilemmas.

Confusingly the various goals kept blending. Even the particularist currents of black power and its sequels carried elements of universalism. For the emphasis on cultural difference began largely as a revolt against the inferior state forced upon the lower caste by a system of white supremacy. If we believed in a single standard, why should it look like straightened hair and thin noses? If history was a unified story, why were the heroes of song and story so disproportionately white? Cultural separatism was fueled by discriminations long in the making. Reformers hardened partly because they reveled in powers freshly achieved, partly because the establishment resisted further reform. Boundaries rigidified. Late-coming reforms are the breweries of excess.

Eventually, in the nature of the case, it would become necessary to choose: Was one obligated to the whole people (or the whole world)? To the oppressed caste? To one's own group, however defined? To one's higher (or lower) self? Once civil rights had been achieved in principle, with the Civil Rights Act of 1964 and the Voting Rights Act of 1965, was there to be solidarity with all the poor, as the organizers of Students for a Democratic Society believed, trying to instigate community organizations that would federate into an "interracial movement of the poor"? Or black Americans? The whole "Third World"? One's own ethnic group? In the latter-day sixties, as the cry of "Black Power," was generalized, the choice was increasingly that of one's tribe, one's own people: Chicanos, American Indians, Jews, Italians, Slavs, gays, women (or at least feminists). . . .[9] This is not the occasion for even the most casual attempt to unravel the philosophical issues entailed in these choices. The point here is double: that amid a tangled history, universalist and particularist tendencies were not identical, and it would have been miraculous if American racial history had been susceptible to a gentle, gradual resolution.

Thus Cass Sunstein is right that the civil rights movement was conservative, aiming as it did to conserve the universalism of the Declaration of Independence. And Randall Kennedy is right that "the most effective and exemplary campaigns for racial change in America were not organized . . . under the banner of black power." But the civil rights movement so casually invoked today—a combination of apple pie and mother's milk—was far from conservative in its means. It vigorously disrespected institutions that sustained a segregationist way of life. The tradition it wanted to conserve was that of universal rights, not that of white supremacy and paternalism. The defense of restrictions on property proposed by Madison and cited by Sunstein felt to many Americans like a violation of *their* traditional principles, and that defense did not go quietly. The young George H. W. Bush, then running for the Senate from Texas, was one of many respectable figures who viewed the Civil Rights Act of 1964 as a transgression against more important rights.[10] The civil rights movement knew that to conserve a value, it is frequently necessary to threaten the comfortable and to challenge, disrupt, defeat, or transform institutions. To have reform, we would have to reach for more than reform. We would need to disrupt an established way of life.

Freedom from desperate need remains the issue that dares not speak its name. The conventional wisdom today is that if the poor shall always be with us, they should do us the favor of getting out of our pockets and out of our faces. Respectable opinion takes for granted stupendous inequality, while identity groups quarrel over the question of who, exactly, ought to be most miserable. What it would take today to free a sizable minority from desperate need is a politically potent majority. In an antiutopian time, when the ceiling of possibility is set low, chances seem slight to mobilize a potent coalition across race and class lines to recognize a common stake in ending poverty, raising the minimum wage, establishing jobs, child care, affordable housing, and universal medical coverage. There is apparently a consensus on "ending welfare as we know it," but very far from a consensus on paying taxes to the hated government to secure those rights for which governments are instituted among women and men.

The growth of global competition and the consequent sense of scarcity are major obstacles to a resumption of the egalitarian spirit. Another is that one of the strongest legacies of the sixties' movements is distrust of the very government that used to be liberalism's preferred vehicle for reform. Gingich's legions give no credit to the New Left critique of centralized power when they claim it for Republicanism. When Republicans claim they want the poor to make their own decisions rather than suffer the whims of Washington bureaucrats—never mind that these are precisely the bureaucrats who would have to enforce any serious campaign against discrimination in housing, jobs, and lending—this is exactly the program of the democratic left in the sixties, which believed that "people should make the decisions that affect their lives," in the words of that organization of premature counterculture McGoverniks, Students for a Democratic Society. ("Maximum feasible participation of the poor" was the Great Society version enshrined in the Economic Opportunity Act.) The antibureaucratic, libertarian, and communal strands of the sixties did not want to be folded, stapled, or mutilated. They too wanted to live free or die.

In particular, it is hard to exaggerate how deeply the course of the last third of the American twentieth century was diverted by the Vietnam War. The activists of course were profoundly shaken by the government's entrenched commitment to this atrocious expedition. Liberals, even moderates, had to take note that four presidents, two of each party, pursued this egregious display of state power for more than a decade. Congress acquiesced, for the most part. But it was not only activists who were shaken. The popular distrust that has dragged down faith in virtually every American institution for the past quarter century has a root in the war. Imagine the sixties without the acceleration of the Vietnam War in 1965, and you can imagine an enduring era of reform. You can imagine a reasonably successful wave of racial integration, a modestly successful War on Poverty, a weakened black power strain. The Democrats might well have recovered from the loss of their racist right because they would not have lost their left at the same time. The New Left would have grown incrementally but not explosively. It would have been the radical, decentralist edge of liberal reforms in the welfare state, reforms that might well have continued under Lyndon Johnson and either Hubert Humphrey or Robert F. Kennedy. Furious alienation would have remained on the fringe, a harsh chorus just offstage from affluent Moloch. Despite growing global competition and Cold War pressures, the country might have made a soft landing into a Newer Deal. Might does not make would, of course. History is full of missed opportunities that stay missed.

What remains from the sixties? Extraordinary improvements in the position of many blacks, women, and gays, great advances in dignity, and the abandonment of the weak. Suspicion of state power. Democratic vistas and apocalyptic militias. Pursuits of happiness, some bright, some self-destructive. Good thought and bad. Fashion shows and compact disks. And disappointments, extremities, recoils. It is early for balance sheets. It is late for delivering on dreams deferred.

NOTES

The author wishes to thank Michael Kazin, Jeremy Larner, and Richard Rothstein for valuable criticisms and suggestions.

1. Fred Barnes, "Revenge of the Squares," *New Republic* (March 13, 1995), p. 29.
2. Ibid. Could it be that the former assistant professor of history failed to get tenure at West Georgia College because he omitted slavery and Indian wars from his tour of the "core pattern" of "how we did it"? But then perhaps not, since slaveowners too liked the sound of the slogan "Don't Work, Don't Eat," and come to think of it, the Europeans did tell the vanquished tribes that their salvation was spiritual and that if they didn't like it, they could bite the dust on the reservation.
3. In the fifties some of the McCarthyist right did of course campaign against the Communist strand of the thirties, but even they did not reject the New Deal *tout court* or think there was mileage in denouncing the CIO or the mass marches of the unemployed.
4. Quoted in David Broder and Ruth Marcus, "Marilyn Quayle, Martin Paint Clinton as Unfit for Presidency," *Washington Post*, August 20, 1992, p. A1.
5. Conservative culture warriors tend to believe that government policy is responsible for the rot in the national moral fiber—for example, the mores of the murderous mother Susan Smith. But in the October 1995 issue of *Commentary*, which rounds up conservative opinion about "The National Prospect," Nathan Glazer and Diane Ravitch, among others, are notably skeptical whether government intervention can make significant changes in American culture.
6. Irving Kristol, "My Cold War," *National Interest* (Spring 1993), p. 144.
7. Quoted in Michael Duffy, "What's on Jesse's Mind," *Time* (December 5, 1994), p. 35.
8. Between 1970 and 1991 the divorce rate rose from fifteen to twenty-three per thousand married women in the United States, from eight to eleven in Denmark, and from seven to twelve in Sweden. It tripled, from three to nine, in France, and doubled, from one to two, in Italy. U.S. Bureau of the Census, *Statistical Abstract of the United States, 1994* (1994), Table 1357, p. 858.
9. I discuss this trajectory in the development of identity politics in *The Twilight of Common Dreams: Why America Is Wracked by Culture Wars* (1995), pp. 134–45.
10. Bush said that the bill would "make further inroads into the rights of individuals and the states, and even provide for the ultimate destruction of our trial by jury system." And: "The new civil rights act was passed to protect 14 percent of the people. I'm also worried about the other 86 percent." Quoted in Jefferson Morley, "Bush and the Blacks: An Unknown Story," *New York Review of Books* (January 16, 1992), pp. 20, 21.